ASSORTED PROSE

John Updike

ASSORTED PROSE

New York: Alfred · A · Knopf

1 9 7 9

Grateful acknowledgment is made to the following magazines and
publishers, who first printed the pieces specified:

THE NEW YORKER: Eight of the ten "Parodies"; all of "First Person
Plural"; "Hub Fans Bid Kid Adieu"; "Outing" and "Mea Culpa";
and nine of the eighteen "Reviews."

THE SATURDAY EVENING POST: "The Lucid Eye in Silver Town," "My
Uncle's Death," and "Eclipse."

THE NEW REPUBLIC: "Poetry from Downtroddendom," "Snow from
a Dead Sky," "No Use Talking," and "Grandmaster Nabokov."

THE NEW YORK TIMES BOOK REVIEW: "Franny and Zooey" and "Credos
and Curios."

THE AMERICAN SCHOLAR: "Honest Horn" (under the title "The Classics
of Realism").

CONTACT: "What Is a Rhyme?"

AUDIENCE: "Why Robert Frost Should Receive the Nobel Prize."

DOUBLEDAY & COMPANY: "The Dogwood Tree: A Boyhood" from *Five
Boyhoods,* edited by Martin Levin.

THE MACMILLAN COMPANY: "A Foreword for Young Readers," Foreword to *The Young King and Other Fairy Tales by Oscar Wilde.*

L. C. catalog card number: 65-13460

THIS IS A BORZOI BOOK,
PUBLISHED BY ALFRED A. KNOPF, INC.

Published May 17, 1965
Reprinted Once
Third Printing, November 1979

TO WILLIAM SHAWN

FOREWORD

In the ten years that I have written for a living, I have published a certain amount of non-fictional prose; this book collects all of it that I thought anyone might like to reread. Several baseball fans have asked me to put the "Williams article" in permanent form. My wife's aunt once expressed a fondness for a paragraph of mine on Grandma Moses. Another woman declared herself peculiarly moved by "The Unread Book Route." Otherwise, these pieces have been assembled here on my own initiative, as one more attempt to freeze the flux of life into the icy permanence of print.

Concerning the first section: I wish that there had been enough parodies and humorous sketches to make a book of their own. My first literary idols were Thurber and Benchley and Gibbs; these few *feuilletons* are what remains of my ambition to emulate them. They were written between 1956 and 1961, when I was young at heart. I leave it to the percipient reader to deduce, where appropriate, that Eisenhower was still President and that Robert Frost was still alive.

From August of 1955 to March of 1957 *The New Yorker* paid me to gad about, to interview tertiary celebrities, to peek into armories, and to write accounts of my mild adventures for its insatiable department "The Talk of the Town." Who, after all, could that indefatigably fascinated, perpetually peripatetic "we" be but a collection of dazzled farm-boys?

When New York ceased to support my fantasies, I quit the job and the city, though from time to time since, revisiting, I have made contributions to "Talk," as well as intermittent editorial "Notes and Comment." In sifting through the yellowing batch of my anonymous offerings, I have eliminated all those that, by mention of brand names, might give comfort to any public-relations outfit and tried to retain those paragraphs with some flavor, touch, or lyric glimpse of the city in them. The long "fact" pieces on pigeons and Antarctica I kept because they represent some honest research work. "Old and Precious," besides being typical of the "visit" pieces I did by the dozen, supplied some crockery to a poorhouse fair of my own. The editorial comments seem a kind of collaboration between my own voice and a voice more confident than mine —more assured of the liberal verities, more serenely facetious.

"Hub Fans Bid Kid Adieu" was a five days' labor of love executed and published in October 1960. For many years, especially since moving to greater Boston, I had been drawing sustenance and cheer from Williams' presence on the horizon, and I went to his last game with the open heart of a fan. The events there compelled me to become a reporter. Without much altering the text, I have added, as footnotes,* some additional information not then available to me.

The fourth section contains six items that at the least have as common denominator a first-person narrator. The first and longest was composed at the invitation of Mr. Martin Levin, for a collection of seven boyhood accounts, one to a decade; the number of boyhoods dropped to five, but a book did appear, published by Doubleday, and quickly disappear. Howard Lindsay, Harry Golden, Walt Kelly, and William K. Zinsser

---

* In the matter of footnotes: notes added in the preparation of this book publication are indicated by asterisks and allied typographic devices; footnotes originally part of a text (e.g., the Eliot parody) are numbered.

were the other boys. Though there are some tenderly turned passages, my reminiscence in general, I fear, has the under-cooked quality of prose written to order, under insufficient personal pressure. The next two pieces, about uncles, are really short stories that took so long to get into print that they lost their place in line and must lodge forever here. The publica-tional history of the "The Lucid Eye in Silver Town" is espe-cially devious. Written, rejected, and set aside in 1956, it was revived and revised eight years later for a *Saturday Evening Post* "Special New York Issue" and, shortly thereafter, for reasons that a trip to Russia did not clear up, was reprinted, abridged, in the June 21, 1964, number of *Pravda*. The other three accounts do not claim to be untrue. The eclipse occurred on July 20, 1963.

Of the books reviewed, some (the Sillitoe, the Aiken, the Agee, the Hughes) sought me out while others (the Salinger, the Spark, the Nabokov) were sought out by me. The Barth article, like the Williams piece, was written in acknowledgment of a debt, for Barth's theology, at one point in my life, seemed alone to be supporting it (my life). The theory of rhyme set forth in "Rhyming Max" is possibly totally wrong-headed; though on rereading it I was, curiously persuaded anew. Mr. Warner Berthoff, a professorial friend, suggested to me on a postcard that pronounced meter and rhyme are dancelike; and perhaps there is a rigidity which is not comic, the rigidity of ecstasy, of rite. But rhyme, I would say, with our present expectations of language, aspires to this intensity vainly. On the other hand, my expressed doubts about de Rougemont's theories of Occidental love have faded in importance for me. His overriding thesis seems increasingly beautiful and pertinent; corroborating quotations leap to my eyes wherever I read:

Some obstacle is necessary to swell the tide of libido to its height; and at all periods of history, wherever natural barriers

in the way of satisfaction have not sufficed, mankind has erected conventional ones in order to be able to enjoy love.
—*Freud, "The Most Prevalent Form of Degradation in Erotic Life" (1912)*

Once upon a time there was a little fish who was bird from the waist up and who was madly in love with a little bird who was fish from the waist up. So the fish-bird kept saying to the bird-fish: "Oh, why were we created so that we can never live together? You in the wind and I in the wave. What a pity for both of us!" And the bird-fish would answer: "No, what luck for both of us. This way we'll always be in love because we'll always be separated." —*Vassilis Vassilikos, "The Well" (1964)*

Beauty is the marking-time, the stationary vibration, the feigned ecstasy of an arrested impulse unable to reach its natural end.
—*T. E. Hulme, epigraph for the poem "Mana Aboda" (c. 1912)*

Myths are the souls of our actions and our loves. We cannot act without moving toward a phantom. We can love only what we create. —*Paul Valéry, "A Fond Note on Myth" (1928)*

CONTENTS

PARODIES

FIRST PERSON PLURAL

CONTENTS

Parodies

THE AMERICAN MAN:
WHAT OF *HIM*?

(An Editorial Left Out of Life's *Special 35¢ Issue:*
"The American Woman")

EVER SINCE the history-dimmed day when Christopher Columbus, a Genoese male, turned his three ships (*Niña, Pinta, Santa María*) toward the United States, men have also played a significant part in the development of our nation. Lord Baltimore, who founded the colony of Maryland for Roman Catholics driven by political persecution from Europe's centuries-old shores, was a man. So was Wyatt Earp, who brought Anglo-Saxon common law into a vast area then in the grip of a *potpourri* of retributive justice, "vigilantism," and the ancient Code Napoléon. Calvin Coolidge, the thirtieth Chief Executive, was male. The list could be extended indefinitely.

Things were not always easy for the American Man. He came here in his water-weathered ships and did not find broad thruways, "cloud-capped towers," and a ready-made Free Way of LIFE. No, what he found confronting him in this fabled New Land was, principally, trees. Virgin, deciduous, hundreds of feet taller than he, the trees of the Colonization left their scars on his mental makeup in the form of the high rates of alcoholism, suicide, and divorce that distinguish him from the men of Continental Europe or Australasia. While his brethren of the Old World were dandling perfumed coquettes on their silk-garbed knees, he was forging inward, across the Appalachians to the Great Prairie, where his woods-tested faith, tempered in the forge of Valley Forge and honed on the heights of Montcalm's Quebec, took on a new austerity and became Evangelical Methodism. The Chevaliers of France didn't give him pause, nor the wetbacks of Mexico. But he did not emerge on the spray-moistened cliffs of California the same man who sailed from Southampton, Brussels, or Rügen. As Robert Frost says, in his quietly affirmative lines:

> The land was ours before we were the land's. . . .
> Possessing what we still were unpossessed by,
> Possessed by what we now no more possessed.

What is it that distinguishes the American Man from his counterparts in other climes; what *is* it that makes him so special? He is religious. He is quietly affirmative. He is trustworthy, loyal, helpful, friendly, courteous, kind, obedient, cheerful, thrifty, brave, clean, and reverent. He carries his burdens lightly, his blessings responsibly. Unlike the Oriental mandarin, he shaves his upper lip. Nor does he let his fingernails grow. Unlike the men of England, he does not wear gloves. Generally, he is taller than the men of nations (e.g., Nepal, Switzerland) where the average height is, compared to ours, laughable. All over the world, coolies and fakirs are picking themselves up out of the age-old mire and asking, "How can we become like Yanqui men?" Our State Department, cleansed of intellectual southpaws, works night and day on the answer.

The American Man has his faults, too. He loves speed. Is speed, in every case, desirable, per se? The editors, no strangers to speed themselves, wonder, for "the race is not [always] to the swift, nor the battle to the strong." The American Man tends to swagger—understandably. He enjoys bowling. He spends more money on bowling each year than the entire income of the Grand Duchy of Luxembourg since the Hapsburgs. Our critics in India, perhaps with justice, lift their eyebrows at this. But he is big, *big*—a big man—and he does things in a big way. He smokes too much and laughs too hard. The popcorn alone that he devours every year would outweigh Mont Blanc. He has more insidious shortcomings, too, but space limitations preclude our listing them.

He can look back over a hundred and eighty years of steady betterment with forward-looking pride. Today, men are active in every walk of LIFE. Politics: Several of our ablest senators are male, and men like John Foster Dulles, Charles Wilson, and Dwight David Eisenhower figure prominently in Washington's innermost councils. Religion: Reinhold Niebuhr has just this year delivered a sermon. Industry: Men are infiltrating the top levels of management, and already dominate such diverse fields as structural engineering, anthracite development, track and field events, and fire control. The Arts: Individual men like Herman Wouk and Archibald MacLeish have authored works in every way comparable to the best of Willa Cather or Mary Roberts Rinehart, the Queen of American Mystery Fiction.

The American Man can be proud of his sex. In the home, though still docile, he cunningly gets his way. In the community, he is a model for all young boys, as to what manhood means. In the state, he pays income tax or sales tax, depending. In the nation, he makes up only slightly less than half the population. Perhaps most importantly, he has solved the millennia-old riddle of the sage:

What is Man, that Thou art mindful of him?

ANYWHERE IS WHERE YOU HANG YOUR HAT

Ralph C. Jones
25 Main St.
Anywhere 2, U.S.A.

　　　　　　to　Mr. Henry Smith
　　　　　　　　901 State Street
　　　　　　　　Anywhere 3, U.S.A.

—Envelope shown in a subway poster, to illustrate the judicious use of postal-zone numbers.

May 18, 19—

Dear Mr. Smith:

"Howdy." Guess you think this is peculiar, my writing you this letter when we live in adjacent postal zones, with only the Everyman General Merchandise Store and the All Souls' Non-Denominational Church and the width of State Street separating us. But what with no mail coming in to Anywhere from the outside (except in December for Santa Claus), John Postmaster, our postmaster, is grateful for whatever jobs we can give him.

Well, the point is (1) to welcome you to Anywhere, the only town in the U.S.A. located on both the Continental

: 6 :

Divide and the Mason-Dixon Line, and (2) to get acquainted, which is only natural, since between the Joneses and the Smiths most of the local population is accounted for, and we better make the best of it, or there won't be no peace for anyone. (joke).

We think of ourselves in these parts as pretty average American. There's one industry on the east side, Acme Mfg., owned by A. Employer, and some foreign element work there, but by and large the fertile prairie all around keeps us white Protestants going. Since we aren't located in any state, we're pretty dependent on federal aid, and as a result the school is poor and the streets full of potholes and like the District of Columbia we can't vote in national elections, but when you average it out each family has an income of $5,520 and 1.3 children, so we can't kick. My own guess is you'll like it fine here. The "Life" photographers come around pretty often so it isn't as dull as it could be.

Well I've just about filled two sides of my medium-wt. stationery, so I'd better say what I have to say, which is, "Come over sometime and let's get acquainted." All of the houses on Main St. are numbered 25, or 1, or 77, or something memorable, so my address won't help you much, but mine is the big rambling house with the shady old elm out in front and the white picket fence.

Best & again "welcome"
Ralph C. Jones

(Of the ensuing correspondence only the letters received by Smith, a shy, methodical man forever making small bundles of his private papers, have been preserved. We may presume that Smith's replies were, like his person, colorless.)

May 30, 19—

Dear Henry,

Rcd. yr. letter and enjoyed same v. much. That was quite a misadventure you had. I should have specified, I guess, that mine was the big rambling house with the old elm and picket fence *and* the porch swing out front. The people you blundered in on, to hear it from the neighbors, were the Does. Nice folks, pretty typical of what you'll meet around here, when you're better accepted. John does "clerical work" for Acme, and his wife Mary used to sell linen goods for the Ajax Dept. Store when she married him. She was far along in her 20s when that luckily happened. He's a conscientious citizen, always filling out income tax forms and money orders and loan applications to show others how it's done. They go to about a movie a week and have dinner out once a month. You probably noticed another woman, bony and slow-moving like John, with the throaty Doe laugh. That was his sister Miss Jane J. Being a spinster doesn't seem to bother her much, I mean very much. She teaches third grade and has Social Security No. 000-00-0000. They let her stay in two tiny rooms over in the west wing.

Depending on how long you made your welcome last, you probably noticed when the two Does get to laughing throatily together Mary looks a little anxious, her eyes shuttling from one to another and her teeth nibbling her lower lip. We always thought that maybe if Mary did something *different* with her mouth, but I guess the truth is her face is one of those clean wide-browed ones that all along the line—childhood, adolescence, young womanhood, and now what they call for politeness maturity—just miss being pretty. Most of us have known little Mary ever since her first Sunday school dress. Her maiden name was Smith, like yours. Maybe she's a relation. In which case you'll probably be as concerned as the rest of us with her happiness. Not to imply it doesn't suit her to a "T," to have John's fond sister Jane living with them.

Well at any rate you'd know best since you've been in the house most recently. John is all right without being the friendliest. Let's you and I meet sometime and talk it out. Since you don't know your way around yet, I suggest some place in downtown Anywhere.

See you then,
Ralph Jones

June 4, 19—

"Hank"——

Sorry you saw fit to skip our appointment. I waited it must have been three hours, but I guess in vain, which doesn't matter to me, who loves nothing more than to sit idle for a stretch in the middle of a day. No hard feelings, no doubt you're keeping pretty busy with the Does.

Would it suit you better in front of the First Peoples Bank some noon? So you won't have any excuse this time, in front of the First Peoples Bank with the big cardboard check for $6.98 made payable to Anyone U. Wish and signed O. U. R. Depositor.

There's an interesting story behind that. Without knowing, you might think it was *Mr*. Depositor, but then Olive always *was* mannish, so you aren't too far off. Her place on the south edge of town was a farm when she was a little girl and when her father died so young, she was left with the land. Selling it off, piece by piece, offended her memory of her Dad (not that he had ever had a kind word for her when he was living —always wanted a boy) and it seemed the only way she could make it up to him was to become more like him, using his expressions of speech, getting his old furniture down from the attic and sitting in it, wearing plain clothes, and eventually just using her initials. Erasing her sex, as it were. But don't go saying I said she's a fool. Every acre she sold, she got hard money for—some think she loves a dollar more than is healthy. That $6.98 to her wasn't what a nickel would be to you or me. To me, at any rate. Maybe you're another of those whose sending our mean national income spiralling up, causing inflation. (joke).

Anyway you can bet that $6.98 meant a lot to Anyone Wish. He just can't hold a steady job, though he has an uncanny way with the mechanical aspect of things. Ever since a kid he's been willfull. "Short, short-sighted, and short-tempered" is what they say of him. He does these odd jobs when he isn't sick, or sleeping—we often wonder if there's a difference, though to be fair, as a youngster, he was puny. The $6.98 must represent something he fixed around the old Depositor house. God knows it's been falling down for years. It's almost disrespectful to her deceased father, the way Olive has let the upkeep of that place go hang.

That's *one* reason why she *might* have written him that check. There's some local speculation about that. It doesn't seem natural, for a woman to coop herself up thirty years and never take a fancy to a man, even a sorry little scrap of rag like Mrs. Wish's youngest boy.

In strict confidence,
"Ralph"

P.S. See you soon. I'll be wearing an everyday suit and have regular features.

June 7, 19—

Smith:

Let's be on the level with each other. Your snippy postcard about waiting by the bank rings about as true as a zinc penny. Saying that everybody you saw looked alike is almost an insult, which better not get around town, which it won't, thanks to my good offices. I don't suppose you'd say that *Jane J. Doe* looks like everybody else. Or is it Mary you're chasing? Reports differ. You live your own life, but it isn't smart (not to mention the ethics of it, I'll leave that to Parson Brown, not that he's any saint) to cross me now, when there's a storm brewing and you'll need every friend you can rummage up.

The Does aren't too popular around here. John is more than a bit "uppity" and there is an opinion that he gets far too much publicity for the size of his hatband, with the rest of us being called in for just an occasional insurance ad or "SatevPost" cover. What's so average about the name Doe anyway? And we aren't too happy about the way he's treated little Mary Smith either. But you pick your own friends, and if I'm not among them O.K., but let's not play the hypocrite Henry. You better see me promptly—your true ally in spite of all—because the rumor is they're going to change the postal zones again and in that case you'll never be able to find me, by mail or otherwise.

Olive Depositor looked at me funny the other day along Shady Lane, down by the Golden Mean Drug Store. I don't suppose you've been breathing a word to her. Oh no Henry. Butter wouldn't melt in your mouth as they say.

You're playing a cagey game, all right, and if you can pull it off, more power to you. Otherwise, I recommend you pack

your cardboard suitcase and leave Anywhere and go back to
Elsewhere, where you came from. We have twenty Henry
Smiths in town already, and one more or less won't make
much, I mean *no* difference.

With your best interests at heart,

R.C.J.

WHAT IS A RHYME?*

*(T. S. Eliot, with Customary Equanimity,
Confronts Mother Goose)*

I DO NOT KNOW whether all childhoods are painful. My own,
or that drastically edited set of snapshots which is all that remains to me of my own, did (or does) not seem especially so.
There is, for example, a beard, attached to one of my grandmother's brothers and perhaps more spade-shaped than not,
the contemplation of which seldom failed to inspire me as a
child with an indeterminate 'enthusiasm'; any attempt on my
part further to particularize this emotion would no more serve
my present purpose than an attempt by Shakespeare to acquaint
his Elizabethan audience with the details of Othello's fascinating travels as thoroughly as Desdemona had been acquainted
with them would have served his dramatic, and different, purpose. It is enough, I think, to be aware that such 'enthusiasm'
somewhere exists. To allay the suspicion that by invoking the
shade of my great-uncle's beard and whatever attendant ecto-
plasm, *inops inhumataque*, its wake includes, I have so far
abused your hospitality as to appoint you my partners in the
type of séance that is best conducted, if at all, in the privacy

---

* An address delivered before the Fifth Form of the High Wycombe
Episcopal Academy in 1952 and subsequently developed for delivery
before a polylingual audience in Prague in 1954. It was published in the
trimonthly magazine *quarto* and issued in hard covers under the title *The
Uses of Assonance*.

of one's flat, it should at the outset be made clear that as I understand the question, 'What is a rhyme?' (and the most zealous attempt to provide answers is necessarily stopped short, like Virgil at the rim of Paradise, at the limits of one's comprehension of what has been asked), it is to an extent inseparable from another: 'What is a child?' I as well wish to affirm that it is not part of my purpose to inspect *all* dictionary senses of the word 'rhyme,' or to decide for once and all if 'fade' *rhymes* with 'said' or 'said' with 'hedge.' The vexing issue of *genres* we shall also skirt. It shall be assumed that a riddle, however ingenious, is not a 'rhyme,' and neither is an epic, even one which jingles—as does, to my ear, *The Curse of Kehama.*

When we read such lines as

> Diddlty, diddlty, dumpty,
> The cat ran up the plum tree,[1]

we must inquire of ourselves not only 'What is our response?' but also 'Is it *right* to respond in such a way?' For the responses of a child are not those of a mature person. You will readily perceive that I have presupposed something which more properly might be phrased as yet another question: 'Were "rhymes" *in fact* composed for "children"?' Here we discover, with mixed apprehension and delight, that we have placed at least the forepart of one foot into the bustling and comforting realm of textual scholarship, whose inhabitants produce a highly valuable form of literary baggage which I have previously determined, however, to make this trip without. For our purpose I believe it is sufficient to say that if 'rhymes' are *not* intended for 'children,' they appear to be failures, whose only interest for the adult can lie in somewhat morbid con-

---

[1] I have used for this and following quotations the Frederick Warne and Company (London) edition. Neither authoritative nor complete, and furnished with illustrations by Miss Kate Greenaway that invariably afford me a shudder, the book was the nearest to hand.

cern with *how far* such efforts are situated beyond the pale
of those canons of judgment which—by their subversion as
well as in their advocacy—have shaped the European, that is
to say, the Christian, tradition.

I confess that when I come upon lines such as those quoted
my reaction is not merely one of disappointment but one
of astonishment, that such a couplet has found its way into
print, and found its way so often. Nor does it seem that the
Mother Goose 'rhymes' (that Elizabeth Goose is the actual
author of *all* rhymes is of course as dangerous an assumption
as *any* assumption about, say, the *Anacreontea*) belong in that
species of composition that makes its effect by *bulk*. Lord
Byron and spaghetti are two examples. Read *in continuo*,
'rhymes' produce a baffling impression of ups and downs, heed-
less spillings, petty chores indifferently performed, and of little
maids and naughty boys who though present in large numbers
quite fail to achieve any sort of union, carnal or conversational,
of which we might approve. This is not to deny that there
are pretty[2] (though far from transcendent) touches: I offer

> All around the green gravel,
> The grass grows so green,

where the repetition of 'green' invites us to share in the difficulty the poet had in grasping the concept of the color. We
should perhaps beware, however, of extending forbearance—
Dante's *amore*—so indiscriminately that it becomes, by the
laws of diffusion, as devoid of true virtue—Virgil's *virtus*—as
the Deity fitfully visible in the tracts of the Theosophical
Societies, or as the eventual universe presented for our consideration by students of thermodynamics. It is our duty, if
Western civilization is in any sense to linger on, to differentiate

---

[2] As to 'prettiness,' I can only recommend the reader to conceive of a
sunflower seed placed next to Wren's original designs for the Cathedral
of St. Paul.

between the excellent, the second-rate, and the fake. These
lines do not seem to me to be fake; but they fail to be so, I
would suggest, by default. In their presence we experience
not even that fear of being hoodwinked which is the *least* with
which verse can enrich our lives: rather, we seem to stand on
the edge of a Limbo where

> secondo che per ascoltare,
> non avea pianto mai che di sospiri
> che l'aura eterna facevan tremare.

Here I wish to make explicit what in the preceding paragraphs I permitted to remain implicit. If we are to consider a
rhyme a variety of poetry which appeals to a child, this sub-
stantially affects our definition of 'child.' And when we suppose a 'child' is that which enjoys rhymes, we run the risk of
correction by experts. If I may bid you to trespass with me
into an area where I myself never venture unless thoroughly
disguised as a deferential amateur, I recommend on this point
Le Réel et l'imaginaire dans le jeu de l'enfant, by that tireless
researcher Jean Château; also Fritz Kunkel's helpful *Jugend-
charakterkunde*. To resort to terms more suited to our concerns, a child is a creature fated, in time and under Providence,
to appreciate Virgil, Dante, and Shakespeare. But

> All around the green gravel,
> The grass grows so green

would lead, insofar as it led anywhere, toward the 'simplistic'
poems of Wordsworth, a very great poet indeed, if 'great' means
anything at all (which Mr. A. J. Ayer tells us it may not), but
one vigorous appreciation of whom, I would suggest, is somewhat peripheral to what seems to me to be (and perhaps here
I perform a pratfall while grimly clutching a goat-bladder de-
pleted of wind) *human responsibility*. Indeed the question is
real, whether Wordsworth or John Cleveland has more just

claims upon our attention at this moment of history; certainly Cleveland, though the smaller poet, was the larger man. In short, 'rhymes' answer less the needs of the child, which are articulate and distinct, than the inchoate needs of the parent who is compelled to purchase 'books for children.' The nature of the compulsion and the definition of 'parent' are in themselves likely topics for another study, which I hope someone else will pursue. It would be beyond the terms of my programme as announced to suggest anything further than that both are products of the unfortunate *fragmentation of sensibility* which occurred, as near as we can tell (in leafing through old magazines I have been puzzled to discover that the critic who most firmly fixed the chronology was, apparently, myself), somewhere within the dotage of Andrew Marvell; and that in the one consists the penitential rock borne by the other, who, his gaze welded to his feet, must travel for many years the circuit of barren terraces:

> Cosi a sé e noi buona ramogna
>   quell'ombre orando, andavan sotto il pondo,
>   simile a quel che tal volta si sogna,
> disparmente angosciate tutte a tondo
>   e lasse su per la prima cornice,
>   purgando la caligine del mondo.

DRINKING FROM A CUP
MADE CINCHY

(After Reading Too Many Books on How to Play Golf)

IN MY TOURS around the nation I am frequently asked, "Have you *ever* broken a cup?" Of course I have. Don't let anybody kid you on that score. *Everyone* who regularly drinks from china, no matter how adept he has become, has had his share of ruined tablecloths and scalded knees. *No human being* is born with the ability to take liquid from a cup successfully; you can easily prove this by trying to feed a baby. Those of us who have attained some proficiency have done so at the price of long hours of systematic application. Without these long hours our natural grace and poise would never have evolved into *skill*. I would not say that everyone is endowed equally; I *do* say that everyone, no matter how clumsy, can reduce his accidents to a minimum that will amaze his wife and friends. He can do this by rigorously adhering to a few simple principles that I have discovered through painful trial-and-error. Had these principles been available in legible form when I was young, my present eminence would have been attained by me *years ago.*

I have analyzed drinking from a cup into three three-part stages: (1) Receipt, (2) The Cooling Pause, and (3) Consummation. However, bear in mind that in practice these "compartments" are run together in one fluid, harmonious social action.

I. RECEIPT

(1) Address the cup by sitting erect, your chest at right angles to the extended arm of the cup-offerer, or "hostess." Even if this person is a spouse or close relative, do not take a relaxed, slouching position, with the frontal plane of your rib cage related obliquely to the cup's line of approach. Such an attitude, no matter how good-naturedly it is assumed, has the inevitable effect of making one of your arms feel shorter than the other, a hopeless handicap at this crucial juncture, where 30% of common errors occur. The reason: *Both hands should move toward the saucer simultaneously.*

(2) In seizure, first touch, with feathery lightness, the rim of the saucer with the pad of the index finger of the right hand. (Left-handers: Read all these sentences backward.) A split second—perhaps .07—later, the first knuckle of the middle, "big" finger, sliding toward the center of the saucer's invisible underside, and the tip of the thumb *must* coördinate in a prehensile "pinching" motion. *This motion must occur.* The two remaining fingers of the right hand of necessity accompany the big finger, but should not immediately exert pressure, despite their deep-seated instinct to do so. Rather, the wrist is gently supinated. This brings the two passive fingers into contact with the underside of the saucer while at the same time the cup is drawn in toward the body by a firm, but not angry, forearm.

Meanwhile, the left hand is not just "taking Sunday off." Fingers and thumb united in one scooplike unit (an imaginary line drawn through the knuckles should intersect your foot), the left hand hovers, convex without being "balled" into a fist, an inch or two (whichever feels most natural) to the left of the inner left edge of the saucer. What is it doing there? Many beginners, having asked this question and having not received an adequate answer, keep their left hands in their pockets and fancy that they are achieving insouciance. They are just being foolish. The left hand, in its "escort" role, performs many functions. For one thing, its being so close by gives the right hand confidence and eases its fear. For another, the index and middle fingers are in a position to snap over and hush the distressing but frequent phenomenon of "cup chatter," should it develop. Thirdly, if the spoon, with its eccentric center of gravity, begins to slither from the saucer, the left hand is there to act as a trap. Fourthly, if worst comes to worst and the cup tips, the left hand is able to rush right in and make the best of a bad situation, whose further ramifications take us into the psychological realm discussed in the chapter "To Err Is Human."

Throughout, keep your eyes travelling rapidly around the rim of the cup.

(3) The saucer is held by your right hand, the "executor." Your left hand, the "guardian angel," cruises in the air inches away. A napkin—the "landing field"—has been previously spread on your right knee. *Now*, softly *constrict*. By this I mean, with one impulse, bring your forearms in toward your sides, bend your spine forward, bow your head, and touch your knees. Without any thought on your part, this syndrome of actions will lead the cup and saucer to descend along a parabolic line whose equation on Cartesian coördinates is $2x = y^2$. At $x = 0$, the tea will be on your knee. Your left hand will have automatically joined the right *under the saucer* and as automatically glided away. You will find that your thighs have become firm flat surfaces. For the first time since your index fingertip touched the icy edge of china, you may smile.

II. The Cooling Pause

(1) The key to this phase—in point of time the longest of the three—is *immobility*. Only the fingers, eyelids, and tongue move at all. Resolutely maintain your bent position over the cup. Think of yourself as "mothering" the beverage. Let your stillness be placid, vegetal, and Olympian, rather than rigid, electric, and Byzantine. Be diffident and amiable in conversation. Some of my fellow pros advise beginners not to speak at all, but such total exclusion is apt to be in itself unsettling. However, *do* avoid anecdotes requiring much facial or other animation, and arguments whose logical structure must be indicated by any action of the hands, whether in drawing diagrams in the air or ticking off points on the fingers.

(2) Resist the temptation, once the saucer seems secure, of straightening up in the chair (or worse, sofa), thereby placing a long diagonal hypotenuse between your nose and the cup. Any hauteur is felt throughout the body. Dignity of bearing is no substitute for muscular control, An obsequious, attentive hunch will not be thought rude as long as you are able to raise your eyes to your hostess fitfully. Indeed, the distention of the eyebrows needed to glimpse her lends to many people an arch charm of mien they otherwise would lack.

(3) Rotate the broad part of the spoon—*not* the handle—in the liquid. Do not splash. Do not toy with the fascinating ripples individual droplets make. Do not attempt to return liquid from the saucer to the cup. Be still.

III. Consummation

"My goodness," I can hear many readers asking, "will we never get a taste of the brew?"

"Yes, you will" is my answer—"especially if you have followed my advice up to now." The reason I have outlined the procedure with such meticulousness is this: Having come so far without a blunder, the "clean" feeling you now have will give you crispness to go on. Success succeeds. If I am wrong, see the chapter titled "There's Many a Slip."

(1) Steam has ceased to arise from the liquid and you are certain it is cool enough to drink. Restore the spoon to the saucer, pinning it with the left thumb. Look around and make sure no one is about to jostle you, either in fun or by accident. The gesture of bringing food to the mouth is so ancient, so fundamental to Man, that a detailed description would be mere padding. The one ticklish decision that remains is the Separation of Cup and Saucer.

(2) The two possible extremes—leaving the saucer on the knee or bringing it with the cup all the way to the chin—are too contemptible to denounce, though I have seen both done. In fact, the problem is self-solving if, contrary to instinct, you pick up the saucer with the left hand, gripping the cup handle with the right. They begin the ascent together, but the inequality of their strength soon tells; in the powerful yet delicate grasp of the right hand, the cup completes its flight to the lips, while the left hand weakly halts at the level of the sternum, where the saucer, braced against your necktie, acts as a tacit bib.

(3) Be conscious that, as you consume the beverage, the weight of the cup diminishes; otherwise the hand may, in reflex, snap it over your shoulder. Never hang on to an empty cup. *Get rid of it.* In replacing the unit on the table or tray presumably provided, a jaunty clatter need not be avoided, if it can be induced without force. When your hands are at last free, sigh and say, "That was delicious," or "I needed that."

Congratulations. You have just drunk from a cup.

Appendix: Helpful Hints

1. Don't be tense.

2. Don't be "loose."

3. Think of yourself not as an assembly of hinged joints inflexibly connected by rods of calcium but as a plastic, pliant animal, capable of warmth, wit, and aspiration.

4. Think of the cup-and-saucer complex, from the instant it is received into your hands to the instant it leaves, as a charge delivered to your care and toward which you feel the maternal emotions mentioned above (II.1). Imagine yourself "crooning" to it, recognizing hereditary resemblances to your own face in *its* face, etc.

5. The angle made by the forearms should never exceed 110° or fall below 72°, assuming the room is at less than body temperature. If it is not, you need my companion work, "The Elements of Sipping Through a Straw."

ON THE SIDEWALK

(After Reading, At Long Last,
"On The Road," by Jack Kerouac)

I WAS just thinking around in my sad backyard, looking at those little drab careless starshaped clumps of crabgrass and beautiful chunks of some old bicycle crying out without words of the American Noon and half a newspaper with an ad about a lotion for people with dry skins and dry souls, when my mother opened our frantic banging screendoor and shouted, "Gogi Himmelman's here." She might have shouted the Archangel Gabriel was here, or Captain Easy or Baron Charlus in Proust's great book: Gogi Himmelman of the tattered old greenasgrass knickers and wild teeth and the vastiest, most vortical, most insatiable wonderfilled eyes I have ever known. "Let's go, Lee," he sang out, and I could see he looked sadder than ever, his nose all rubbed raw by a cheap handkerchief and a dreary Bandaid unravelling off his thumb. "I know the WAY!" That was Gogi's inimitable unintellectual method of putting it that he was on fire with the esoteric paradoxical Tao and there was no holding him when he was in that mood. I said, "I'm going, Mom," and she said, "O.K." and when I looked back at her hesitant in the pearly mystical UnitedStateshome light I felt absolutely sad, thinking of all the times she had vacuumed the same carpets.

His scooter was out front, the selfsame, the nonpareil, with its paint scabbing off intricately and its scratchedon dirty words and its nuts and bolts chattering with fear, and I got my tricycle out of the garage, and he was off, his left foot kicking with that same insuperable energy or even better. I said, "Hey wait," and wondered if I could keep up and probably couldn't have if my beltbuckle hadn't got involved with his rear fender. This was IT. We scuttered down our drive and right over Mrs. Cacciatore's rock garden with the tiny castles made out of plaster that always made me sad when I looked at them alone. With Gogi it was different; he just kept right on going, his foot kicking with that delirious thirtyrevolutionsasecond frenzy, right over the top of the biggest, a Blenheim six feet tall at the turrets; and suddenly I saw it the way he saw it, embracing everything with his unfluctuating generosity, imbecile saint of our fudging age, a mad desperado in our Twentieth Century Northern Hemisphere Nirvana deserts.

We rattled on down through her iris bed and broke into the wide shimmering pavement. "Contemplate those holy hydrants," he shouted back at me through the wind. "Get a load of those petulant operable latches; catch the magic of those pickets standing up proud and sequential like the arguments in Immanuel Kant; boom, boom, bitty-boom BOOM!" and it was true.

"What happens when we're dead?" I asked.

"The infinite never-to-be-defiled subtlety of the late Big Sid Catlett on the hushed trap drums," he continued, mad with his own dreams, imitating the whisks, "Swish, swish, swishy-swish SWOOSH!"

The sun was breaking over the tops of Mr. Linderman's privet hedge, little rows of leaves set in there delicate and justso like mints in a Howard Johnson's roadside eatery. Mitzi Leggett came out of the house, and Gogi stopped the scooter, and put his hands on her. "The virginal starchblue fabric; printed with stylized kittens and puppies," Gogi explained in his curiously

: 25 :

beseechingly transcendent accents. "The searing incredible *innocence!* Oh! Oh! Oh!" His eyes poured water down his face like broken blisters.

"Take me along," Mitzi said openly to me, right with Gogi there and hearing every word, alive to every meaning, his nervous essence making his freckles tremble like a field of Iowa windblown nochaff barley.

"I want to," I told her, and tried to, but I couldn't, not there. I didn't have the stomach for it. She pretended to care. She was a lovely beauty. I felt my spokes snap under me; Gogi was going again, his eyes tightshut in ecstasy, his foot kicking so the hole in his shoesole showed every time, a tiny chronic rent in the iridescent miasmal veil that Intrinsic Mind tries to hide behind.

Wow! Dr. Fairweather's house came up on the left, delicious stucco like piecrust in the type of joints that attract truckers, and then the place of the beautiful Mrs. Mertz, with her *canny* deeprooted husband bringing up glorious heartbreaking tabourets and knickknacks from his workshop in the basement, a betooled woodshavingsmelling fantasy worthy of Bruegel or Hegel or a seagull. Vistas! Old Miss Hooper raced into her yard and made a grab for us, and Gogi Himmelman, the excruciating superbo, shifted to the other foot and laughed in her careworn face. Then the breathless agape green space of the Princeling mansion, with its rich calm and potted Tropic of Cancer plants. Then it was over.

Gogi and I went limp at the corner under a sign saying ELM STREET with irony because all the elms had been cut down so they wouldn't get the blight, sad stumps diminishing down the American perspective whisperingly.

"My spokes are gone," I told him.

"Friend—ahem—*zip, zip*—parting a relative concept— Bergson's invaluable marvelchocked work—tch, tch." He stood there, desperately wanting to do the right thing, yet always lacking with an indistinguishable grandeur that petty ability.

"Go," I told him. He was already halfway back, a flurrying spark, to where Mitzi waited with irrepressible womanwarmth.

Well. In landsend despair I stood there stranded. Across the asphalt that was sufficiently semifluid to receive and embalm millions of starsharp stones and bravely gay candywrappers a drugstore twinkled artificial enticement. But I was not allowed to cross the street. I stood on the gray curb thinking, They said I could cross it when I grew up, but what do they mean grown up? I'm thirty-nine now, and felt sad.

WHY ROBERT FROST SHOULD
RECEIVE THE NOBEL PRIZE

ONCE PER FORTNIGHT or so a letter comes to this column accusing its author of the sin of "fuddyduddyism." While such charges, phrased as they usually are in the quasi-literate elisions of what I believe is termed "hip" slang, and signed as they are as often as not by a gluey scrawl in the latest mode of "action painting" (or whatever such dribble is dubbed by its dupes), do not by any means undermine the calm of one who has been steeped since youth in the broadening classics of post-Homeric literature, nevertheless perhaps the charge should be disposed of once and for all before I set forth a proposition which I believe will contribute no little toward world sanity.

For one thing, I have always been a friend of modern literature, and continue to be. My quarrel with it arises only where it seems to me diffuse and decadent, as in Proust, or obscure and obscene, as in Joyce. I have for thirty years, much against the advice of my more expediency-minded friends, refused to board the bandwagon of T. S. Eliot, with all the aridity of spirit and religious obscurantism it represents, and neither have I embraced the megalomaniacal political systems of two much overrated versifiers, William Yeats and E. Pound. Indeed it is my conviction that there is less sense and fun in all five of these above-mentioned writers than exists on any random page of *Penrod*, by Booth Tarkington. No, while

I am in full sympathy with the mainstream of present-day writing, I by no means subscribe to its eccentric fringe manifestations, and if this makes me a "rogue and petty slave" to the peddlers of the latest symbol-bloated bosh, so—to paraphrase the Latin—be it.

I confess that I feel most at home amid the lusty wits and wise hoydens of the eighteenth century. There I find human content *ad profusio*. By Dickens' time the disease has already started of which Henry James is to be an agonized paralytic victim, and Joseph Conrad another (though some of his descriptions of salt-water are good)—the disease of endlessly pecking like nervous chickens at the wonderful and unified fabric of human experience. The question proper to the narrative artist is not *Why* do we do things? but *What* do we do? In asserting that this century has not yet produced another *Pamela* I am not quarrelling with its modernity; rather I am saying that it is not modern enough. I do not think that one who (as has been my honor to have been) was among the first to hail the talents of Mrs. Buck and Somerset Maugham need have any self-doubts as to being retrograde.

In sharp contrast to the twitching spectres of what I have heard amusingly described as "era-itis" stands Robert Frost. His craggy snow-capped figure puts me in mind of the splendid quatrain of Karle Wilson Baker:

> And there is healing in old trees,
> Old streets a glamour hold;
> Why may not I, as well as these,
> Grow lovely, growing old?

—lines that Frost himself would doubtless be proud to claim as his own. Frost's poems do not always rhyme, and in fairness this may be objected to them. But we must balance this defect with larger considerations. His English is always intelligible and rarely contains ill-digested scraps of some fashionable foreign tongue. While there is nothing in his vision as grotesque and ungainly as the God of orthodox theology, yet his poems at their eloquent best provide the vague sense of reassurance which this God at *His* best provided. Finally, he is thoroughly American; in his works we seem to perceive the humanism of Jonathan Edwards, the pragmatism of Fenimore Cooper, Thoreau's bile, Whitman's effluvia, and Hamlin Garland's choler. Frost as a man combines the tang of wood smoke with the flexible strength of cantilever construction; I can think of no better way for the Nobel Prize Committee to make amends for the carnival of French Existentialists and Mississippi stream-of-consciousness purveyors who have recently degraded this award than to award it to him. It will strike a blow for healthy sanity in literature and in life. I offer this advice to so august a committee with my diffidence considerably bolstered by the knowledge that in this opinion, at least, I have the eminent company of J. Donald Adams, Orville Prescott, Maxwell Geismar, and Henry Seidel Canby, to name but a few.

CONFESSIONS OF A WILD BORE

PITY THE POOR BORE. He stands among us as a creature formidable and familiar yet in essence unknowable. We can read of the ten infallible signs whereby he may be recognized and of the seven tested methods whereby he may be rebuffed. Valuable monographs exist upon his dress and diet; the study of his mating habits and migrational routes is well past the speculative stage; and statistical studies abound. One out of three hundred and twelve Americans is a bore, for instance, and a healthy male adult bore consumes *each year* one and a half times his own weight in other people's patience. But in all this vast literature (and this is not to disparage the scientists who have selflessly carried forward their research, nor the generous philanthropic foundations that endowed their gleaming laboratories) one grave defect persists: the bore is always described externally, in a tone of distance and distaste. Hence the central question—what makes a few people bores when the rest of us are so fascinating—remains cloaked in mystery. Yet bores, unlike Red Indians, were not here to greet the Pilgrims. They do not, like rabid bats, come up from Mexico. No: the shameful truth, suppressed by both the public press and the spokesmen of our federal government, is that bores are created *out of our own number*. Each year, a few healthy Americans, whether by alchemy, infection, or unscrupulous recruiting methods among the alumni, are converted into bores. How can this happen? The riddle of borogenesis has defied solution for several reasons. For one thing, by their very natures bores are the most difficult and unappetizing class of society to interview, and have been shunned where prostitutes, alcoholics, and juvenile delinquents have been (sociologically) embraced. For another, bores have themselves *heavily infiltrated* the very psychological sciences that should be grappling with the problem! But the chief, and most impressive, obstacle is that *bores are oblivious of being such.* A mature, fully feathered bore absolutely believes that he is just like anybody else—if anything, cuter; so he has no recollection of becoming one. Hence superstition continues to hold court, and what is actually a disease is still widely regarded as a vice.

I have been prompted to these reflections by a remarkable document pressed upon me, with a wild, pleading look of apology, by an insufferable person as I was leaving a dinner party he had utterly ruined with his ceaseless prattle. Though it will strike some tastes, no doubt, as too morbid for print, I submit it in the interests of sunlight, reason, and mercy:

HOW INNOCENTLY [*the document, written in a fluent hand on several hundred sheets of lawyer's yellow foolscap, begins*] it all began! I noticed a faint, not disagreeable itching in the back of my throat whenever anyone else talked for as long as two or three minutes. I would shake my head vigorously, and think that the sensation would pass, but by the fourth minute the itching became so unbearable that I *had* to interrupt. At first, my remarks bore a deceptive pertinence to the topics under discussion, and I flatter myself that in those early months no one but my wife, whose canny blue eyes developed a defensive narrowing tic, noticed anything amiss.

My first total blackout occurred toward the end of August.

It had been a very warm August, but that evening a little breeze sprang up off the bay, and my wife and I attended a dinner party with a few of our dearest friends. Never, I thought, had the food been so delicious, the wine so subtle, the ladies so lovely, and the gentlemen so sturdy, acute, and wry. Our conversation on the veranda seemed a veritable dance of ideas, counterthrusts, and graceful laughter. I was dazzled to think that here, in this specific house on the North American continent, Mankind's tortuous climb toward civilization had at last borne fruit. Imagine, then, my amazement when, in the private closeness of our car, as I hummed a popular air in celebration of a perfect night, my wife turned to me and snapped, "Why did you talk so much? You bored everybody silly."

"I?" I protested. "I said little, but that little, well."

"Stuff!" she snapped. "Your tongue didn't stop for four hours. You drove poor Maggie Wentworth absolutely to sleep. And as for Horace, you brought on a bilious attack that had him hiccuping like a cricket." [*Several pages of such dialogue are here expunged.*—ED.] Even now, I find it difficult to believe that her impression of the evening is the correct one. One piece of evidence, however—admittedly circumstantial—emerged to support her case. The Wentworths never had us back, though *they* owe *us*.

After this seizure I was more watchful of myself. I deliberately curtailed my conversational offerings, even in relation to subjects upon which I was plainly the best informed and possessed the most lively and intricate opinions. I made myself, as it were, a mere supplier of footnotes, and artificially withheld from my fellow-humans the riches of information and nuance I knew to be within me. I was on the verge of shucking this (as I thought) foolish and inhibiting cocoon when late one night, as I was briefly qualifying something someone else had said—scarcely, indeed, qualifying; merely restating his gist in more lucid and understandable terms—I noticed, to my horror, that a delicate but distinct glaze had overspread the faces of my auditors. It is impossible to convey the macabre effect. It was not so much that their eyes had gone out of focus (for some eyes were staring fixedly at me) or that their mouths had sagged open (for some mouths were rigidly clamped shut): It was the curious uniformity of complexion, as if with one swipe their faces had been painted with the same lacquer, an impalpable coating whose emotional color, translated into visual terms, was the yellow of distant wheat fields seen through a grimy train window. And, though I paused, gagging on my terror at this disgusting omen, *I went right on talking*. It was then that I realized that I was a hopelessly ill man.

My subsequent decay was not without its pretty phosphorescences. One of the most vivid, and in a way mystical, sensations is that of *repetition*. As words issue from one's mouth, one is conscious of having said them before, but with no idea of whether it was an hour ago, a week ago, or in another world altogether. The feeling is not unlike the universally experienced intuition of having been in a strange place at a previous time, which offers to some a comforting proof of the doctrine of reincarnation. The bore's repetition wears a kindred nimbus of romantic reassurance; though I know I have pronounced these words before, perhaps to this identical company, yet I have no inclination to stop. Indeed, the words seem enhanced by repetition, as in some aesthetic credos furniture and utensils are improved in beauty by the marks of wear left upon them by humble thumbs.

Becoming a bore is far from a simple, simultaneous decline of the mental and sensory faculties. On the contrary: some are unhealthily heightened. As one's stock of anecdotes and topics dwindles to a precious few, one's ability to relate these obsessive subjects to a running conversation increases. It is truly astounding with what ease the mind of the bore creates an illusory relevance! If, as has been said, the mark of the rational mind is the ability to perceive connections between unlike things, then the bore is truly in the forefront of rational beings. For instance: I am oppressed by a peculiar vague emotion, or circular set of propositions, about my home town that, boiled down to its essence, might go as follows: "It seems extraordinary to me that the town where I was born, and spent all my formative years, had nothing extraordinary about it. Yet is not this, in a sense, extraordinary?" Not that I ever state it so baldly. My effort to unburden myself of this strange message usually takes the form of a sentence beginning, "In the town where I grew up," and going on to describe some innocuous condition like the way the mailman walked up one side of the street and then down the other. Non-bores can have no conception of how many opportunities I perceive in the course of an hour to intrude this kind of information. A conversation on, say, cybernetics seems to my deranged but active brain an immense sieve full of holes crying to be plugged with a sentence beginning, "In the town where I grew up." The glaze on the faces around me is no longer a deterrent, since that particular varnish is applied now the moment I enter a room. I am indifferent to it; I am indifferent to sniggers, to yawns, to the creeping net of ostracism that is tightening around me and my family. There is one delight left in my life, one music toward whose enchanted strains my whole being is bent. My throat itches, my larynx inflates with air, my tongue contorts; and I am drowned in bubbling syllables of bliss.

Yet, between the luminous day of normality and the ecstatic night of boringness there exists a twilight, brief for some, agonizingly long for others, in which the sufferer flitters ambiguously among phantasmal shapes of embarrassment and shame. While his tongue happily lopes along, a remote corner of his mind involuntarily observes the dismal effects he is producing; in intervals of extreme lucidity he is even bored himself. It is in such a twilit moment that I have sat down to pen, before the black curtain falls finally, these hasty words, this quick cry. In the town where I grew up. . . . [*The remaining hundred and eighty thousand words of the confession, while of indubitable interest to the specialist, are well in excess of the needs of the general reader.*]

THE UNREAD BOOK ROUTE

Imagine two rectangles, representing the first and second stories of my home. Each contains an angular flux, clockwise and counterclockwise respectively, of arrows, lettered, at various elbows, A through G. This is the unread book route. Over the last eighteen months I have charted it by means of patient observation, phosphorescent tracing dyes, electronically tripped cameras, factory-tuned logarithmic tables, and some inspired —as they say in the scientific quarterlies—guesswork. While I dare not claim for my investigations an importance equal to the more publicized researches of the I.G.Y. (researches that have conclusively demonstrated, according to my reading of *Life*, that the ionosphere is shaped like a macaroni's cravat, that the continents are merely large irregular cherries in a wobble of silicon Jell-O, and that the Pacific Ocean bulges toward Tahiti whenever you leave the hot water running), nevertheless The Unread Book Route is one more piece fitted into the puzzle of the mysterious and irresistible currents that do so much to make our terrestrial existence discomfiting.

The books enter at A, which is the letter slot. I cut the slot myself, working with a bent keyhole saw, so that the inner lip of metal juts above the ragged wood and effectively blocks whatever letters the mailman attempts to insert. After rattling the brass flap angrily for up to five minutes, he rams his shoulder against the door, losing his powder-blue cap and twenty-five pounds of *National Geographics*, and throws everything into the foyer, including four dividend checks for the lady next door. After delivering the checks, and running after the mailman with his cap, I return to my house and find that the children have already torn open the Jiffy book envelopes, an operation that has left the floor evenly coated with iron-colored fluff.

At Point B, next to our four-sided three-legged table, the books are presented to me. I gratefully inhale the fragrance of the bindings, slice all uncut pages, and even read a few paragraphs. I am especially apt to begin reading if the book is one for which I have sent. For instance, *A History of Japan to 1334*, by George Sansom (Stanford University Press): the physical presence of this book, so substantial, so fresh, the edges so trim, the type so tasty, reawakens in me, like a Proustian talisman, the emotions I experienced when, in my youth, I ordered it. "About time I knew something about Japan up to 1334," I say again to myself, and again seem to stand overlooking a vast landscape bathed in lifting mist. Soon that distant line of trees, that vague row of Fujiwara regents, will embower my marching strides; that remote cottage, that Hōryūii monastery, will house me tonight. Then the dinner bell, or the doorbell, or the alarm bell, rings, and the unread book takes up its first station, at C, on top of the television set.

Here it resides for an indetermine period. As new arrivals pile in, the stack grows irregular, and by osmotic pressure they reshuffle themselves so that the largest are on the bottom, for stability. They withstand a constant sidewise pressure from a vase of pussy willows, and spasmodic tremors when the children manipulate the volume dial. Sometimes, even, a few of the upper, lighter books fall behind the set into the morass of wiring; but by and large they are secure here, in the shade of the pussy willows, on a high ledge where ashtrays and coffee cups and broken crayons seldom climb. So it always startles

me when, suddenly one night, they pull up stakes, spattering
the wallpaper with phosphorescent dye, and take a new stance,
at D, the top of a bookcase.

Here you would think they would find peace. This is a bookcase, after all, and they are books. But it is a bookcase in which
several years ago I scrupulously arranged, in chronological
order, shelves of American literature, English literature, Russian, Spanish, and Irish (a pretty triplet, I thought) literature
so neatly and tightly that our purchases in all of these categories have had to stop. True, there is more flexibility in the
top shelf, containing French books and "little, cute" volumes
like Peter Pauper editions of Malayan aphorisms, and in the
bottom shelf, reserved for big, strikingly uncute books—Belloc's
biography of Danton, the bound reports of the Rhode Island
Audubon Society, and college anthologies scribbled with insane notes like "Marvellous!," "Micro-macro," and "Cf. Romantic *Angst*"—but time with its relentless neap tide has
wedged even these catch-alls solid. So the unread books re-
cline uneasily on top, still on their sides, suffering the company
of porcelain figurines, water glasses full of dripping daffodils,
and children's drawings, which move around the house in a
sort of counter-swirl to the unread books. I have often noticed
how at this stage their jackets, though untouched, begin to
tatter with despair.

One night, when we are all asleep and except for the twitching of the thermostat the house is still, the unread books leap
into the air, sail through the kitchen door, bank jauntily over
the stove, and coast at a smart cant into the library (E), where
they settle, fluffing and cooing, on chair arms, sofa backs, hi-fi
speakers, and the space where my wife is supposed to write
letters. At first, I believe, they batter their wings against the
bookcase, but it is as futile as pigeons trying to roost on the
side of the U.N. building, for they meet a sheer wall of Bernard

Shaw, Penguin classics, paperbound theology, and other books too odd for the bookcase at D. Once, years ago, a few unread books found a purchase here, and it may be a racial memory of this that drives them into the room; but they find the meadows sere, the once-open range strung with barbed wire, and the rivers polluted with radioactive silt. It is not long before the more enterprising of the unread books are stomping up the stairs, and creeping into our bedroom.

F is a tiny table that stands beside our bed. I bought it at an auction, having failed to see that it was not a table at all but a stand in which to hold a large flowerpot. Accordingly there is a circular hole in the top, which we have patched with a slim volume of paintings by Paul Klee. The painting on the cover shows a bright pink face with three or four eyes, and it makes an unsteady, wrinkling surface. Now, *A History of Japan to 1334* is a tall, solid book; it needs firm support. The sides of the flowerpot stand are too low; *A History of Japan* keeps being shoved over the edge by *Black Lamb and Grey Falcon*, by Rebecca West, in one volume, a book so hefty I sprained my latissimus dorsi lifting it in and out of bed. Furthermore, the other unread books, hearing us scuffling around overhead, come pouring up the stairs and jump on the little table—that was never meant to hold anything except a flowerpot in the first place—and keep falling off and jumping again, like shipwreck survivors around the one lifeboat that got free of the rigging. Sometimes a whole dozen squeeze on at once, and then the Klee collapses, and they fall through the circular hole. Their bodies, after a mysterious subaqueous passage, come to surface at G.

G is a tiny room, once titled "the study," which I tricked out with shelves to hold papers, stamps, athletic trophies, rubber bands, and similar proofs of my masculinity. Unfortunately, the influx of broken toys, cracked mirrors, defunct light bulbs,

cranky children, sewing machines, and other things that puzzled my wife became so great that I was flooded away, and
was forced to abandon the shelves, which have become the
terraces of the Afterworld of unread books. Here they stand,
upright at last, in rigidly packed rows. There is no exit; the
unremitting arrival of new immigrants puts them under terrific
pressure, and, like the countless microörganisms that dedicated
their corpses to our petroleum deposits, like the millions of
once-green leaves compressed into the coal fields underlying
Wilkes-Barre, they form a rich resource for future ages.

ALPHONSE PEINTRE

*(An Interview Not Utterly Unlike Those in
"The Artist in His Studio," Text and Photographs
by Alexander Liberman)*

THE SQUALID HUT, near Rouen, whence issue the cryptically
dabbled bits of canvas that have soothed five generations of
art dealers is approached by an unspeakable dirt road winding
among depressingly dusty lime trees and appallingly tawdry
livestock. How true it is, I reflected, that artists are slovenly
about their environments! So deeply rutted was the road that
as I bounced to a stop in front of the master's residence a stack
of *Vogues*, which I had brought as my recommendation to the
reputedly inaccessible sage, leaped from the back seat of my
convertible and flew into the air like assaulted chickens. Or perhaps they were real chickens; I was amused to discover that
several lice-infested fowl had become fatally entangled with
the grille of my Mercedes.

I had been prepared by my Paris friends for the fact that
Peintre's living quarters were not commensurate with the elegance of his productions; but I had not been warned that the
shack was mounted on ten-foot stilts. The only access to the
hovel was by means of a movable ladder which, to judge from
the sounds of altercation within, someone was reluctant to put
down. At last, however, after I had nearly exhausted my battery
in beeping the horn, a cheery red female face appeared at one
of the windows, and a diaphanous old derelict clad in baggy

blue coveralls, grumbling in a language I could not understand, lowered the rickety steps into place. This grim wraith was Alphonse Peintre.

I had an excellent opportunity to study his face when, as I carried my cameras up the ladder, a rung snapped and to preserve my balance I seized his Orientally long, silken beard. His face was eroded by wrinkles as if by some never-ceasing geological process. His lips were thin and hard with peasant cunning. His ochre cheekbones suggested a possible Mongol strain in his blood. He wore a drab puce beanie on his abundant but unkempt locks, clotted with snaffles and burrs. But it was his eyes that held my attention. They were round with astonishment, their blue bleached as if by a sudden infusion of pain, and an indignant glint flashed deep in their lucid, oddly youthful depths.

His wife rushed forward to lift us both into the cottage. As I felt her broad crimson hands, roughened by homely labor, tighten around my abdomen, I realized who of the couple provided the physical strength. This faithful helpmate was *de la terre*. I perceived a paradox in so airy an art loyally sheltered by such powerful, earthy muscles. Mme. Peintre cradled her husband like a child and set him in the room's one furnishing, a worm-riddled rocking chair. "You have brought us luck," she confided to me. "You will pay for the chickens?"

It was a dispiriting room. A little wan light dribbled in across the thatched windowsills. Pots, peanut-butter jars, dried tubes, twisted coat hangers littered the floor. An icon hung cockeyed in one corner. The walls were entirely of canvas, punctured here and there where the good wife had snipped out pieces to sell to the American museums. Through these rents I saw a landscape from which all color had been drained by the vivid fancies of the artist's remorseless imagination. Some sections of the shabby wall writhed with superimposed scribbles, like the magic caves near Lascaux.

The venerable eremite slowly allowed a few words to escape his canny reserve. Though he had been a contemporary of Balzac, his words were not those of a senile man. How remarkably old these visual sorcerers live to be! It must be the relaxed work hours. "Giotto . . . blotto," he said, in response to a question of mine. "Michel Agnolo . . . a little dude." He called him "Agnolo," as you would a childhood friend. "Monet . . . *nada*. Poor Cézanne . . . a grind. He seemed always to be preparing for an examination that was never scheduled. Art is not like that. Art is like baby shoes. When you coat them with gold, they can no longer be worn. Do not take down my words," he protested with a sudden sly wave of his beautifully withered hand, encrusted with Byzantine rings, the ancient ascetic's one luxury. "They are foolish. Art is foolish. Since Watteau, *nada*. And myself. I try. The moon is coming closer. I am not afraid. It is no bigger than a pie plate. Do you have enough?"

We ate peanut-butter sandwiches—a typical meal of this *pays de Caux*. Mme. Peintre, a girlish grace imprisoned in her heavy body, adroitly usurped the rocking chair and fell asleep. Peintre scowled and squatted on the floor and began to twist coat hangers into unique and exquisite shapes. Absentmindedly he spat on my tripod, near my shoes. I assured him it was an accident. In the mysterious way of genius, he seemed to have retreated into himself. My conversational gambits fell unanswered, as if into an inscrutable primeval pool. Regretfully, I took my leave; in going out the door, I forgot—so charming and intense was the atmosphere of this consecrated interior—about the ladder, and fell ten feet with all my equipment. Looking up from my position on the foul ground, I saw Peintre's remarkable countenance framed in the crude portal, and was rewarded in a most unexpected way. The Olympian *hauteur* of his visage cracked, and the immortal smiled.

MR. EX-RESIDENT

(Assuming, Unlikely Though It Seems at First Blush,
That Harry S. Truman, Author of "Mr. Citizen,"
Also Wrote Adam's Memoirs)

A LARGE NUMBER of people have expressed curiosity as to how
Eve and I like residing out of Eden. The answer is very
simple. We like it fine.

I began as a farm boy, so the thorns and thistles of the
"outer world" are not news to me. We thoroughly enjoyed
our years in Eden, but now that they are over we find many
things to enjoy elsewhere. Pleasant as it was, Eden always had
the disadvantage for me personally of being a little too lush
and orderly. As the saying goes, I like some grit to my mash.

So many contradictory accounts of what happened have
been published that I think the time has come to set the record
straight. Now that my grandson Enoch has builded a city of
the same name, I know there is a firm watertight place where
the records can be kept. I think it is very important, whether
or not it causes embarrassment in Heaven, for the First Man
to set down in his own words his side of the story so that the
generations succeeding him in this world can understand their
present condition and why things are the way they are.

When the matter first came up of eating of the tree of
knowledge of good and evil, I consulted with Eve and with the
serpent and their consensus seemed to be that it could do no

harm and might do a lot of good. It is easy to identify mistakes in hindsight, but at the time this was the best available information I could get, and it was my responsibility to act upon it. And I did.

The following day, God came to me and asked, "Hast thou eaten of the tree, whereof I commanded thee that thou shouldest not eat?"

I thought this was a curious question, since if He were omniscient as supposed He must have already known that I certainly had. But I have never had any trouble keeping the reins on my temper. With the utmost patience and courtesy I explained the situation.

When I was done, He simply told me, "In the sweat of thy face shalt thou eat bread, till thou return unto the ground." I felt lucky at that, since what He said to Eve and the serpent was far worse.

We wasted no time getting out, once the circumstances had become definite. I expected no fanfare, so it was one of the deeply moving experiences of my life to see all the cherubim waving goodbye with their flaming swords. I had not in any way asked them to do this. It was a truly spontaneous demonstration.

Two things need to be cleared up, for the reason that there has been a lot of improper and inaccurate speculation written concerning them.

The first is this. At no time, then or since, have Eve and I exchanged recriminations. She was produced from my rib and I have never for a moment wanted my rib back. In my opinion, she did a wonderful job raising Cain and Abel in an environment that was necessarily unsettled and far from ideal. If the boys did not turn out exactly the way we had hoped, this is no excuse for the disproportionate publicity that has surrounded their quarrel. It is of course a tribute to the office of

First Man that everything that happens within his family circle attracts widespread comment.

Secondly, a lot of well-meaning—I will give them the benefit of the doubt—souls have expected us to resent how the serpent has insinuated himself into the good graces of subsequent administrations and is in fact enjoying a good deal of present prosperity. This shows they have no knowledge of the nature of the cosmos. It is the essence of the system that the serpent, having served his term with us, should seek "greener pastures." While I cannot feel that his advice was always in the best interests of my family, he was by his own lights successful and must be admired for it. History has been created by just this type of personality.

I have been called, among many other things, an optimist.

I do not think of myself as a optimist or a pessimist but as a normal human individual blessed with 100% excellent physical health since the day of my creation. At the time, a certain number of angels whom I do not wish to name doubted my ability to serve as First Man. I showed them that they were wrong. It is my sincere belief that any healthy man, placed in that position, could have done the job.

Though there is a lot wrong with the state of the world as we know it, I think entirely too much is made of the Fall. Eden just could not have accommodated all the men and women who now enjoy the blessings, qualified though they are in some instances, of earthly life. I lived in Eden many years and I flatter myself that I know more about its dimensions than most of the theological journals I make it my habit to read. These are written by good men, but their morbid preoccupation with Original Sin rubs me the wrong way, though I don't mind in the least whatever they say about me. I have no regrets. And I recommend that you have none either.

First Person Plural

Central Park

March 1956

ON THE AFTERNOON of the first day of spring, when the gutters were still heaped high with Monday's snow but the sky itself was swept clean, we put on our galoshes and walked up the sunny side of Fifth Avenue to Central Park. There we saw:

Great black rocks emerging from the melting drifts, their craggy skins glistening like the backs of resurrected brontosaurs.

A pigeon on the half-frozen pond strutting to the edge of the ice and looking a duck in the face.

A policeman getting his shoe wet testing the ice.

Three elderly relatives trying to coax a little boy to accompany his father on a sled ride down a short but steep slope. After much balking, the boy did, and, sure enough, the sled tipped over and the father got his collar full of snow. Everybody laughed except the boy, who sniffled.

Four boys in black leather jackets throwing snowballs at each other. (The snow was ideally soggy, and packed hard with one squeeze.)

Seven men without hats.

Twelve snowmen, none of them intact.

Two men listening to the radio in a car parked outside the Zoo; Mel Allen was broadcasting the Yanks–Cardinals game from St. Petersburg.

A tahr (*Hemitragus jemlaicus*) pleasantly squinting in the sunlight.

An aoudad absently pawing the mud and chewing.

A yak with its back turned.

Empty cages labelled "Coati," "Orang-outang," "Ocelot."

A father saying to his little boy, who was annoyed almost to tears by the inactivity of the seals, "Father [Father Seal, we assumed] is very tired; he worked hard all day."

Most of the cafeteria's out-of-doors tables occupied.

A pretty girl in black pants falling on them at the Wollman Memorial Rink.

"BILL & DORIS" carved on a tree. "REX & RITA" written in the snow.

Two old men playing, and six supervising, a checkers game.

The Michael Friedsam Foundation Merry-Go-Round, nearly empty of children but overflowing with calliope music.

A man on a bench near the carrousel reading, through sunglasses, a book on economics.

Crews of shinglers repairing the roof of the Tavern-on-the-Green.

A woman dropping a camera she was trying to load, the film unrolling in the slush and exposing itself.

A little colored boy in aviator goggles rubbing his ears and saying, "He really hurt me." "No, he didn't," his nursemaid told him.

The green head of Giuseppe Mazzini staring across the white softball field, unblinking, though the sun was in its eyes.

Water murmuring down walks and rocks and steps. A grown man trying to block one rivulet with snow.

Things like brown sticks nosing through a plot of cleared soil.

A tire track in a piece of mud far removed from where any automobiles could be.

Footprints around a KEEP OFF sign.

Two pigeons feeding each other.

Two showgirls, whose faces had not yet thawed the frost of their makeup, treading indignantly through the slush.

A plump old man saying "Chick, chick" and feeding peanuts to squirrels.

Many solitary men throwing snowballs at tree trunks.

Many birds calling to each other about how little the Ramble has changed.

One red mitten lying lost under a poplar tree.

An airplane, very bright and distant, slowly moving through the branches of a sycamore.

No Dodo

November 1955

LATELY, we've been pondering the pigeons in Bryant Park. It seemed to us that they showed a decided preference for the paving, and trod the grass gingerly and seldom. Only once did we see one roost in a tree. It was an awkward, touching performance, like that of a man tying the bow of an apron behind him. Why should the common pigeon be embarrassed in the presence of vegetation? Because, research showed, he is a descendant of the blue rock dove. *Columba livia* is a native of the cliffs and rocky islands of western Europe and northern Africa, with subspecies ranging from the Canary Islands to India and Japan. The American branch stems from some of the English colonists' domestic pigeons, who flew the coop, went wild, shed their fancy shapes (the shapes of domestic pigeons can be very fancy), reverted to the parent type, and headed for the cities. Pigeons, or doves, have never made much of a distinction between natural and man-made crannies. Song of Solomon 2:14 apostrophizes "my dove, that art in the clefts of the rock, in the secret places of the stairs." Homer speaks of "Messe's towers for silver doves renowned," and Juvenal describes "the tiled roof where the gentle pigeons leave their eggs." Tibullus asks, "Why need I tell how the sacred white pigeon flutters unmolested about the numerous cities of Syrian Palestine?" No other bird has been as widely revered. Disturbing their nests in the Mosque of Doves, Istanbul, is blasphemy. In 1925, the Bombay Stock Exchange was closed and riots were threatened because two European boys had ignorantly killed some street pigeons. Kama, the Hindu god of love (a minor deity), is sometimes depicted riding a dove. In Christian iconography, the dove represents the Holy Ghost. And, of course, there's Noah. The Arabian version of the Deluge contains a pretty touch. When the dove returned to the ark the second time, its feet were stained with red mud. Noah, realizing that this meant the waters were receding, prayed that the messenger's feet might remain that color. They have. There is a Filipino legend that, of all birds, only the dove understands the human tongue.

Pigeons have been the most faithful of man's feathered friends. Records of the bird's domestication extend back to the Fifth Egyptian Dynasty, around 3000 B.C. Homing pigeons have been used as messengers through the centuries from Cyrus the Great, of Persia, to yesterday's bootleggers. How they home is still something of a mystery. Keen eyes and a good memory just don't quite explain it, and neither do theories about magnetic or electro-magnetic control, sensitivity to light rays, the effect of air currents on the nasal passages or the semicircular canals, or "celestial orientation." Ancient Romans and medieval monks bred pigeons. Mary Queen of Scots and Queen Victoria were fanciers. The hobby is conjectured to be of Indian or Persian origin, and the results are so elaborate that it took Darwin ninety-eight pages to prove that jacobins, satinettes, barbs (the ideal barb's head resembles a spool), turbits, dragoons, fantails (when the fantail strikes his favorite pose, he can't see over his chest), visors, pouters (the pouter looks like a tennis ball stuffed into a glove), long-faced tumblers, inside tumblers (the inside, or parlor, tumbler is prized for his inability to fly a few feet without taking a backwards somersault), priests, nuns, monks, archangels, etc., etc., were all artificial variations of one bird. The difference noticeable in the markings of street pigeons is a vestige of their earlier domestication. Because their feather-color patterns provide an external record of hereditary influences, and because they are docile and hardy, pigeons are a favorite laboratory animal of modern geneticists.

Pigeons are social, somewhat timid, strong, and monogamous. Once mated, they customarily stay so for life. The cock as well as the hen broods the eggs, the hen working all night, the cock relieving her around ten in the morning and mooching off at four in the afternoon. The same schedule applies to the feeding of the young; both sexes secrete "pigeon milk" in their crops. Before coition, at the bonbon stage of courtship, the male feeds a regurgitated substance to the female. Maeterlinck called *Columba livia* "the most sedentary, most homekeeping, most habit-ridden of bourgeois." Fire will not budge a brooding pigeon. If a female leaves her nest before an egg has been laid, the male marches behind her, pecking at her head, until she returns or faints. A male will fight to the death defending the sanctity of his hearth. The nests are simple affairs—flat arrangements of twigs, feathers, straw, any old thing. The Museum of Natural History once possessed one made of paper clips; it was found near Wall Street. Are pigeons stupid? It is true that they will inadvertently trample their young to death in the nest; they carry only one twig at a time, whereas the sparrow carries two or three; and a pigeon will make romantic overtures to a bit of broken glass. But, pigeon boosters reply, pigeons have big feet and small fledglings; the sparrow makes a sloppy nest; and what's wrong with looking in a mirror? Certainly the bird is very eager to survive, unlike his cousin, the passenger pigeon, and his great-uncle once removed, the dodo.

New York City is a good town for pigeons. The health officials of London kill a third of the pigeon population each year. In 1945, Philadelphia started an anti-pigeon campaign, and it trapped twenty-six thousand birds before it admitted that pigeons are irrepressible. In 1930, the superintendent of the State Capitol in Albany poisoned a batch around the building, and the stirred legislators promptly passed the following law: "Pigeons shall not be killed within the limits of any city except for food purposes, or unless sick or injured beyond recovery." The only major local violation of the statute occurred in 1937, when an unknown fiend, in two sessions (August 10th and November 17th), fed a hundred Broadway pigeons strychnine pellets. The uproar, including a *Times* editorial entitled "St. Francis Must Weep," was huge. Building owners wage cold war against pigeons with spikes, prongs, metal netting, and lye-strewn or electrified ledges. The absence of filigrees, cornices, and other nook-rich ornamentation from the newer buildings is partly an anti-nesting device, though the pigeon theory of modern architecture should not be pursued to the exclusion of Frank Lloyd Wright. The bird's main Manhattan enemy, strange to relate, is the duck hawk, who swoops from bridges and skyscrapers. When Dr. Harry

Emerson Fosdick suggested that the predators nesting in the steeple of Riverside Church be wiped out, the city's falcon lovers raised a strenuous outcry. Not quite as strenuous, though, as that which greeted Magistrate Anthony Burke, who in the same month (July, 1936) handed down the opinion that people who feed pigeons are morons. This hit a lot of citizens, for upward of fifty thousand pigeons live in Manhattan on handouts plus garbage. Pigeons cannot vote, and only five are in the phone book—two Edwins, two Georges, and one Pete.

Voices in the Biltmore

April 1956

EVER ON THE LOOKOUT for a feasible means of rejuvenation, we took ourself to the Biltmore Hotel one afternoon during the college Easter vacations. As we had hoped, the cocktail lounge, that pond of perpetual youth, brimmed with high spirits, forced laughter, and expressively exhaled smoke. The room—"room" is a weak word for a volume of space enclosed by Babylonian veils of palms, pillars, and mirrors, and vertically limited by a ceiling with a truly supernal apogee—seemed quite overheated. Every bright, smooth face we saw was flushed. Whether the room was warming the youngsters or the youngsters the room is a conundrum we were too hot to unravel. We watched a forward-looking hat precede the pink face under it across the public view; noticed large numbers of Alexanders and whiskey sours—easy transitions, both, between orange pop and gin; dodged six boys, four of whom were shaking hands and two of whom were carrying tables; savored the overhead fragment "*I* say he's an Existentialist. *He* says he's a Jesuit"; and scuttled into a nook near a table of burly youths who were bringing a great weight of attention to bear on two pretty girls with slender necks. Their conversation, as we caught it, was only slightly less confused than this transcription, here printed for its value as an American document:

"Hello. Hello, this is Harry Belafonté." Laughter. (All voices, unless otherwise specified, are male. We were unable to sort out the four or five boys, who looked exactly alike, though of graduated sizes, like boxes of breakfast food.)

"Man, you're fantastic."

"And he said, 'Are you going to be a host tonight?' I said, 'Host tonight?' and just looked at him."

"She needed a *draft* card—always what I wanted."

"Hello, this is Morey Amsterdam."

"Let's go up to Two Hundred and Forty-second Street."

"Fantastic!"

"I have a car."

"Stop that."

(The above interchange we took to be the warmup. Now they began to address the girls directly.)

"Wouldn't you all [inaudible]?"

"No." (Female voice.)

"Waiter! *Wait-er!*"

"Allo. Allo. This is Bridey Murphy."

"Hey, Les, this is good."

"What?"

"Your whiskey sour."

"What's *this?*" (Female voice.)

"My *name*. What's the matter, you don't like it?" (Tones gruff with embarrassment.)

"We're calling for you if we knew where to call for you."

"No, she's leaving her boy friend." (This was the other female voice, one with a titter in every other syllable.)

"Hey, you know where Atlas holds up the world?"

"Maybe." (Female.)

"Right in front of that statue."

"There's going to be fourteen boys and eight girls."

"Carol's your *last* name?"

"Ann, meet Bob, Joseph, Jack, and Lester the Fester. Ann."

"No, no. We're asking you out for the *evening*."

"Cut it out."

"That's O.K. They're roommates."

"In Scranton?"

"Don't they dig coal in Scranton?"

"Oh, your father's a coal miner."

"Hello, this is Audie Murphy."

"Good old New York."

"You know anybody from the Philippines?"

"This is the most honest girl at the table. You hear what she just said?"

"Two girls from Vietnam! Please stand up, girls." (Voice raised in mock-ceremonial manner.)

"We are gratified to have with us two girls from the free state of Vietnam."

"We have a car."

"I'm singing my way into your heart."

"Come with us now to the Biltmore." (Girlish laughter.)

"Am*bass*ador, boy."

"This *is* the Biltmore, dope."

"We have a car parked in Kinney's parking lot."

Suddenly the boys, as if harking to an ultrasonic whistle, left, marching out in single file, their stride jouncy. The girls (there seemed to be three now) made superior little noises with their tongues and teeth. The following voices are all female.

"No, I didn't like him *at all*."

"He was *très* peculiar."

"I like the one who sat here."

"This one had only one side of his collar buttoned, did you notice?"

"No, I wasn't embarrassed. I've got very hardened, believe you me."

"I thought Tony was *nice*?"

"I used to get *so* embarrassed."

The three girls stood up, fastened capes around the chaste white collars of their dresses, became women, and were heard no more.

Our Own Baedeker

March 1956

In ANTARCTICA, everything turns left. Snow swirls to the left; seals, penguins, and skua gulls pivot to the left; the sun moves around the horizon right to left; and lost men making a determined effort to bear right find they have made a perfect left circle. Sunlight vibrating between white snow and white clouds creates a white darkness, in which landmarks and shadows disappear. A companion three feet away may vanish, and moments later rematerialize. On the other hand, whales and ships appear inverted in the sky. The sun may appear to rise and set five times in a day. Mountains actually over the horizon seem to loom close at hand. Minor irregularities in the ice tower like steeples. All these illusions are created by a combination of the oblique solar rays, the refraction and reflection of light among strata of warm and cold air, and the appalling lucidity of a dust-free, nearly vaporless atmosphere. In unclouded sunshine, the eye can follow an observation balloon for sixteen miles of its ascent into an inky-purple sky. Sudden veils of intense blueness fall over the world and in a few minutes are mysteriously lifted. When the sun is low, the sky appears green. Men exhale, in their crystallized breath, iridescent rainbows. Weather rainbows are white. The wind-driven snow charges men's noses and fingertips with static electricity, which is given off as a phantom luminescence.

For centuries, the continent itself was a phantom. From the time men first recognized that the earth was spherical, a great land mass in the south was imagined. In 1539, Emperor Charles V, of the Holy Roman Empire, appointed Pedro Sancho de Hoz governor of an area shown on maps of the period as stretching from the tip of South America across the pole to China. European scholars equated southerliness with fecundating warmth. Alexander Dalrymple, an eighteenth-century hydrographer for England's East India Company, predicted that the human population of the unknown continent would be found to exceed fifty million. In 1768, Lieutenant James Cook was sent by the British on a secret mission to locate the southern land mass and "to observe the genius, temper, disposition, and number of the natives and endeavour by all proper means to cultivate a friendship and alliance with them." Cook was unable to penetrate the ice pack, and concluded that if a continent lay beyond it, it was uninhabitable and inhospitable. How true! Antarctica more nearly resembles Mars than the earth we live on. It has no trees, no rivers, no land animals except a few degenerate insects, no vegetation other than some doughty moss and lichen, and no political or economic significance, though it may have some any day now. Permanent bases are being established by scientists of many of the nations involved in the antarctic aspect of the International Geophysical Year 1957–58. Russia thus far has not pressed the claims that the offshore explorations of Czar Alexander I's Admiral von Bellingshausen might justify. In 1948, though, the Kremlin ominously resurrected and published his report. Hitler once dropped thousands of swastika-stamped darts into a mammoth stretch of ice, named it New Swabia, and left it at that. Britain, France, Norway, Australia, New Zealand, Chile, and Argentina profess to own wedges of the pie. The United States has recognized no claims. Our antarctic policy, reportedly due for an overhaul, was established by Secretary of State Hughes in 1924, when he asserted that the *sine qua non* of territorial rights is permanent settlement.*

Rain and disease are practically strangers to the antarctic. The air is sterilized by ultraviolet rays, which are present in enormous quantities. Penguins, tough birds in other ways, have no resistance to germs. Expeditions never catch cold until they return to civilization. In a sense, the continent lacks even time. In 1947, members of Byrd's expedition visited the hut of the English explorer Scott. In thirty-five years, nothing had

---

* This remains our policy. In 1959 the United States proposed a treaty, accepted by twelve nations, which would preserve Antarctica as a territory of scientific research free from national claims. Though several nations, including the United States and the Soviet Union, have established year-round bases, Antarctica remains the most amicable of continents. Russo-American amicability has a long history here: Captain Nathaniel Palmer's claim to be its discoverer (in November, 1820, he sighted a strange coastline still named the Palmer Peninsula) was obligingly reinforced by von Bellingshausen, who habitually referred to the land mass as "Palmer's Land." Since 1956, scientific exploration, besides collecting much meteorological data, has discovered several striking mountain ranges and unexpected warm patches. The thesis that the continent is divided, beneath the bridging ice, by a strait between the Ross and Weddell seas has been advanced and generally rejected. Admiral Richard Byrd, whose lifelong devotion to the antarctic spanned the eras of individual heroism and of massive mechanized assault, died in 1957.

changed. The London magazine on the table could have been printed the day before. There was no rot in the timbers, no rust on the nailheads, no soot on the windowsills. Outside, a sledge dog that had frozen while standing up still stood there and looked alive. Explorers have no qualms about eating food that was cached decades previously. Admiral Byrd, the world's leading Antarcticophile, has suggested that the land might be used as a refrigerator for the world's food surpluses. Books could also be stored there, out of geopolitical harm's way and in an air where even the tabloids would not yellow. Were it not for the lung-scorching effect of sub-zero temperatures, this highest and driest of continents would make an excellent tuberculosis sanatorium. Antarctica is a plateau. Its mean altitude is six thousand feet—twice that of Asia, its tallest competitor. Its land area equals that of Australia and the United States combined. The seas surrounding it are not only the roughest but the richest in the world, with a greater weight of diatoms and plankton than tropical waters have. The land probably contains all the baser metals. Its resources of coal are judged to be the largest in the world—a geological puzzle, since there is no reason to assume that the south-polar region was ever warm enough for luxuriant vegetation. The most prominent thesis, supported by glacier scratches and the wide-ranging fossils of the primitive fern Glossopteris, posits Gondwanaland—a vast continent in the southern hemisphere two hundred million years ago, when the flat, swampy earth supported gigantic tree ferns, abundant mosses, and the earliest vertebrates. According to the "continental drift" theory, this mass of land shifted around a good bit, the surface of the earth being as loose as a puppy's skin, and eventually fragmented into the pieces now called Africa, South America, Australia, New Zealand, and Antarctica—the last a once tropical realm brought to rest at the bottom of the world and buried in ice.

Ice—of two sorts, white (compressed snow) and blue-green

(frozen water)—is what Antarctica has lots of. Ten quadrillion tons, say, plus a few billion created by the lack of centrifugal force near the poles. A man weighs almost a pound more at the South Pole than he does at the equator. Glaciers, sliding on water melted by the pressure of their own weight, flow away from the pole, squeeze through notches in the rim of mountain ranges, and extend themselves over the sea in the form of ice shelves. The largest shelf, the Ross, has the area of France. Chips as big as Manhattan crack off the shelves. These icebergs are carved by wind and waves into the shapes of palaces, cathedrals, pagodas, men, and angels before dissolving in temperate waters. In 1927, one was measured and found to be a hundred miles square—the size of two Connecticuts. The snow precipitation does not equal the ice lost in the form of bergs, so a recession of the icecap is believed to be taking place. Were it to melt completely, seeds held in suspension millions of years might germinate. Strange viruses and bacteria could be unleashed on the world. New York City would be under three hundred feet of water. This is not likely to happen in our time.

Postal Complaints

October 1956

UP TO NOW, nobody has breathed a word in defense of the dip pens Postmaster General Summerfield is ousting from post offices across the nation, and if we don't speak up the pens will go out thinking they didn't have a friend in the world. (Nobody said much when the mailboxes were made as garish as beer advertisements, or when the noble series of Presidential profiles on our postage stamps gave way to an ill-engraved gallery of lifeless mugs, but let it pass, let it pass.) We liked the old pens; the ink flowed from the nibs dark and luminous, the faint scratching was an agreeable accompaniment to composition, the cork holder felt airy and suave between the fingers, and even the most abject handwriting took on an angular distinction. We are thinking especially of the square-tipped nib, though the bowl-shaped, too, induced more real penmanship than any flow-forever, jet-styled pen. True, some post-office pens were splayed, split, and encrusted, and some wells dry, but seeing a herd of scrawny cattle we do not curse the suffering animals. Few people are fit to tend a cow, and fewer are competent to hold a pen. To seize, to press, to frown and crush was for many the exercise of their certificated literacy.

The pens, like modern poetry and Dean Acheson, were abused in a tone of impregnable smugness. We once overheard, in a Vermont post office, a woman rest the case for democracy on their wretchedness. "Compare these pens with the bank's," she instructed the child with her. "The Post Office is a state-run monopoly; you take what it gives you. The banks operate in a competitive system, and have to please their customers." The bank, as will happen in Vermont, was right across the street, and we found there the ball-point instruments usual in local temples of deposit, insultingly chained to their tuberous sockets. We hope the child's conversion to the free way of life did not hinge on this lesson alone. Ball-point pens began as a vulgar novelty for subaqueous scribes. The industry's publicists have shown great vigor, and thanks to them ink may become as quaint a liquid to the next generation as kerosene is to this, but their product still unrolls a pale, dull line, whose total lack of the thin-and-thick elements that quicken calligraphy is not redeemed by an erratic splotchiness.

Perhaps the inverse ratio between beauty and efficiency is

rigid and not to be bucked. The candle was a graceful, ardent, and numinous method of illumination, but fluorescent tubes in gawky casings are no doubt easier, in the optometrical sense, on the eyes. We consent to hideous brightness. However, it seems that Progress, in order to maintain the appearance of itself, must sacrifice to the dumb god Era its own best fruits. The roll-top desk was the most functional desk ever devised; Functionalism swept it away. The customary resident of that desk, the dip pen with metal nib, retained the eloquence of the goose quill and saved the geese. When Summerfield moved, the geese stood idly by.

March 1958

POSTMASTER GENERAL SUMMERFIELD is that rare combination, a man of ideas and a man of action. No sooner did he conceive of red-white-and-blue mailboxes than they twinkled from every street corner. One minute he learned that dogs bite postmen; the next, he was hurling thunderbolts of excommunication at impenitent owners. Congress dared balk at budget time last spring; Summerfield declared Saturday a legal holiday. And, with a divine imperiousness, he stamped his own Christmas cards with four-cent stamps. In view of this dynamic record, we have no hope that he will be frustrated in his scheme to impose two billion dollars' worth of improvement upon post offices across the nation. We mourn, nevertheless. It used to be that in any town from Bangor to Fresno the heartsick stranger could find honesty, industry, piety, and free reading matter in two places: the post office and the public library. Since Andrew Carnegie couldn't be everywhere, in many hamlets the post office was the sole repository of our traditions. It rises before the imagination now: the village post office, with its quaint grilled windows, its ink-stained floors, its hideous orange writing shelf, its curiously nibbled blotters, its "wanted" posters for Dillinger and Aaron Burr, and its twin letter slots dividing the world into two great halves, "Local" and "Out of Town." Framed by the window marked "Postal Savings" (another of Summerfield's victims, along with the nib pen), the postmaster himself is seen—his shirtsleeves secured by elastics, his glasses hung on the tip of his nose—alternately dispensing gossip and stamped envelopes. Beside him stands his wife, a pencil in her hair, weighing packages. Some are enormous; she forces a grin as she lifts them. Over by the wall, next to the radiator, the town idler lingers, pretending to fill out money-order blanks. Uncle Sam gesticulates from the bulletin board; a W.P.A. mural, executed with Assyrian dignity, fades above the transom. The laughter of the sorting clerks filters in from the back room. . . . The vision fades.

Instead, we see a cinder-block cube, painted indigo, scarlet, and ivory. Within, a loudspeaker murmurs cocktail music as shoppers promenade along clearly marked lanes, between pyramids of sanitarily wrapped Defense Bonds, postcards, and stamps. A sign proclaims, "5¢ STAMP SPECIAL—1,000 FOR $49.98." Another importunes, "SEND A PACKAGE TO BRITAIN FOR JUST 20¢ DOWN." At the door sits a young man in white, hammering a cash register; $2,000,000,000.00 is the sum he has just rung up.

Old and Precious

March 1957

UP AT THE THIRTEENTH ANNUAL NATIONAL ANTIQUES SHOW, held in the not undingy basement of Madison Square Garden, we saw more old and precious things than you could shake a stick at. For that matter, a person shaking a stick in among all those Staffordshire inkwells, Baccarat chandeliers, hurricane lamps, crystal *bobêches*, Japanese *netsukes*, *doré* bronze candelabra, Zuñi necklaces, Bohemian tankards, vellum music sheets, bisque clocks, Basque jugs, and specimens of dragware, creamware, queen's ware, stoneware, pearlware, and colored, cut, blown, pressed, and authentic milk glass would doubtless be removed from the premises—quite properly, too. All the booths—and they were legion—were numbered. We paused by F-15, distinguished by a huge green metal cow, a hideous brittle pillar about the size of an umbrella stand, and an 1807 sampler upon which a childish artisan had inscribed, "May I with equal art engrave each gentle Virtue on my heart and as Life wears away may I grow wiser and better each Day. The Ways of Wisdom are ways of pleasantness and all her paths are peace." Anxious to set off on the pleasant ways of wisdom, we asked F-15's proprietor, a tall, elegantly turned-out gentleman, what the cow was. "A weather vane," he said, in a tone of who-doesn't-know-that.

"It looks heavy for the purpose," we said.

"On the contrary, it's light. It's hollow," he said, and rapped the creature's resounding flank, then punched its head. "They always weighted the head, for balance, so it would turn."

"Oh. And that?" We indicated the umbrella stand.

"Hungarian. Made in Budapest. Eighteenth-century."

"Uh, what does it do?" we asked.

"Do? It doesn't do, it *is*," he replied. "It's a pedestal. Something stood on it. Now, *that* is a stein." He pointed at a ponderous mug decorated with drunken trolls doing the Germanic version of the light fantastic in the convex confines of a bas-relief tavern, and waved us off.

At G-5, we studied a *fin-de-siècle* painting of a child with elevated eyeballs. The nineteenth century, to judge by the relics recovered from its ruins, had a much keener *Innigkeit* toward animals than toward human beings. The innocence of the child's face was so vacuous, so total, that it gave us a queer, embarrassing impression of nudity. In fact (forgive us if we sermonize), the Victorian era was, in its sly way, appallingly naked. Gladstone's minions made lamp bases out of the bodies of young marble girls and covered footstools with cloth the pink of painted skin. Even the vases—florid, nippled, with provocative concavities—are scarcely fit for twentieth-century eyes. Seeking chastity, we turned to the consoling Puritanism of a whalebone swift, which expanded, with mathematical flexibility, at a touch.

The Carlebach Gallery has established a display of Burmese, Chinese, French, and Hindu chess sets. Rooks were, variously, pagodas, castles, and howdah-heavy elephants. My Sister and I, Stein Specialists, had assembled vessels of wood, china, silver, brass, and opaline, in the shapes of skulls, roosters, monkeys, monks, Bismarck, nuns, foxes, George Washington, slaves, fops, Churchill, and a woman's bare legs. In one nook were some old maps of the American Northeast, with strange nations like Pensylvania, Nova Jersey, Nova York, and Pars Aouanushionigy squeezed in between the Atlantic and Lake Ontario. In another, the Sons of the American Revolution had arranged George Washington's sugar-loaf crusher, bleeding knives, fob seal, telescope, dress sword, sextant, and shoe-measuring scale for our edification, along with Martha Washington's lace needle and formal slippers. She had tiny feet. Speaking of feet, there was the Joseph Burger collection of footwear, which proved that the poorer the wearer, the more sensible the shoe. The Mexican peasant's leather sandals, the Chinese coolie's "bird's-nest" boots, and the Norwegian yeoman's woven shoes set a norm of comfort and simplicity from which sophistication could only depart, tweaking the toes upward (Turkey and Syria), adding square flaps to the front (Bohemia), piling on width (dunderbludgeons, popular under Henry VIII), adding height (Japanese clogs), and, in a frenzy of civilization, withering the foot itself into a pitiful flipper that could fit into a five-inch envelope of flowered cloth (China).

Our own feet began to ache. We hastily glanced at a Bible owned, each in his time, by Charles I and Benjamin Franklin; at aboriginal vacuum cleaners, their sucking action created by metal pumps (1905), scissor bellows (1907), and accordion bellows (1911); and at the American Museum of Photography's array of stereoscopes, crystallotypes, graphascopes, daguerreotypes, melainotypes, ambrotypes, and ferrotypes. On the way out, we experimentally opened what we took to be a fancy toothpick holder. Inside, there was a miniature buttonhook for a baby's shoes. How precious. How old.

Spatial Remarks

November 1957

LAST WEEK we passed several anxious days tending the man in the moon, for whom previously we had never much cared. "The moon," a third-grade teacher once told us brusquely, "is a stone. A mammoth stone." That seemed to sum it up. Debunked as a deity, stripped of its authority to cause madness and promote crops, nervously plucking at the tides like an old pensioner perpetually adjusting a blanket, the satellite (to use the word in its primitive sense) was a heavenly deadhead. Yet when we read that the Russians might celebrate their birthday party by splashing a red stain across a breadth of lunar craters, it could have been our own face they were planning to spatter with ink, so great was our indignation, alarm, and shame.

The rumor seemed plausible enough. The handy phrase "Red Moon" had been bouncing through the headlines for the past month. And any man or bear intent on showing off his muscles will go for the biggest rock he sees. On the night before the day that in Russia would mark the ruby anniversary of the Bolshevik Revolution, we were in a country house, so the sky was much with us. It had cleared for the first time in November; the moon was brilliant and a hair less than full. The pure and venerable disc, tastefully touched with shadows named by the homely astronomy of a more deferential time Aristotle, Plato, Copernicus, Newton, Hell, Beer, and Mare Serenetatis, suddenly seemed precious, like one coin we had saved never to spend. Bidding the moon good night, we wondered in what shape it would rise again—with one cheek meretriciously rouged, or perhaps with the entire head split in two by a festive cobalt bomb or even fragmented into a cloud of triangular asteroids. There was as yet no burlesque, however brutal, of the celestial landscape that seemed beyond the youthful powers of our companion in world leadership.

Troubled, we woke when it was still dark, and went to the window, to see, through a screen of leafless elm branches, the moon half submerged on the horizon—bloated, cockeyed, and, in the orange dawn, transparent. Lord, we thought, the moon has foundered! Our wife, also awake now, assured us the moon was merely setting in its accustomed manner, and together we watched it sink from view, plunge on its way, poor, blind, dumb thing, to the other side of the earth, where an eclipse and heaven knew what strange assault awaited it. How reluctantly it abandoned the obsolescent safety of the American sky!

The next night, the mammoth stone returned unharmed—indeed, augmented and completely full. We were grateful. Whether it was the honor of the universe or of our country that had survived a crisis we are as yet too addled by moonbeams to declare.

September 1959

TWENTY-TWO MONTHS AGO, we wrote in this space of our deep, primeval fear that Soviet Russia would celebrate the revolution's fortieth anniversary by splashing red paint on the face of the moon. This threat of heavenly vandalism was in the wind, you may remember, shortly after the first sputnik violated the azure serene of our national vanity. Since that innocent awakening, sublunar space has become as crowded with peculiar missiles as a panel of "Krazy Kat"; the phrases "in orbit" and "launching pad" have entered our advertising slang; the fizzles at Cape Canaveral have blended with the friendly sizzling of breakfast bacon; and the United States government, in all seriousness, has selected seven young fathers from dreamy towns like East Derry, New Hampshire, to colonize the circumambient vacuum. Perhaps television comedians and the backs of Kix boxes have made this whole awesome business too familiar to all of us. At any rate, the Soviet flag has pricked the moon, and we feel no pain.

March 1963

SCIENCE takes away with one hand what it gives with the other. No sooner do Russian scientists claim that they have revived two lizards that had been frozen in the Siberian tundra for five thousand years than American scientists announce that there is no life whatever on Venus. In a way, we're relieved, for there's so much life in France, Cuba, and the subway these days that it's a comfort to know there are still a few underdeveloped areas in the universe. But in a way we're sorry, for the tendrilous, polyoptical Venutian was, along with the wispy, transparent Lunite and the green-skinned, snaggle-toothed, canal-building Martian, a childhood friend. How vivid the populations of other planets once seemed—far more imaginable than the residents of Cambodia or Chicago! The people on Jupiter were terribly squat and slow, because of the intense gravity; when they moved, it was like lava pouring, and when they talked, it was like furnaces grumbling. The inhabitants of Saturn always wore wide-brimmed hats and hoopskirts, whereas the folks on Neptune swam everywhere they went, carrying tridents. Pluto, so remote, cold, and small, seemed the planetary poor relation, and we pitied the cosmic hillbillies who had to live there, clad in rags, drinking cheap sulphates, and trying to warm their shivering limbs in the rays of a sun no bigger than a star. At the opposite end of the system, but somewhat kindredly underprivileged, were the almost Caribbean individuals sweltering out their lazy days on Mercury, which always kept the same side toward the sun, and where everything this side of silicon melted, making machinery impossible and architecture unstable.

Now they tell us this is all fancy. Venus, far from being a tropical paradise beneath its mantle of perpetual clouds, is a baking limbo of eight hundred degrees Fahrenheit. Though there is still hope that a bit of moss enlivens Mars, the planets have, in effect, been given a clean slate. They are innocent of life, and the earth, which is so guilty of it, can feel a little safer, and a little lonelier.

August 1964

WE LOOKED FORWARD with avidity to the pictures of the moon sent back by Ranger VII, but now that they are in *Life*, between Lyndon Johnson and the Vanderbilts, we confess ourself disappointed. What did we expect? Not, really, a gridwork of streets and the tops of little bald horned heads. But some message, some brief scrawl from God, a legible graffito on that invitingly blank and conspicuous surface. Instead, we got the same old pockmarks and smears we'd known were there all along: a riddled, wrinkled old celestial hide spattered with craters idiotically round and arbitrarily disposed. From four hundred and eighty miles away, the moon still has a semblance of terrain and wears a kind of face. At two hundred and thirty-five miles, the ridges and splotches are smoothing into a milky, speckled blandness. At eighty-five miles, the blandness is growing tasty, and the curdled circularity of the holes begins to remind us of—yes, the closer we get to the moon, the more it looks like cheese, presumably green.

Dinosaur Egg

April 1958

EASTER WEEK made us think of (a) eggs and (b) how old we are getting, which two preoccupations naturally led us to a concern with the oldest egg in New York—a dinosaur egg a hundred and twenty million years old. This egg rests in that catch-all of the ages, the Museum of Natural History, whose Curator of Fossil Reptiles and Amphibians, Dr. Edwin H. Colbert, told us, "We acquired it in a trade with a little museum in southern France—Aix-en-Provence. They found quite a few of these eggs not far from the surface near the mouth of the Rhone. Harvard University has another. Dinosaurs made nests and deposited eggs in them, much as alligators and crocodiles do today. For some reason, these didn't hatch. In time, they cracked, and the goo—the albumen and yolk—ran out, and mineral-bearing water and sand flowed in and solidified into rock."

A woman with harried hair and anxious eyes burst into the office where we were talking and exclaimed, "Dr. Colbert, there's a man from Guatemala waiting downstairs with some strange bones he wants you to look at!"

Dr. Colbert's shell, unlike the egg's, didn't crack; he calmed the lady and said to us, "While this egg is the oldest in the city, far older ones have been found. Our egg is Jurassic—that is, in the vicinity of a hundred million years old. The oldest existing vertebrate eggs were dug up in Texas and date from Permian times—about twice as long ago. They are at Harvard. We have some eggs from Mongolia that are Cretaceous. A few bits of what may be embryonic bone can be glimpsed in them. These are smaller than the Jurassic egg, and so are the Permian eggs. We don't know what creature laid the Permian eggs; our Jurassic egg is pretty certainly from a sauropod dinosaur that was about forty feet long. The egg is twice the size of an ostrich egg, which, of course, is small in relation to the size of the parent. That's how reptiles are; they lay many smallish eggs. Our egg is about as big as they come."

We thanked Dr. Colbert and went downstairs to look at this wonder. The egg sat alone in a glass case, thousands of miles and millions of years from Mother. She was pictured, in white ink, above her egg; she looked like a tadpole evenly mounted on four lumpy legs resembling an elephant's. Her head was a mere cursory termination of a long and rather lovely neck. The expression in her eye was faint but earnest; she was probably not very bright, but good. Beneath the picture was written "*Hypselosaurus priscus.*" The egg was mostly a smooth yellowish-gray stone, much wider than it was high, like a partly deflated volley ball. The stone was cracked and chipped yet clearly ovoid. To sections of the surface clung curving flakes of the shell, its texture delicately stippled, its color a blackened but still fairly lambent reddish-brown. The shell was less than an eighth of an inch thick; its fragments adhered to the rock with a gentle, even tender convexity.

The little children in their Easter clothes, emerging goggle-eyed from under the horrors of the adjacent Tyrannosaur Hall, tended to pause by the egg.

"There's an egg!" a mite cried.

"I *wanted* you to see this," a schoolteacher told her brood.

"It's shaped funny," a little boy complained.

Most of the onlookers rushed up to the case, gazed a long moment, and walked away silently. Nearby were Iguanodon footprints a yard square; bones the size of boulders littered the wall. Comparatively, the egg was a pebble. The emotions of its viewers seemed to be, in sequence, expectation, surprise, readjustment, a certain ineffable content and pleasure, and, lastly, disappointment.

A man and his son, dressed in matching lumberjack shirts, came up. "There's the dinosaur egg," the father said, with a pride almost paternal.

The boy, plump and saucy, stared and said, "It doesn't look like a dinosaur egg to me."

"That's what they look like," said the father.

Upright Carpentry

May 1958

WE RECENTLY had a carpenter build a few things in our house in the country. It's an old house, leaning away from the wind a little; its floors sag gently, like an old mattress. The carpenter turned his back on our tilting walls and took his vertical from a plumb line and his horizontal from a bubble level, and then went to work by the light of these absolutes. Fitting his planks into place took a lot of those long, irregular, oblique cuts with a ripsaw that break an amateur's heart. The bookcase and kitchen counter and cabinet he left behind stand perfectly up-and-down in a cockeyed house. Their rectitude is chastening. For minutes at a stretch, we study them, wondering if perhaps it isn't, after all, the wall that is true and the bookcase that leans. Eventually, we suppose, everything will settle into the comfortably crooked, but it will take years, barring earthquakes, and in the meantime we are annoyed at being made to live with impossible standards.

Crush vs. Whip

June 1958

APPARENTLY, the St. Louis Cardinals are much more friable than they used to be, for a paper in San Francisco recently ran the headline "GIANTS CRUSH CARDINALS, 3–1." Now, we don't want to suggest that our city's eldest franchise has got in with a group of orange squeezers who don't know real pulverization when they see it. There's been too much of such carping already. When a boy leaves home, a mother's duty is to hold her tongue, we always say. While voices around us cried that the West Coast was, variously, a vile limbo, an obscure religious sect, a figment of Walter O'Malley's fevered imagination, and a tar pit of busherism certain to fossilize whatever it enveloped, we kept mum. As a reward to ourself for restraint, therefore, we *will* offer some advice about the science or art of baseball-headline verbs. These we have seen evolve from a simple matter of "WIN" and "LOSE" into a structure of periphrasis as complex as heraldry in feudalism's decadence. New York City, now a quaint port known principally for her historical monuments, once boasted three—we swear it, *three*—baseball teams and a dozen daily newspapers. The lore accumulated here should be passed on to headline writers in all the fresh, brash towns likely to be visited as the major leagues, driven by a dark fatality, continue their migration toward Asia.

The correct verb, San Francisco, is "WHIP." Notice the vigor, force, and scorn obtained, quite without hyperbole. This table may prove helpful:

3–1—WHIP
3–2—SHADE
2–1—EDGE
1–0—(Pitcher's name) BLANKS[1]

Turning back and working upward, we come to 4–2, known professionally as "the golden mean," or "absolute zero." The score is uniquely characterless. The bland terms "BEAT" and "DEFEAT" are called in from the bullpen (meaning an area in

---

[1] Below, in smaller type, you may have "Twirls 3–(4–, 5–) Hitter." Two-hitters are "spun." For a one-hitter, write "Robbed of No-hitter."

which pitchers not actually in the game may "warm up"). However, 4–1 gets the coveted verb "VANQUISH." Rule: Any three-run margin, *provided the winning total does not exceed ten*, may be described as a vanquishing. If, however, the margin is a mere two runs and the losing total is five or more, "OUT-SLUG" is considered very tasty. You will notice, S.F., the trend called Mounting Polysyllabism, which culminates, at the altitude of double digits, in that trio of Latin-root rhymers, "ANNIHILATE," "OBLITERATE," and "HUMILIATE." E.g., "A's ANNIHILATE O's, 13–2."

Special cases:

1. If the home team is on the short end of the score, certain laws of mutation apply. "SHADE" becomes "SQUEAK BY." For "OUTSLUG," put "WIN OUT IN SLOPPY CONTEST." By a judicious exploitation of "BOW," the home team, while losing, can be given the active position in the sentence and an appearance of graciousness as well.

2. Many novice banner writers, elevated from the 2-col. obscurity of Class A ball to the black-cap. screamers of the big leagues, fumble the concept of "SWEEP." It *always* takes a plural object. Doubleheaders and series can be swept, but not regulation single games. (The minimal "WIN STREAK" is three games long; five makes a "SURGE.") A team that neither sweeps nor is swept splits. A headline familiar to New Englanders is "SOX SPLIT."

3. Which brings up the delicate matter of punning, or paronomasia. Each Baltimore journal is restricted by secret covenant to one "BIRDS SOAR" every two weeks. Milwaukee, with a stronger team, is permitted twelve instances of "BRAVES SCALP" before the All-Star game. "TIGERS CLAW" and "CUBS LICK" tend to take care of themselves. As for you, San Francisco, the lack of any synonyms for "giant" briefer than "behemoth" and "Brobdingnagian," together with the long-standing failure of

New York's own writers to figure out exactly what giants *do* (intimidate? stomp?), rather lets you out of the fun. In view of this, and in view of the team's present surprising record, you may therefore write "GIANTS A-MAYS." But don't do it more than once a month: moderation in all things, S.F.

Métro Gate

January 1959

LA RÉGIE AUTONOME DES TRANSPORTS PARISIENS—The Paris Transit Authority—has very generously given the Museum of Modern Art a battered old entrance gate to the Métro, the French capital's subway system. The Museum has no less courteously installed the thing in its garden, and there we went to see it. The gate, of cast iron, and one of many produced from a design by Hector Guimard, an exponent of the curvilinear, vegetative style that was known as Art Nouveau in 1900 and that, curiously, is still known by that name in 1959, has been rooted in concrete near the windowless gray brick tower built by the Museum after its fire. The garden, cold and sere within its high walls, was loud, as it always is, with the strange murmur (Traffic? Air-conditioners? The End of the World?) that so strongly resembles the protest of a sea-shell against your ear. The *objet d'art* we had come to view proved to be an inverted U of scabby green metal fifteen feet high and six strides wide. We stood between its legs and looked up, and received the disconsolate impression we usually receive underneath the brontosaurus in the Museum of Natural

History. The metalwork is less foliate than we expected—indeed, there's not a leafy line in it—and the organic principles informing its contours derive less from branches than from bones. Anticipating the tapering, strenuous grace of arboreal imitation, we found instead the stubborn little knobs and puckers of bones, an impression to which patches of blood-color scumbled through the vile green paint added an explicit grisliness. These were not even clean bones bolted and welded together but dirty bones, the remains of a too hasty feast, partly wrapped in awkward whorls and wrinkles: crushed napkins of iron. These clothlike ridges, especially at the base of the columns, suggested the ascending folds of French cathedral sculpture, but the aspiring eye was led upward not to the serene face of a stone saint but to a brown bulb, a lamp—an ant's abdomen magnified. This abdomen, this sac of stained glass, was grooved so that it took on, as we gazed upward, the aspect of an inhuman face, eyeless and cruel. The lamp bulb was gone from the opposite upright, as if the one had eaten the other. With tentacles of metal, the two posts reached out and interlocked, and in the center of their embrace was hung a sign that, in the neo-Turkish lettering once used to advertise ice cream in this country, proclaimed "METROPOLITAIN."

We were virtually alone with the gate. A woman wearing a foreign face and a furry coat, pursing her lips with that affectionate vehemence peculiar to Gauls, paused briefly, and a young couple, whom we knew to be French because the backs of their heads looked exactly alike, came and mooned a moment. These persons had clearly arrived at the end of a pilgrimage such as our own expatriates in Paris might make to see the water cooler in the American Express office. Otherwise, the scene was devoid of human content, and we resorted to asking the statues in the garden their opinions of their new neighbor.

The nearest, Rodin's lumpy monument to Balzac, replied

by staring rigidly at the roof of the Hotel Dorset. "I haven't seen the gate," he confessed. "The idiot sculptor hewed my neck with such a heroic roughness that it cannot be turned."

Lipchitz's "Figure," however, could look at nothing else. Words came with difficulty out of his (or her) intricate but regular convolutions. "I am puzzled," it admitted at last. "Is that really how you spell 'Metropolitan'?"

Renoir's "Washerwoman" was, as we had hoped, more amiable and optimistic. "It will be lovely," she sweetly promised, "in the spring, when it blossoms."

The Haida Indian totem pole, all fangs and nostrils, offered the most aggressive judgment.

"I
T
'
S

U
G
L
Y,"

the pole said, with typical totemic unkindness.

Cancelled

July 1959

HERE, with the best will in the world, we go up to the grand opening of the Hudson Celebration Theatre-in-the-Park, on the site of the Wollman Memorial Skating Rink, in Central Park, and it's cancelled, because of rain.

"But it's not raining now," we protested.

"The performance is cancelled," the young man in the box office repeated, staring stonily ahead, waiting for the next in line.

He had been saying the same words so often that his entire body had grown rigid around the thought of cancellation; his brain had coagulated, causing a fine sweat to break out evenly on his face. The phone rang. He picked it up, listened a moment, said "Cancelled," and replaced the receiver. He looked up, and saw us still standing there; a spark of anger flicked across his features. "Next," he said.

The lady behind us was very short and held on to her ticket as if it were the end of a rope that would pull her to a greater height. "Somebody said tonight's tickets would be good tomorrow," she began.

"That is correct, Madam. Tonight's performance is cancelled." He glanced away, to the next in line.

"But," the short lady said, and her hat trembled a bit, "tomorrow night my daughter's coming over from New Jersey."

"Do you want a refund?"

"She's coming over with my grandchildren, and I don't see how I can do both."

While she was saying this, he looked at the color of her ticket and took two dollar bills and some change from a drawer and passed them toward her, turning his palm upward for the ticket. She held on to her ticket and her thought tightly. "I don't see how I can come; the papers said the opening was tonight."

"The performance is cancelled," he said.

We moved away. The circumambient trees, soaked off and on all afternoon by rain, smelled fresh and looked dark in the twilight. The octagonal paving around the rink was spottily damp. The amphitheatre, airily designed by Edward Stone, was a thick ring of red canvas chairs surrounding a circular platform lit by four tall towers of lights. It was gaudy as a circus, without the sawdust sadness. A few lithesome young people, clad in informal, patchy-looking ballet outfits, bounded about on the stage in time to the remote jangle of a piano. The slithering footsteps made a sound infinitely faint in the center of that silent scarlet circle of chairs. We put our elbows on a wall whose concrete was exhaling a delicate damp scent, and watched. The last time we leaned on this wall and watched, there had been skaters down below, gliding, weaving, tottering, tumbling. A priest, we remembered had brought some children, and was himself ravishing on skates, black against the white ice, his arms folded behind him, skimming on one foot, then the other, with the incisive, irresistible grace of a medieval proof. Behind this elegant crow, his childish flock, a muffled bunch of sparrows and chickadees, fluttered along as best they could, extending stumpy wings for balance, chirruping with delight.

What we saw now was equally fine. A long-throated girl in a snug patchwork of black and gray pirouetted, leapt, and crossed her pale hands on her breast, and bowed her head. Despair? Shy stirrings of love? Without a program, we could not tell. A young man, as the piano rumbled into a masculine octave, pranced up a ramp and extended his arm. The prince? Her lover? Her accuser? Without costumes, they were clothed in mystery. More dancers joined them as the invisible plot thickened under the deepening stars. Their motions, cut off from explicit interpretation, enacted upon the precarious surface of music—the spaces between the lone piano's notes were sealed with the whisper of their feet—possessed a power beyond beauty, a power existential in the sense that, stripped of the smart paint of art, they shone with the bare, non-committal luminosity of fact. It was as if, walking through the Park, we had come upon people dancing out a personal incident in their lives. The young man, the perhaps prince, balanced on one foot and urged his face forward. An older man, gray-haired and in tights—the director, certainly—posed opposite him in the same position, so that the two of them became reflections in an imperfect mirror. The older man strained forward to lead the younger into greater urgency, to bring him to fill with his body the emotion to the brim. A few curt words, the scene collapsed, and now the girl flew in a great scissoring circle around the rim of the stage, a smile flashing on her twirling face. Happy. She was conveying happiness.

"Why doesn't she bend her body a little?" a female voice asked near us along the wall. The wall was crowded with people. Almost uniformly, the people who had not been clever enough to phone ahead had walked over from the box office to watch the rehearsal. Their burning cigarettes hung like an uneven string of small lanterns. Their talk made a harmless complement to the pantomime below. "When I was in the restaurant business, the cops . . ." The young prince made a mistake with his legs; the music stopped; a gentle laugh ran along the wall; he went back to the far edge of the stage. ". . . this cop said to me, he said, 'Boy, this is the greatest; I recommend it,' he said. He said, 'For ten years, you know, I had a lot of jobs and I was nuthin'. Nuthin'. Now,' he said, 'when I walk down the street, wearing my gun, I'm king. I'm the king,' he said. I said to myself, 'This man's a psychopath. *This man is a psychopath.*' "

The dancers ceased; there was brief clapping. The lights dimmed into a red tint. The girl, talking to the director, put her hands on her hips and laughed. Everybody along the wall hushed at the laugh. We all held silent, waiting for another. There wasn't another; she walked away, flat-footed, and the gray pattern that decorates the stage was vivid now that the platform was empty. The crowd that had attended the cancellation was slow to leave. Above the trees, the buildings along Fifth Avenue and Central Park South burned with a great cool wealth of fluorescent tints. The city is lovely from within the Park after dark; it's a view we don't see often enough. The crowd lingered, smoking. An out-of-town voice behind us insisted, "No, I loved it. Listen, in the winter I make sacrifices to see this stuff." The crowd—perhaps three hundred or more—wandered away, east, west, and south, long lines silhouetted under the lamps heavily caged against vandals. We ourselves went back to the path along the pond, where the ducks were sleeping.

Morality Play

October 1959

THE MYSTERIOUS AND AWFUL THING about the television quiz scandals is not that the jaded souls who ran the show were hoaxers but that dozens, and perhaps hundreds, of contestants, almost all of whom must have applied in the simplicity of good faith, were successfully enrolled in the hoax. Now, as we remember the flavor and ethos of that innocent era, the contestants, aside from their freakish passion for Hittite history or skeet-shooting statistics, were meant to be us—you and me and the bright boy next door. This was America answering. This was the mental wealth behind the faces you saw in a walk around the block. The appeal of the programs, with the rising challenge of Soviet brain power as a backdrop, was ultimately patriotic; the contestants were selected to be a cross-section of our nation just as deliberately as the G.I.s in a war movie are. There we bravely sat in our living rooms, sweating it out with this or that Shakespeare-reading poultry farmer or chemistry-minded chorus girl, and there they were on the other side of the blurred little screen, patting (not wiping) their brows with handkerchiefs, biting their tongues as instructed, stammering out rehearsed answers, gasping with relief at the expected cry of congratulation. And we sat there, a nation of suckers, for years. It's marvellous how long it went on, considering the number of normal Americans who had to be corrupted to keep the cameras whirring. In all this multitude, not one snag, not one audible bleat, not one righteous refusal that made the news. The lid didn't blow off until, years afterward, a winner, disgruntled because he had not won more, was moved to confess and purge his guilt.

We are fascinated by the unimaginably tactful and delicate process whereby the housewife next door was transmogrified into a paid cheat. We picture her coming into the studio, a little weary still from yesterday's long plane trip, a bit flustered by the noise and immensity of the metropolis—Dorothy Dotto, thirty-eight, happily married for nineteen years, the mother of three, a member of the Methodist Church, the Grange, and the Ladies' Auxiliary. She lives, and has lived all her life, in the town of Elm Corners, somewhere in the Corn Belt; as a child, she won seven consecutive pins for perfect Sunday-school attendance, and she graduated with good grades from a public school where the remarkable truthfulness of George Washington and the durable axioms of Benjamin Franklin were often invoked. Her father, Jesse, who is retired but still alive (bless him), for forty years kept above his desk at the feed mill a sign declaring, "Honesty Is the Best Policy."

Our heroine meets the show's producer, dapper, dimpled Leonard Blough (pronounced "Bluff"), who takes her into a little room walled with aluminum and frosted glass:

BLOUGH (*smiling and lifting from her arms a bundle, containing her lunch, that she has been clutching awkwardly*): Well, Mrs. Dotto, you did very well on the qualifying tests. Very well indeed.

MRS. D. (*blushing*): Thank you. My dad always told me I had a good head for books; he wanted me to go on to normal school and be a teacher, but then I met Ralph, and—well, one thing led to another . . . (*Blushes more deeply*)

BLOUGH: Ah, yes. Young love, young love. Well, Dorothy— You don't mind if I call you Dorothy?

MRS. D.: Sakes, no!

BLOUGH: We look forward to having you on our show. We know you're going to be a wonderful contestant.

MRS. D.: Well, I hope so. It's a wonderful honor for me. When I think of all those folks back in Elm Corners watching, I'm afraid I'll get so nervous I won't be able to make a word come out of my mouth. We all watch, you know, every day, fair weather or foul.

BLOUGH (*dimpling profusely*): That's the kind of tribute we value most. Dotty, I know you won't be nervous; we're a very close and friendly family on this show. By the way, the capital of Paraguay is Asunción.

MRS. D.: Eh?

BLOUGH (*consulting a paper on his desk*): A-s-u-n-c-i-o-n. Asunción. Better practice the Spanish accent in your hotel room tonight.

MRS. D. (*flustering*): But— But— You think I might be asked that?

BLOUGH (*his eyes narrowing thoughtfully*): Let's put it this way, Dot. The odds on your being asked the capital of Paraguay are as good as the odds on your being asked anything else. Do you follow me?

MRS. D.: I— I— I'm not sure.

BLOUGH (*looking her right in the eyes—a devastating effect*): I think you do. And—oh, yes—an animal that carries its young in a pouch is a marsupial. M-a-r-s—

MRS. D.: Yes, I know that. But why are you telling me?

BLOUGH (*leaning back in his chair and staring at the ceiling, which is one great fluorescent panel*): Let me try to express myself. I like you, honey. I think you have what it takes.

MRS. D.: But you mean that all this is a fake—that all those people answering questions are told the answers ahead of time?

BLOUGH: Come, come, let's not be nai-*eev*, dear. That's show biz.

MRS. D.: But I thought— The whole idea— I mean what made it interesting—

BLOUGH (*cunningly*): It *is* interesting, isn't it? I mean it's a good show. Now, it wouldn't be a good show if the clucks out there *knew*, but they don't *know*, so they're *happy*. Aren't they?

MRS. D.: Well, but my daddy always had this sign over his desk—

BLOUGH: And we don't want them to be *un*happy, do we? We don't want them, say, to have their own Mrs. D. show up as a dope tomorrow, do we? Listen, Sister, we can lace questions into you you won't even know what they *mean*. Now, listen to reason. Be a doll.

MRS. D.: Well, I've come all this way—

BLOUGH (*jubilant*): That's the girl! You're on! And when the time comes to take your dive, you'll take it, won't you? Huh?

MRS. D. (*growing fairly cunning herself*): Not this side of three grand I won't.

BLOUGH (*standing up, arms spread wide*): Baby! It's a deal! (*They embrace, and, as the Curtain Falls, the West Declines noticeably.*)

Obfuscating Coverage

July 1960

AFTER A WEEK of attending closely to the news coverage of the Democratic Convention, our chief impression was of the obfuscating, eclipsing, and molesting action of the news coverage itself. In nuclear physics there exists an "uncertainty principle," which states that beyond a certain threshold atomic phenomena become hopelessly obscured by the interference of the observing process itself. It seemed to us that newsmen, or at least television interviewers, reached a comparable threshold at Los Angeles, and zoomed across it into an ugly chaos where nothing was visible except their own drawn, pale, bleating faces.

The essence of a news gatherer, like the essence of a window, is transparence. But the window on the convention that the television networks let into our living room was so badly besmirched by the shoulders, smirks, rudeness, and cynicism of the reporters that the actual proceedings were glimpsed fitfully, through momentary—and, indeed, reluctant—intermittances of news *gratia* news. We were asked to witness the apotheosis of the newsman as his own hero. Television, unlike anything that has gone before it, puts him in front of the camera. Nothing was clearer, in the wavery image piped into our poor old set, than the broadcasting apparatus itself. The men who used this apparatus, growing increasingly conscious through five days that their own presences were on the television screen and as big as anybody else's, became increasingly clownish, aggressive, sarcastic, and self-important. The harassment of the politicians reached an obscene pitch. Senator Kennedy, trying to hack his way through the jungle of thrusting mikes and brazen importunities that grew up in the corridors of his hotel, was physically pushed into a panicked anger that for a moment marred even his extraordinary composure. Senator Jackson, to name one of the lesser fry, not only was compelled to produce the magic words "I don't know" a dozen times running but was persistently teased, by an especially pert microphonist, about his facial expression. With the disappointed candidates, the game seemed to be to goad them into sobbing. As for delegation chairmen, several of them were reduced to open-mouthed, staring silence by the forwardness of their tormentors, each of whom wore little electronic wings that presumably made him as exempt as an angel from mundane considerations like courtesy. These interviews, which were countless, not only looked ugly and were devoid of factual content but had the additional disagreeable effect of forcing good men to lie. Under the barrage of gouging inquiry, many of the political leaders retreated from the well-worn ground of politic discretion and took up positions that were plainly false. This was especially noticeable in the protestations of innocence and ignorance that surrounded the jockeying for the Vice-Presidential nomination.

Furthermore, the whole show was mangled by a policy of ad-lib interruption that allowed the bored and disconsolate ringmasters to break into any speech they considered dull with hot tips, chitchat, or yet another scabrous interview. It was as if a telecast of a baseball game were to be patched out, in the quiet innings, with shots of beneath-the-stands scuffling and film clips of last fall's pro-football season. We submit that a person who wants baseball wants all the innings, and that a person who wants a convention wants the convention in all its quaint tedium, right down to the last soybean statistic, evocation of natural grandeur, and tribute to Southern womanhood.

Bryant Park

July 1960

THE OTHER DAY, we went over to Bryant Park and sat down, on the steps in front of the statue of William Cullen Bryant. The steps, though this was early evening, were warm. Behind us Bryant, in bronze robes, slumped on a bronze throne; he looked like a very wise and dignified man who has been draped in yards of curtain material and then wetted down with a fire hose. A quadrangle of maples enclosed our lower vision. On our right, through the trees, peeped the peppermint-aqua of Stern's awnings, saying "COOL COOL COOL." Higher, on the sides of the old-fashioned skyscrapers that rim the Avenue of the

Americas here, signs spoke loudly of far-off places. "ACAPULCO One airline all the way AERONAVES DE MEXICO." "MILLER HIGH LIFE Brewed *Only* in Milwaukee." "AMBASSADOR World's Lightest Scotch." Sombreros, tortillas, the Braves, bonnie braes, and bagpipes jumbled together in our mind. By shifting our vision slightly, west by southwest, we treated ourself to a delightful antique jumble of high architecture. Granite gingerbread, pseudo-cathedrals, tessellated brickwork, grilled windows, that Babylonian wall decoration native to the thirties— all these dear ghosts, so thoroughly exorcised by Mies van der Rohe and the glass marvels of the new Park Avenue, still reign untroubled above the southwest corner of Bryant Park. Only the tips of the trees, at this hour, displayed any sunshine; it raked their tops like an ethereal hedge clipper. In the canyon of Forty-first Street—a trough open all the way to Jersey— golden-white, on top of that blue-white, and, topmost, blue, an ebbing blue, were the sky's colors. Behind a few of the windows a desultory secretary could be seen tidying up the final carbons of the day, and the first neon lights were glowing weak red.

Inside Bryant Park it was quiet. Cars swished and cursed, an airplane muttered, a child cried, but it was, on the whole, quiet. No zoos, no Shakespeare, no banjo-playing beatniks here. The people who come to this park, we decided, are the quiet people —lovers, thinkers, newspaper readers, derelicts, the retired, the out-of-work, the sleep-it-offs, and the dying. We looked at our fellows in the park; they were, we estimated, about four-fifths male, one-third colored, and two-thirds solitary, with a median age of fifty-one. In front of us, on the steps, a girl with chestnut hair that she could have sat on arrived, carrying books. This wonderful hair was done up in a long pony-tail, and she sat not on it but on a newspaper that her companion spread on the steps for her. She arranged herself and her books with a touching care. She moved not with the jerky, spiked walk of a secretary but with the languid calm of a student, on sandals of soft leather and thonged thought.

No, the secretary kind of girl was nowhere in the park, or was just passing through, like her counterpart the businessman. The businessmen, always in pairs and always talking, in creased suits of a cunning summer weave, strode by on the flagstones, on their way to somewhere else. We admired them, these children of the morning, these creators, but they did not admire us in turn. We were, we residents of Bryant Park, a quiet, uneasy, twilight lot. Those of us who could not find seats stood or wandered in foreboding little circles, facing in different directions and often looking up, as if a catastrophe—our own mortality or something vaguer—were faintly screaming toward us from beyond the tops of the maples. For some of us, catastrophe had already come: a young man with bright-carrot hair lay stretched out face down on a bench; a child kept crying; an old man in clothes too big for him stared blindly with alcohol-gutted eyes at the scuttling pigeons.

It abruptly occurred to us that we were near the center of the world. Within a few blocks of us, Fifth Avenue and Forty-second Street made their celebrated intersection. Times Square hoisted its gritty emblems, the greatest public library in the world reared its wisdom, the densest shopping area in the country offered its wares, and, in a show window two blocks away, the crown jewels of England in all their splendor were assembled to advertise one more airline. Where but here, in Bryant Park, was the bull's-eye of our city? As surely as if we were in the Forum of 160, on the Ile de la Cité in 1260, or in Piccadilly Circus in 1860, we sat, now, in 1960, in the center of Western civilization. Not quite; we sat to one side of the middle of the steps. To our right, in the exact middle, was a weary old man in a dusty blue sweater sitting on a tabloid, chewing a cigar, and blinking like Tiresias.

John Marquand

August 1960

JOHN P. MARQUAND wrote many good books and one for which we cannot be grateful enough. *The Late George Apley* is many things. It is a sentimental novel that fully satisfies the expectations aroused in us when we approach a professional product. It is the finest extended parody composed in modern America, the stately, cloying, and somewhat melodious prose of Mr. Willing, "Boston's Dean of Letters," being so surely wedded to its subject that it can be overlooked as a continuous invention of high literary irony. It is a detailed valentine to a city, Boston, and an admirably wrought fictional monument to the nation's Protestant elite. Once Marquand had made, with a satire no less ferocious for being urbane, the point that the Apleys are not better than other men, he went on, more remarkably, to suggest that they are no worse. At the end of a life bounded on the south by Providence and on the north by Portland, a life laborious and timid, smug and mean, George Apley sits down and writes his son a farewell letter in which snobbery, generosity, pomposity, and courage ecstatically merge. And when, having settled the last formality of his own funeral, he writes, "During the last week I have been working on several plans to rid the attic of those gray squirrels, I think now the only thing to do is to keep watch near the limb of the elm tree and to shoot them as they enter by that hole under the gutter," centuries are stripped away, the woodsman at the marrow of the Brahmin stands revealed, and we can all go about our business with refined hearts.

We ourself met Mr. Marquand twice, both times briefly. He was, perhaps, an author who aspired to earthly dignity rather than unearthly glory. Dignity he had achieved, and he wore it well, but he was the creator of the "Marquand hero," and not this hero himself. His evenly rosy complexion seemed distinctly French, and his remarks, delivered to a stranger among the diffident courtesies of a cocktail party, had a flattering precision and pertinence. The second time we saw him was five days before he died. He seemed in excellent health. It was the week of the Democratic Convention, and he surprised us (for we had understood that he was a Republican) by announcing his intention to vote for Senator Kennedy and by contributing, as his share of the talk (he contributed no more than his share; he still had, impressive in an honored, elderly man, the writer's habit of listening), a personal anecdote about the nominee's grandfather, whom he called Honey Fitz.

Two Heroes

December 1960

NEWSPAPER READERS pick up their daily catalogue of villainies partly in the expectation—never completely dulled—of finding heroes, yet when heroes appear, the river of print whisks them past us in such unexpected poses that we scarcely have time to recognize them. Last week, a man and a woman, the Reverend Lloyd A. Foreman and Mrs. James Gabrielle, were glimpsed in the act of escorting their daughters to a New Orleans elementary school. By the time these lines appear, both may have been removed from view by events making their heroism either unnecessary or hopeless, but at this moment there they still are, holding the hands of wide-eyed, white-faced little girls named Pamela and Yolanda, while behind them segregationist banshees scream obscenities and police grimly offer protection.

We have become familiar, callously familiar, perhaps, with the heroism of the Negro children who each autumn carry the tide of equal rights a little deeper into the South. There has been so much of it, and there is so much more to come. To be a Negro, James Baldwin has recently said, is to be "a fantasy in the mind of the republic." Living, as we do,* a few miles from the most populous and notorious Negro ghetto in the world, threading our life through a multitude of polite and unspoken segregations, we have not earned the right to sympathize fully with those Negro children, to suffer with them. We watch them helplessly from a distance, and, indeed, we are equally helpless in regard to Mr. Foreman and Mrs. Gabrielle; we have no more power than their abusive neighbors to lessen or increase by a step their stubborn walks to and from the William Frantz School.

Together, the two schools blasphemed by the presence of four small colored girls had a normal enrollment of a thousand pupils. This means, then, close to two thousand parents. Of those two thousand, how many sincerely believe that racial separation is divinely ordained, how many think that it is circumstantially prudent, how many don't really care, how many think that it is wrong and would like to be brave, we do not know. One way or another, under the harsh and ingenious pressures that a community can apply, all have been chipped away, leaving, for us to see, two people—a Christian minister and an ex-WAC whose husband, she has told reporters, spent three years in a foxhole in New Guinea and wasn't going to let a mob of women tell him what to do. Out of two thousand, two. Strangely, it seems enough.

---

* A poetic fiction, unsteadily maintained, is that the writer of "Talk of the Town" lives in Manhattan. In many cases, of course, he does.

Doomsday, Mass.

November 1961

A NEW MOTEL in Danvers, Massachusetts, is to be equipped
with an underground shelter large enough to house for six
months a community capable of creating the world anew in the
event of holocaust. The community is to be composed of (a)
the sixty motorists lucky enough to be stopping at the motel
on Doomsday, and (b) a group of about fifty persons selected
in advance, presumably from the locality. The brave new
world, from Cape Town to Nome, will speak with a Danvers
twang—a sobering thought. The selected group will include
(and we quote from the Boston *Herald*) "one surgeon, obstetrician, nurse, veterinarian, lawyer, estate planner, social
director, machine-gunner, bulldozer operator, teacher, horticulturist, cook, twenty municipal officers, civil-defense officials,
dietician, fisherman, radio operator, carpenter, clergyman,
mechanic, plumber, dentist, electrician, chemist, radiologist,
and others." It is an interesting list, especially when compared
with the older scheme of having the animals walk in two by
two. The order of listing presumably reflects the order of
importance, or at least the order in which the professions occurred to the provident motelkeeper as he talked to the news-
paperman. The first four professions are medical, as well they
might be, since even if everybody gets into the shelter unharmed, six months of scuffling around in the earth is apt to

generate a few bruises. The "obstetrician" immediately after "surgeon" is a reassuring touch, implying that not all the scuffling will be aimless. "Lawyer," next in line behind the veterinarian—who has, the article explains, "a cow, a bull, chickens, and rooster" to supervise—is a bit of a stopper, though, and "estate planner" stopped us completely. The opportunities for litigation at the end of the world would not appear to be great, and the need for estate planning seems at first blush negligible. The wealth of these hundred or so souls when they emerge into a world they have entirely inherited is apt to be considerable, however, and some sound investment counsel, Boston style, will doubtless be welcome. Continuing down the list, we encounter a series of happy pictures: the social director organizing square dances and pinochle tournaments in the shelter; the machine-gunner busily mowing down the interested crowds that have come up from Lynn; and the bulldozer operator, off in a corner with a dummy gearshift, keeping his reflexes sharp for the glad moment when he will be let loose to purify the landscape of all those crunchily empty houses. From a bulldozer's point of view, the next post-war world will certainly be paradise.

We envision, in those cozy concrete caverns, the teacher teaching (Readiness, Righteousness, and Radioactivity), the horticulturist tending his meagre salvage of seedlings, and the cook cooking. Indeed, we wonder why the cook wasn't placed at the top of the list. But those twenty—*twenty!*—municipal officers, and those civil-defense officials, who would seem to have their responsibilities behind them. Here is some excess fat for someone—the dietician, perhaps—to trim. The remainder of the list, especially the fisherman and the dentist, seems unobjectionable, though we wonder if perhaps, as at Presidential inaugurations, three or four clergymen might not be required for reasons of tact. Certainly the need for tact will be very great, what with that bull running around and those sixty motorists itching to get on with their trips. Their vacations will have long since expired, and possibly their automobile-inspection stickers will have lapsed. Yes, tempers may run short, and for that reason we deferentially suggest that the "others" include a psychologist of conservative cast (non-depth), a sincere, conscientious public-relations man, and conceivably even a writer, who could while away the long cave nights with fabulous tales of the world when men walked upright, in sunshine, only intermittently afraid.

August 1962

Six persons in Boston—three males, three females—were recently asked what they would do if notified that the world was going to end in four days. Why four days instead of the more conventionally apocalyptic three we leave as a mystery forever embedded in the mind of the Boston *Herald* reporter who asked the question. It is not the question that startles us but the answers. Two of the women said they would go to Bermuda. One woman answered that she would move up the date of her wedding, which is at present scheduled for December 24th. One man, a law-school student, thought he would take his wife on as long a trip as they could manage in so cruelly curtailed a period. "I'd see America first," he said. So, if these six were a fair cross-section, in the last agony of the United States the highways will be clogged with determined sightseers, the telephone wires jammed with the details of hastily rearranged weddings, and the reservations to Bermuda booked solid.

The bars may or may not be full. Another man, an electrician, ventured to guess that he'd "either tie one on or spend four days in church." The law student judiciously estimated, "I don't think drinking would help much." Only one of the six, a Waltham homemaker, unqualifiedly plumped for pleasure. "I'd go out and have a ball. I'd be of the eat-drink-and-be-merry school. I'd go back to Bermuda." The amount of business the churches would do is also uncertain. An insurance agent said, "I guess the best thing to do would be to try to make peace with my Creator." But then he added, "I don't think that would take four days." The second Bermuda-minded woman ("It only takes about two hours to get to Bermuda from here," she pointed out) supposed she would "spend some time in church and try to be natural." Being natural was the insurance agent's keynote. "I think my family and I would stay together and spend the time quietly. Really just go along the way that we always do."

All in all, it was a rather reassuring picture these six conjured up, of a hundred and eighty million doomed souls reaching for their car keys, giving the airport a ring, rather shyly veering between the saloon and the cathedral, quietly keeping natural, and—though no one said this—presumably maintaining that indispensable American virtue, a sense of humor. We tried to picture what we would do, and tended to agree with the Brighton schoolteacher who said, "Frankly, if the world was going to end in four days, I'd like to have it be a surprise."

Grandma Moses

December 1961

THE DEATH of a very old person seems no more natural, no less an untoward incursion, than the death of a young one.

Perhaps death seems natural only to Nature herself—and even she may have some doubts. Yet we cannot think of the life, now concluded, of Anna Mary Robertson Moses without cheerfulness. To live one allotted span as a farm wife and the mother of ten children, and then, at the age of seventy-six, to begin another, as an artist, as Grandma Moses, and to extend this second life into twenty-five years of unembarrassed productiveness—such a triumph over the normal course of things offers small cause for mourning. If we do mourn, it is for ourselves; she had become by her hundredth year one of those old people who, as old buildings civilize a city or spindly church spires bind up a landscape, make the world seem safer. Shaw and Brancusi were examples; Churchill and Schweitzer still are. They pay the world the great compliment of being reluctant to leave it, and their reluctance becomes a benediction. Little is said nowadays about the wisdom of age. Perhaps such wisdom is dreaded, for there is melancholy in it. Yet even awkward truths can be gracious and cheering in their expression. Describing her method of painting, Mrs. Moses once said, "I paint from the top down. First the sky, then the mountains, then the hills, then the houses, then the cattle, and then the people."

Spring Rain

April 1962

As THE SKY is pushed farther and farther away by the stiff-arms of this and that new steel frame, we sometimes wonder if what is reaching us is really weather at all. Whenever we have looked down at the street this spring, the perpetually rain-coated figures have appeared to be marching, jerkily fore-shortened and steadfastly downstaring, under a kind of sooty fluorescence bearing little relation to the expansive and variable light of outdoors. The other day, as if at the repeated invitation of all those raincoats, it *did* rain, and we ventured outdoors ourself; that is to say, we made our way down several corridors and shafts and into a broader corridor called Forty-fourth Street, whose ceiling, if one bothered to look, consisted of that vaguely tonic, vaporish semi-opacity old-fashionedly termed the Firmament. On this day, the Firmament, which showed as a little, ragged strip wedged between the upper edges of the buildings, seemed in a heavy temper. Water was being silently inserted in the slots between the building tops, and a snappy little secondary rain was dripping from marquees, overhead signs, fire escapes, and ledges. On the street itself, whose asphalt had emerged from the blanket of winter as creased and bumpy as a slept-on sheet, the water was conducting with itself an extravagantly complicated debate of ripple and counter-ripple, flow and anti-flow. It looked black but not dirty, and we thought, in that decisive syntactical way we reserve for such occasions, how all water is in passage from purity to purity. Puddles, gutters, sewers are incidental disguises: the casual avatars of perpetually reincarnated cloud droplets; momentary embarrassments, having nothing to do with the ineluctable poise of H_2O. Throw her on the street, mix her with candy wrappers, splash her with taxi wheels, she remains a virgin and a lady.

The breeze caught its breath, the rain slackened, and the crowds that had been clustered in entranceways and under overhangs shattered and scattered like drying pods. We went over to Fifth Avenue; the buildings there, steeped in humidity, seemed to be a kind of print of their own images, a slightly too inky impression of an etching entitled "Fifth Avenue, Manhattan, c. 1962."

No matter how long we live among rectangular stones, we still listen, in the pauses of a rain, for the sound of birds chirping as they shake themselves. No birds chirped, but the cars and buses squawked in deeper, openly humorous voices, and a trash can and a mailbox broke into conversation. CAST YOUR BALLOT HERE FOR A CLEANER NEW YORK, the trash can said, and MAIL EARLY IN THE DAY IT'S THE BETTER WAY, the mailbox beside it quickly responded. Both seemed to be rejoicing in the knowledge of their own inner snugness—of all the paper, folded or crumpled, addressed or discarded, that they had kept dry through the shower.

The façades of the buildings darkened in tint, the lights within windows seemed not merely to burn but to blaze, and abruptly the rain was upon us again. In the instant before it fell, the air felt full of soft circular motions and a silent cry of "Hurry!" Pedestrians hustled for shelter. The search converted Fifth Avenue into a romantic and primitive setting for adventure. Pelted, we gained the cave of Finchley's Tudor arcade, with its patio-red floor and plastic orange tree and California sports jackets. The next instant, we ran on into the green glade of the Olivetti entrance, with its typewriter-tipped stalagmite. Finally, we lodged in the narrow but deep shelter of Brentano's leafy *allée* of best-sellers, and from there we observed how the rain, a gusty downpour now, had the effect of exquisitely pressing the city down into itself. Everything—taxi roofs, umbrellas, cellophane-skinned hats, even squinting eyebrows—conveyed a sharp impression of shelter. Just as in a Miró painting the ovals and ellipses and lima beans of color sail across the canvas, so the city seemed a mobile conglomerate of dabs of dryness swimming through a fabric of wet. The rain intensified yet one more notch; the Fred F. French Building developed a positively livid stain along its bricks and the scene seemed squeezed so tight that it yielded the essence of granite, the very idea of a city. In a younger century, we might have wept for joy.

And when the rain stopped at last, a supernaturally well-staged effect was produced in the north. Owing to the arrangement of the slabs of Rockefeller Center, the low, westward-moving sun had laid an exclusive shaft of light upon the face of St. Patrick's Cathedral. Like two elegant conical bottles, the steeples were brimful of a mildly creamy glow. We hastened toward the omen, but by the time we reached the site the sunshine had faded. Yet, looking up through the skeleton globe upheld here by the grimacing Atlas, we saw beyond the metal framework what was, patchy blue and scudding gray, indisputably sky.

Eisenhower's Eloquence

May 1962

THE AMERICAN PRESIDENCY, it occurs to us, is merely a way station *en route* to the blessed condition of being an ex-President. In office, Herbert Hoover made the nation feel drastically insecure; out of office, he has radiated for thirty years a positively archangelic calm. While Harry Truman was residing in the White House, he gave the impression of being an unnerved riverboat gambler improvising his way through the biggest crap game in Western history; back home in Independence, he gets wiser every year, until in retrospect it seems that we had a combination of von Clausewitz, Macaulay, and Ty Cobb supervising our destinies in that harried era. And now Dwight Eisenhower, who for two terms spoke in long, gray stretches, has become piercingly eloquent. "Only Americans can hurt America," he told a crowd in Abilene, Kansas, according to the paper we read. *Only Americans can hurt America.* We are not quite sure how it fits all the facts, but it has a ring to it that sets the patriotic vertebrae in our spine tingling. It's been a long time since we read a sentence containing the word "America" that made any sense. This sentence seems to us properly proud, taut, mysterious, and true. We propose that it be engraved on a special-issue postage stamp and, in the fullness of time, be allowed to pass into our currency, to keep company with "In God We Trust," "*Annuit Coeptis*," and "This Certificate Is Legal Tender for All Debts Public and Private."

Not content with having delivered himself of a motto, Mr. Eisenhower went on to criticize the Twist. He compared it unfavorably with the minuet. So, no doubt, would have Voltaire. But the more we meditate, the more likely it seems that the Twist, along with Abstract Expressionism, is here to stay. Both were a long time evolving (through rock 'n' roll and Cubism, respectively), and both have attained a rugged, blunt attack that will not yield easily to the next would-be King of the Mountain.* What is a dance? A dance, we suggest, is a socially performed parable of sexual relations. The minuet, with its intrigue-like shifts of position and its subtle homage to a Clockwork Universe, offered the Age of Reason a contemporary frame for this perennial parable. Cool fingers touch, eyes glance, lids lower, fans tilt and quiver, and all the while the little buckled feet tidily slither and patter through the pattern of a secure rationale. Whereas in the Twist a man and a woman, isolated not only from everybody else but from each other, eyes closed, teeth clenched, perform one monotonous

---

* Even as I wrote this, Pop Art and the Frug were kicking in the womb of Culture.

motion to rigorously monotonous music. It is very beautiful. Across the little space between the man and the woman a call goes forth, but the space remains, and they never touch, poignantly acting out the Breakdown of Communications for which our century is celebrated. We live in the Age of Un-consummation, but we cannot be denied our solipsistic ecstasies. It is interesting to us that the Europeans, in taking to the Twist, have endowed it with soft graces and tender intricacies—made of it, in short, a kind of minuet. No, only Americans can understand America. Only Americans can love America.

Mostly Glass

October 1962

IT IS NO DISCOVERY of ours that Park Avenue, which just yester-day was a delicacy of dowagers and poodles between two slices of granite gingerbread, is today mostly glass. Thinking, the other afternoon, that we ought to welcome the future to our city, we strolled over to say hello to the massive, glinting architectural newcomers that have suddenly filled the ten or so blocks north of Forty-seventh Street—and discovered that once "Hello" was pronounced, the conversation threatened to end. For perhaps the first thing to say about the new architec-tural mode is that it leaves one with little to say. It glossily sheds human comment. The old modernism bustled forward, with its squared-off edges and concrete spirals, like a geometri-cal puppy eager to be praised for its successful burial of ob-solete bones. The new buildings on Park Avenue—Nos. 270,

280, 300, 320, 350, 375, 390, 399, 400, and 410, to give them their names—have not so much arrived as seeped through, and they hover on their thin stilts, slightly darker than the sky, like boxy clouds that, the next moment, may shrug and be gone.

Not that they are transparent. No, they are curiously opaque, considering that they are made of glass. The old skyline, the jagged continuum of rosy-ochre stone, was airier, really; its even ground of tint made the individual buildings appear to have more silhouette than mass. Perhaps the opacity of the glass buildings has to do with their refusal to accept atmosphere, to melt, as it were, into a landscape. For while it is true that they reflect, it is also true that they reflect only each other, like actors at a cocktail party who will speak only to other actors. As we observed the windows of Lever House reflecting, with that warp and shimmer so beloved of our photographic journals, the windows of the First National City Bank Building across the street, and then observed the First National City Bank Building courteously reflecting Lever House, we felt trapped beside a conversation that we would never be invited to enter.

Grant these new buildings their aloof good looks. The Seagram Building (375) is, of course, the stately Negro of the group, and Lever House (390) very much the fine lady. The Union Carbide Building, down the street (270), has scope; each side of it is a prairie county in acreage. The stainless-steel verticals are shaped like flanged railroad tracks, and to the man looking up they recede through fifty-two stories as the Union Pacific roadbed receded west a century ago, the dark between-window horizontal bands serving perfectly, in the visual pun, as railroad ties. But, these three buildings somewhat excepted, the group makes an insubstantial and disquieting impression. As our lives in this era all hang by threads, so our buildings stand on sticks. The stilt mode, though it has doubtless liberated some space for pedestrians, heightens the general impression of danger fostered by the newspapers, the stock market, and the Russians. It is disconcerting to see, in those buildings under construction, such as the Bankers Trust Building, at Forty-eighth Street, how importantly what looks like wide Scotch Tape figures in the construction, and how the first story seems to be built last, almost as an afterthought—as if the buildings were, like mistletoe, actually rooted in the air. Certainly the occupants of these new buildings must be teased by the fear that if they slam the lobby door too hard, an entire cosmos of glass and metal webbing will crash down on their heads.

What we miss, perhaps, is hopefulness. These new skyscrapers do not aspire to scrape the sky; at the point of exhaustion, where the old skyscrapers used to taper, gather their dwindling energy, and lunge upward with a heart-stopping spire, these glass boxes suffer the architectural embarrassment of having to house the air-conditioning apparatus, and slatted veiling snuffs out their ascent. Glassy-eyed from contemplation of these buildings made entirely of windows, we walked west feeling as if we had dined on a meal of doughnut holes.

Three Documents

May 1963

WE HAVE ON OUR DESK three thoroughly assorted documents: (1) an edition, published by Penguin Books, of George Bernard Shaw's *Androcles and the Lion* printed in the forty-eight-letter alphabet to whose development and promulgation Shaw willed a major part of his fortune; (2) an account, from the *Times*, of Gordon Cooper's press conference concerning his twenty-two-orbit ride in space; (3) an illustrated catalogue, put out by the Museum of Modern Art, of its fifteen-artist exhibit entitled *Americans 1963*. We have collected these documents in the last week, and have clung to them in the vague yet persistent hope that they are not only individually precious but collectively significant. We feel that somehow, in the translucent corridors of time, a corner has been turned recently. These three bundles we are clutching may well be clues to our own new whereabouts.

The Shaw document has the quaintness of a bygone era. On the right-hand pages, *Androcles and the Lion* is printed in conventional roman type; on the left-hand pages, "ᚾᚦᚱᛞᚳᚻ ᚳ ρ ᚳᚱᚾ " appears in the synthetic alphabet, adopted from designs by Mr. Kingsley Read and printed from unique type fonts owned by the Messrs. Stephen Austin & Sons, Ltd. The alphabet is totally invented; its closest roman relative is the long "o" sound, which is called "oak" and is written ο . All the letters, like runes, have names, rather anticly bestowed— "peep," "tot," "thigh," "bib," "mime," "ha-ha," and the like. There are four classifications—Tall, Deep, Short, and Compound—and the voiced and unvoiced sounds are visually symmetrical; e.g., "p" and "b" are) and (, "t" and "d" are 1 and (, "ch" and "j" are ᘓ and ᘔ . Strictly speaking, there are forty letters (ten Tall, ten Deep, and twenty Short), plus eight Compounds, called "are," "or," "air," "err," "array," "ear," "Ian," and "yew." It is all very orderly, and we have no reason to doubt the claims, set forth in a spirited introduction by Sir James Pitman, that it affords superior typographical compression, speed in writing, legibility, and phonetic logic. For practiced users of the Shaw alphabet, the ambiguities of spelling and capitalization would vanish. Furthermore, the new letters in mass, resembling a kind of stiff shorthand, or loose columns of hitherto undiscovered Arabic numerals, have an electric elegance. The alphabet is handsome, efficient, and ingenious. It is also unmistakably, serenely, and even cheerfully dead. It does not, except formally, exist. It was conceived by the past for the benefit of a future that has not, and will not, come to be. It is Shaw's last brain child, which has outlived him just as he outlived the era when intelligent, benevolent men believed that the world could be bloodlessly revolutionized by the decrees of brute sanity. The alphabet, which at first glance looks crazy, is eminently sane, and if some antiseptic miracle were to foist it on the English-speaking world, it might reduce printing space by a third, reading time by half, and writing time by at least eighty per cent. But the alphabet, unlike the cumbersome set of haphazard marks in which this paragraph is printed, does not embody human blood. It lacks the awkward poetry of the evolved. It has not bloomed from the infinite fumblings of anonymous men. It lacks even the urgent practical excuse of shorthand, and, unlike Arabic numerals, it does not replace a hopelessly inappropriate system of notation. Until we all experience emotions phonetically and fulfill our destinies unambiguously, we will continue to make note of ourselves with ambiguous vowels, silent consonants, and hodgepodge transliterations of abandoned tongues. The stubbornness that resists the smooth banalities of utility is righteous and respectful. Honor the dead—including the extravagantly lucid playwright whose alphabetic bequest to the future seems, today, an amiable curiosity, if not a witting irony.

Gordon Cooper, over a hundred miles above the scorned surface of the earth, saw the smoke from Tibetan villages. Above the Arabian peninsula, he saw a boat going down a river, "creating a wake behind it." He saw his own neighborhood in

Houston, although trees obscured the sight of his own house. On the other hand, Red China, he said, "looks just like it looks on the map." He slept; he ate fruitcake and brownies; he tucked his thumbs into his harness so his arms would stop floating away. When the time came to bring the spacecraft down, the machinery balked and he brought it down himself, looking out the window at the horizon to keep himself upright.

Why is it that the details of space flights grow increasingly homely and comforting? When Alan Shepard went zooming into the airless altitude above the Caribbean, we held our breath, horror-struck. When John Glenn girdled the earth three times one morning, his heroism seemed supernal. It remained for Gordon Cooper to domesticate space; his dozing nonchalance has made the void more habitable. We are glad that he came back safely and that on emerging from the capsule (in his words) "I began to get a little dizzy. . . . After I'd taken a step or two I felt perfectly all right." We are delighted that the man proved himself a better pilot than his machine. And we are especially happy that, from the ghastly height of the future, he could look down and see the smoke of hearth fires kindled by Tibetan peasants.

The catalogue is a souvenir of a show we saw last week, and greatly enjoyed. "Enjoyed," surprisingly, is the word, though the art assembled on the third floor of the Museum of Modern Art, being the work mainly of young artists, presumably should be, if progress means anything, more violent and exacerbating than Abstract Expressionism, which it succeeds. Much of it, certainly, is premeditatedly outrageous—dribbly plaster imitations of hamburgers, sculpture made entirely from old automobile bumpers, imperceptibly tinted canvases of solid black, huge blurred patterns of newspaper ads, exquisitely faithful duplications of billboard lettering, systematic experiments in retinal irritation, wicked three-dimensional satires in wood, plaster, and (at one point) old tennis sneakers. Yet, believe it or not, the show is heartening. Passing through the fifteen rooms, we found grandeur, wit, care, and tenderness—above all, perhaps, tenderness. The man (Jason Seley) who made statues out of car bumpers obviously loved car bumpers; the woman (Chryssa) who fiddled with newspapers and lettering made beautiful things of them, as fond and lyric as any water color of wild flowers you have in your attic. Our impression— to cut short this untoward trespass into the realm of our art critic*—was of an art that, able at last to relent in its fierce, long battle with pictorial convention, was giving God, God the maker of unmade things, the glory. The world is full of blatant trash—industrial, mental, visual. Perhaps the time has come to give this trash the homage that Nature in all her aspects deserves. At any rate, we left the Museum wondering if, in those translucent corridors where history wanders, a homeward turn hadn't been taken, and the future hadn't become, momentarily, the present.

Free Bee-hours

October 1963

THE UNIVERSITY OF ARIZONA's Agricultural Experimental Station, under the leadership of Mr. Charles D. Owens, has

---

* Harold Rosenberg, who a few weeks later, in his review of this show, took testy exception to the enthusiastic paragraph in which his nameless colleague on Talk of the Town "babbled of green fields."

developed a machine that uncaps honeycombs twice as fast as any other honeycomb-uncapper now in use. The news item in the *Times* so reporting goes on to say, "This could be an aid to the nation's half million beekeepers who produce well over $200,000,000 pounds [sic] of honey a year. *And it could save the nearly 300,000,000,000 domestic bees in the land a lot of time and effort*, because the combs can be used over again." The italics are ours. Who are we (to be precise, who is Charles D. Owens) to be saving bees "a lot of time and effort"? What will the country do with yet another leisure class? Consider it arithmetically. Assume that in the old days the average bee (we are averaging the worker bees, who work all the time, with the drones and queens, who incessantly debauch) spent two hours a day repairing the honeycombs ravaged by the nation's half-million beekeepers. This seems modest, and it likewise seems modest to guess that the improved honeycomb-uncapper will cut this time in half. So each day we are releasing into the air a total of three hundred billion bee-hours, which amounts in the course of a year to twelve and a half billion bee-years! Now, Mr. Owens and the beekeepers are living in a fool's paradise if they imagine that the bees are going to utilize that leisure time by improving their humming, or refining their honey, or simply sleeping an hour later. As anyone who knows apian nature could tell them, the bees will spend it watching television, or, worse, going out on golf courses and stinging people. In a few years, the very simile "busy as a bee" will have joined "hot as a firecracker" in obsolescence, and the low-grade honey produced by part-time bees will taste suspiciously like gall.

Beer Can

January 1964

THIS SEEMS TO BE AN ERA of gratuitous inventions and negative improvements. Consider the beer can. It was beautiful—as beautiful as the clothespin, as inevitable as the wine bottle, as dignified and reassuring as the fire hydrant. A tranquil cylinder of delightfully resonant metal, it could be opened in an instant, requiring only the application of a handy gadget freely dispensed by every grocer. Who can forget the small, symmetrical thrill of those two triangular punctures, the dainty *pffff*, the little crest of suds that foamed eagerly in the exultation of release? Now we are given, instead, a top beetling with an ugly, shmoo-shaped "tab," which, after fiercely resisting the tugging, bleeding fingers of the thirsty man, threatens his lips with a dangerous and hideous hole. However, we have discovered a way to thwart Progress, usually so unthwartable. *Turn the beer can upside down and open the bottom.* The bottom is still the way the top used to be. True, this operation gives the beer an unsettling jolt, and the sight of a consistently inverted beer can might make people edgy, not to say queasy. But the latter difficulty could be eliminated if manufacturers would design cans that looked the same whichever end was up, like playing cards. What we need is Progress with an escape hatch.

Modern Art

April 1964

A SHIFTING DISPLAY of modern art, by anonymous artists, is on view these days in front of the Museum of Modern Art, whose interior is closed for renovations. The show as a whole is marked by the slashing style, inflated scale, and promiscuous receptiveness to accident characteristic of Abstract Expressionism, but the ironic precision of Pop Art and even some neo-naturalistic undertones are present as well. The show has been mounted in a deliberately jumbled manner, so that some of the most provocative works are virtually eclipsed, and the complete lack of titles will probably addle museum-goers accustomed to such helpful labels as "Painting No. 4" and "Form No. 5." The narrow board catwalk the directors have provided permits a steady flow of traffic but does not permit much lingering.

Entering the exhibit from the east side, we were first impressed by a generously scaled arrangement, unpainted and stabilized by no binding agent other than its own weight, of hollow cement blocks in two sizes. The eye, roaming the stately surfaces of this elegantly patterned mass, is enchanted by the subtle variations in texture and occasionally startled by some adventure in the form—a pair of blocks laid diagonally, or even (in one instance) a block impudently stood on end. While the proportions of the pile approximate twice those of a sleeping woman, the organic reference is not pressed; rather, the material itself is permitted to speak, and speak it does—of a mineral universe where a kind of silicate transcendentalism replaces the pious fatuities of Madison Avenue and the Marine Corps Band. We hope the unnamed creator of this lovely piece does not too quickly desert his recalcitrant medium for the more facile pleasures of balsa wood and daubed burlap.

High above this sculpture hangs a truly impressive canvas (if that is the word) of metal and glass, the glass panes decorated with long strips forming the letter "X." The "X" motif is repeated the length and breadth of the work, and while the canvas is not the sort of thing a collector of Degas pastels would care to hang in his living room, it convincingly carries its metaphor, which we took to be that contemporary existence is all façade. Moving on, we encountered a more intimate work, playful in spirit, though lethal in wit. Of welded metal, it may best be described as a deep trough mounted on four thin legs (suggesting a spavined horse?), the whole drenched in hot tar and issuing (whinnying?) clouds of steam. While one must admire the ingenuity of this Happening transposed into a mock-equine statue, the danger to passersby can only be deplored.

On the other side of the narrow gallery is a long polytych of wood panels painted a creamy gray and stencilled in white with the repeated slogan "POST NO BILLS." We assume that the same artist is responsible for the smaller work in red cloth, lettered, again in white, "DANGER." The difficulty with incorporating legible words into such abstractions is that the literary content overpowers, as it were, the necessarily diffuse and delicate pictorial content. We responded much more warmly to the ductlike forms of extruded aluminum loosely mounted in a scaffold of unpainted but skillfully splintered wood, and to the stairlike arrangements of granite slabs, reminiscent of the earlier Lipchitz. Finally, we would like to single out for praise the very modest construction of yellow-painted metal, orange glass, and black wire; its effect, of potential luminosity, stood out like a signal in the mass of grandiose and dark dreaming surrounding it. In sum, the exhibited works compensate in energy for what they lack in finish.

The Assassination

November 1963

IT WAS AS IF WE SLEPT from Friday to Monday and dreamed an oppressive, unsearchably significant dream, which, we discovered on awaking, millions of others had dreamed also. Furniture, family, the streets, and the sky dissolved; only the dream on television was real. The faces of the world's great mingled with the faces of landladies who had happened to house an unhappy ex-Marine; cathedrals alternated with warehouses, temples of government with suburban garages; anonymous men tugged at a casket in a glaring airport; a murder was committed before our eyes; a Dallas strip-tease artist drawled amiably of her employer's quick temper; the heads of state of the Western world strode down a sunlit street like a grim village rabble; and Jacqueline Kennedy became Persephone, the Queen of Hades and the beautiful bride of grief. All human possibilities, of magnificence and courage, of meanness and confusion, seemed to find an image in this long montage, and a stack of cardboard boxes in Dallas, a tawdry movie house, a tiny rented room where some shaving cream still clung to the underside of a washbasin, a row of parking meters that had witnessed a panicked flight all acquired the opaque and dreadful importance that innocent objects acquire in nightmares.

What did it mean? Can we hope for a meaning? "It's the fashion to hate people in the United States." This quotation might be from one of a hundred admonitory sermons delivered after President Kennedy's death. In actuality, it occurs in an interview granted in 1959 to a United Press reporter, Aline Mosby, by a young American defector then living in Moscow, Lee Harvey Oswald. The presumed assassin did not seem to be a violent man. "He was too quiet, too reserved," his ex-landlord told reporters. "He certainly had the intelligence and he looked like he could be efficient at doing almost anything." In his room, the police found a map on which was marked the precise path that three bullets in fact took. The mind that might have unlocked this puzzle of perfectly aimed, perfectly aimless murder has been itself forever sealed by murder. The second assassination augmented the first, expanded our sense of potential violence. In these cruel events, democracy seemed caricatured; a gun voted, and a drab Dallas neighborhood was hoisted into history. None of our country's four slain Presidents were victims of any distinct idea of opposition or hope of gain; they were sacrificed, rather, to the blind tides of criminality and insanity that make civilization precarious. Between Friday and Monday, three men died: a President, a policeman, and a prisoner. May their deaths be symbols, clues to our deep unease, and omens we heed.

December 1963

CHRISTMAS THIS YEAR has the air of a birthday party carried on despite a death in the family; the usual garishness that exhilarates and grates is absent, though not visibly so. In search of the invisible difference, we wandered out onto Fifth Avenue last week, and the first thing we saw was the large American flag on the Bank of New York which, because it was hung at half-mast, was beating itself against the windows and the limestone of the building. The flag was, in the brisk wind of that day, like a hapless tricolor bird trying to roost. All up and down the Avenue, the half-mast flags were gray from rubbing against sooty façades.

We were led to notice, through observing the flags, how Christmas tends to stop at the second story. With a few exceptions (the annual festoon at Lord & Taylor, the pipes and choirboys up at Saks), the wreaths and tinsel give out above the display windows, like sea wrack above the high-tide line. And we noticed, too, how little movement there is this year in the Christmas displays. We did see a papier mâché Santa, gift certificate in hand, revolving his torso in the window of the John B. Stetson Company; he seemed to be doing the hula, or the upper half of the Twist. Except for him, the windows were strangely still.

Oh, we saw cheerful things: two nuns, themselves so immaculately packaged, carrying packages; the so-called Dog Bar at Wallachs (a little marble saucer set low to the pavement) splashing as self-importantly as a Neapolitan fountain; a harried lady doubling back to put a coin in a curbside Santa's pot. Saks was a glorious grotto, a super-Antarctica of white stalactites and frosty Spanish moss, where even the floorwalkers' white neckties had a polar primness, like the breasts of penguins. The women shopping were wonderful; this year's high heels do not jounce the face but wobble the ankles, so that women walking have the tremulous radiance of burning candles as, step by step, they quiver in and out of balance.

But a sombre undercurrent persisted. Cartier's wore her strands of dull-gold tinsel like an old woman wearing a mourning shawl. The beards of the Santa Clauses along the street looked transparently false—shiny, ill-fitted appendages of nylon. In the old days, it seemed to us, the Santa Claus beards bristled like the coats of badgers and were as soft as the fleece of lambs. This year, they are palpably pretense; the party must go on. At Rockefeller Center, the tree is hung with two-dimensional balls, and the greenery in the center of the mall is confused with strange artifacts of white and silver wire—giant jack-in-the-boxes, outsize alphabet blocks, huge mock toys. The effect is not entirely fortunate. We kept seeing the green shrubbery through the wire constructions and wondering which we were meant to believe in—which was Christmas and which was Nature.

We walked across the street to St. Patrick's Cathedral. It alone, on all the festive Avenue, seemed totally convinced. We had never so closely observed the central doors, which are usually open or obscured by darkness. The six bronze figures on them we had assumed to be iconographically standard, indistinguishably Biblical. This was not so, and for those as inexcusably unobservant as we are, we will list them, left to right, top to bottom. On the doors of St. Patrick's Cathedral, in full-relief figures about a yard high, are St. Joseph, Patron of the Church; St. Patrick, Patron of This Church; St. Isaac Jogues, Martyr and First Priest in New York; St. Frances X. Cabrini, Mother of the Immigrant; Ven. Kateri Tekakwitha, Lily of the Mohawks; and Mother Elizabeth Seton, Daughter of New York. The Lily of the Mohawks, with her stoic face, her Indian headband, and her Christian cross, seemed peculiarly relevant to the gently forlorn metropolitan flux around us. We do not often enough, perhaps, think of ourselves as successors of the Indians—subsequent tenants, as it were, of a continuing mystery. We went inside the cathedral. A Mass was in progress, and it was well attended. At side altars, banks of candles glowed and wavered like crowds of female shoppers. At the front altar, the priest, the back of his white chasuble shining, seemed the lone passenger on a splendid, house-shaped boat afloat before our eyes. Bells rang. People knelt. Again bells rang. The kneelers rose; the noise of their rising merged with the shuffle and scrape of footsteps around us, in the rear of the cathedral.

Outside on the street, Christmas did seem to have solidified. Cool sunlight was falling unruffled through the wind, and, looking at the crowds, we realized what the difference is this year. People are not determined to be jolly; they do not feel obligated to smile. From the sudden death of our young President, Americans may in time date a great physiognomic discovery: a human face may refuse, or fail, to smile and still be human.

T. S. Eliot

January 1965

THE DEATH of T. S. Eliot deprives the English-speaking world not of a literary master—he exists in his work and will continue to exist—but of a cultural presence that united two literatures and extended the venerable tradition of the presiding poet-critic into the present time. He was our Dryden, our Coleridge, our Arnold; and as long as he was alive our literature seemed in some sense restrained from the apocalyptic formlessness and obscenity that it seeks. Eliot's peculiar authority derived from his own participation in this century's despair;

he was a veteran of anarchy who elected to rule, a great conservative containing a thorough radical. What was most peculiar about his authority, perhaps, was how generally it was acknowledged, considering the modesty, in both tone and bulk, of his production. He was like Valéry in the weight his silences borrowed from the penetration of his utterances. Of the many makers of modern literature, he was the most penetrating, and it is this gift of penetration that makes his poems so strangely unforgettable and his critical judgments, beneath their circumspection, so shockingly right. He had (an optional virtue for writers) an inability to write other than the truth— we mean, of course, the truth as he felt it—so that even the pallor and whimsey of the later plays are rendered supportable by a final earnestness. As a poet, he belongs not with the great verbal impresarios, like Shakespeare and Joyce, but with those great who, like Donne and Wordsworth, arrive in one's imagination somewhat hobbled by an awkward honesty. Like Valéry, Eliot won, for his austerity and precision, that intensity of respect which passes into love. Unlike Valéry, he won it from a people, the English, who customarily reward genial copiousness. If, in the atmosphere of public veneration that attended his old age, in the hundreds of American classrooms where his passionate and enigmatic lines were dutifully charted, there was something stale and falsely official, Eliot's sly gray image evaded incrimination. In trying to frame that image, we see it triangulated by three poets whom he had considered well. We mention, for metrical power, Milton. For impeccability, Marvell. And, for paternal elusiveness, Edward Lear.

Hub Fans
Bid Kid
Adieu

HUB FANS BID KID ADIEU

FENWAY PARK, in Boston, is a lyric little bandbox of a ballpark. Everything is painted green and seems in curiously sharp focus, like the inside of an old-fashioned peeping-type Easter egg. It was built in 1912 and rebuilt in 1934, and offers, as do most Boston artifacts, a compromise between Man's Euclidean determinations and Nature's beguiling irregularities. Its right field is one of the deepest in the American League, while its left field is the shortest; the high left-field wall, three hundred and fifteen feet from home plate along the foul line, virtually thrusts its surface at right-handed hitters. On the afternoon of Wednesday, September 28th, 1960, as I took a seat behind third base, a uniformed groundkeeper was treading the top of this wall, picking batting-practice home runs out of the screen, like a mushroom gatherer seen in Wordsworthian perspective on the verge of a cliff. The day was overcast, chill, and uninspirational. The Boston team was the worst in twenty-seven seasons. A jangling medley of incompetent youth and aging competence, the Red Sox were finishing in seventh place only because the Kansas City Athletics had locked them out of the cellar. They were scheduled to play the Baltimore Orioles, a much nimbler blend of May and December, who had been dumped from pennant contention a week before by the insatiable Yankees. I, and 10,453 others, had shown up primarily because this was the Red Sox's last home game of the season, and therefore the last time in all eternity that their regular left fielder, known to the headlines as TED, KID, SPLINTER, THUMPER, TW, and, most cloyingly, MISTER WONDERFUL, would play in Boston. "WHAT WILL WE DO WITHOUT TED? HUB FANS ASK" ran the headline on a newspaper being read by a bulb-nosed cigar smoker a few rows away. Williams' retirement had been announced, doubted (he had been threatening retirement for years), confirmed by Tom Yawkey, the Red Sox owner, and at last widely accepted as the sad but probable truth. He was forty-two and had redeemed his abysmal season of 1959 with a—considering his advanced age—fine one. He had been giving away his gloves and bats and had grudgingly consented to a sentimental ceremony today. This was not necessarily his last game; the Red Sox were scheduled to travel to New York and wind up the season with three games there.

I arrived early. The Orioles were hitting fungos on the field. The day before, they had spitefully smothered the Red Sox, 17–4, and neither their faces nor their drab gray visiting-team uniforms seemed very gracious. I wondered who had invited them to the party. Between our heads and the lowering clouds a frenzied organ was thundering through, with an appositeness perhaps accidental, "You *maaaade* me love you, I didn't wanna do it, I didn't wanna do it. . . ."

The affair between Boston and Ted Williams was no mere summer romance; it was a marriage composed of spats, mutual disappointments, and, toward the end, a mellowing hoard of shared memories. It fell into three stages, which may be termed Youth, Maturity, and Age; or Thesis, Antithesis, and Synthesis; or Jason, Achilles, and Nestor.

First, there was the by now legendary epoch* when the

---

* This piece was written with no research materials save an outdated record book and the Boston newspapers of the day; and Williams' early

young bridegroom came out of the West and announced "All I want out of life is that when I walk down the street folks will say 'There goes the greatest hitter who ever lived.'" The dowagers of local journalism attempted to give elementary deportment lessons to this child who spake as a god, and to their horror were themselves rebuked. Thus began the long exchange

---

career preceded the dawning of my *Schlagballewusstsein* (Baseball-consciousness). Also for reasons of perspective was my account of his beginnings skimped. Williams first attracted the notice of a major-league scout—Bill Essick of the Yankees—when he was a fifteen-year-old pitcher with the San Diego American Legion Post team. As a pitcher-outfielder for San Diego's Herbert Hoover High School, Williams recorded averages of .586 and .403. Essick balked at signing Williams for the $1,000 his mother asked; he was signed instead, for $150 a month, by the local Pacific Coast League franchise, the newly created San Diego Padres. In his two seasons with this team, Williams hit merely .271 and .291, but his style and slugging (23 home runs the second year) caught the eye of, among others, Casey Stengel, then with the Boston Braves, and Eddie Collins, the Red Sox general manager. Collins bought him from the Padres for $25,000 in cash and $25,000 in players. Williams was then nineteen. Collins' fond confidence in the boy's potential matched Williams' own. Williams reported to the Red Sox training camp in Sarasota in 1938 and, after showing more volubility than skill, was shipped down to the Minneapolis Millers, the top Sox farm team. It should be said, perhaps, that the parent club was equipped with an excellent, if mature, outfield, mostly purchased from Connie Mack's dismantled A's. Upon leaving Sarasota, Williams is supposed to have told the regular outfield of Joe Vosmik, Doc Cramer, and Ben Chapman that he would be back and would make more money than the three of them put together. At Minneapolis he hit .366, batted in 142 runs, scored 130, and hit 43 home runs. He also loafed in the field, jabbered at the fans, and smashed a water cooler with his fist. In 1939 he came north with the Red Sox. On the way, in Atlanta, he dropped a foul fly, accidentally kicked it away in trying to pick it up, picked it up, and threw it out of the park. It would be nice if, his first time up in Fenway Park, he had hit a home run. Actually, in his first Massachusetts appearance, the first inning of an exhibition game against Holy Cross at Worcester, he *did* hit a home run, a grand slam. The Red Sox season opened in Yankee Stadium. Facing Red Ruffing, Williams struck out and, the next time up, doubled for his first major-league hit. In the Fenway Park opener, against Philadelphia, he had a single in five trips. His first home run came on April 23, in that same series with the A's. Williams was then twenty, and played *right* field. In his rookie season he hit .327; in 1940, .344.

of backbiting, bat-flipping, booing, and spitting that has distinguished Williams' public relations.* The spitting incidents of 1957 and 1958 and the similar dockside courtesies that Williams has now and then extended to the grandstand should be judged against this background: the left-field stands at Fenway for twenty years have held a large number of customers who have bought their way in primarily for the privilege of showering abuse on Williams. Greatness necessarily attracts debunkers, but in Williams' case the hostility has been systematic and unappeasable. His basic offense against the fans has been to wish that they weren't there. Seeking a perfectionist's vacuum, he has quixotically desired to sever the game from the ground of paid spectatorship and publicity that supports it. Hence his refusal to tip his cap** to the crowd or turn the other

---

* See *Ted Williams*, by Ed Linn (Sport Magazine Library), Chapter 6, "Williams vs. the Press." It is Linn's suggestion that Williams walked into a circulation war among the seven Boston newspapers, who in their competitive zeal headlined incidents that the New York papers, say, would have minimized, just as they minimized the less genial side of the moody and aloof DiMaggio and smoothed Babe Ruth into a folk hero. It is also Linn's thought, and an interesting one, that Williams thrived on even adverse publicity, and needed a hostile press to elicit, contrariwise, his defiant best. The statistics (especially of the 1958 season, when he snapped a slump by spitting in all directions, and inadvertently conked an elderly female fan with a tossed bat) seem to corroborate this. Certainly Williams could have had a truce for the asking, and his industrious perpetuation of the war, down to his last day in uniform, implies its usefulness to him. The actual and intimate anatomy of the matter resides in locker rooms and hotel corridors fading from memory. When my admiring account was printed, I received a letter from a sports reporter who hated Williams with a bitter and explicit immediacy. And even Linn's hagiology permits some glimpses of Williams' locker-room manners that are not pleasant.

** But he did tip his cap, high off his head, in at least his first season, as cartoons from that period verify. He also was extravagantly cordial to taxi-drivers and stray children. See Linn, Chapter 4, "The Kid Comes to Boston": "There has never been a ballplayer—anywhere, anytime— more popular than Ted Williams in his first season in Boston." To this epoch belong Williams' prankish use of the Fenway scoreboard lights for rifle practice, his celebrated expressed preference for the life of a fireman, and his determined designation of himself as "The Kid."

cheek to newsmen. It has been a costly theory—it has probably cost him, among other evidences of good will, two Most Valuable Player awards, which are voted by reporters*—but he has held to it. While his critics, oral and literary, remained beyond the reach of his discipline, the opposing pitchers were accessible, and he spanked them to the tune of .406 in 1941.** He slumped to .356 in 1942 and went off to war.

In 1946, Williams returned from three years as a Marine pilot to the second of his baseball avatars, that of Achilles, the hero of incomparable prowess and beauty who nevertheless was to be found sulking in his tent while the Trojans (mostly Yankees) fought through to the ships. Yawkey, a timber and mining maharajah, had surrounded his central jewel with many gems of slightly lesser water, such as Bobby Doerr, Dom DiMaggio, Rudy York, Birdie Tebbetts, and Johnny Pesky. Throughout the late forties, the Red Sox were the best paper team in baseball, yet they had little three-dimensional to show for it, and if this was a tragedy, Williams was Hamlet. A succinct review of the indictment—and a fair sample of appreciative sports-page prose—appeared the very day of Williams'

---

* In 1947 Joe DiMaggio and in 1957 Mickey Mantle, with seasons inferior to Williams', won the MVP award because sportswriters, who vote on ballots with ten places, had vengefully placed Williams ninth, tenth, or nowhere at all. The 1941 award to Joe DiMaggio, even though this was Williams' .406 year, is more understandable, since this was also the *annus miraculorum* when DiMaggio hit safely in 56 consecutive games.

** The sweet saga of this beautiful decimal must be sung once more. Williams, after hitting above .400 all season, had cooled to .39955 with one doubleheader left to play, in Philadelphia. Joe Cronin, then managing the Red Sox, offered to bench him to safeguard his average, which was exactly .400 when rounded to the third decimal place. Williams said (I forget where I read this) that he did not want to become the .400 hitter with just his toenails over the line. He played the first game and singled, homered, singled, and singled. With less to gain than to lose, he elected to play the second game and got two more hits, including a double that dented a loudspeaker horn on the top of the right-field wall, giving him six-for-eight on the day and a season's average that, in the forty years between Rogers Hornsby's .403 (1925) and the present, stands as unique.

valedictory, in a column by Huck Finnegan in the Boston
American (no sentimentalist, Huck):

Williams' career, in contrast [to Babe Ruth's], has been a series
of failures except for his averages. He flopped in the only World
Series he ever played in (1946) when he batted only .200. He
flopped in the playoff game with Cleveland in 1948. He flopped in
the final game of the 1949 season with the pennant hinging on the
outcome (Yanks 5, Sox 3). He flopped in 1950 when he returned
to the lineup after a two-month absence and ruined the morale
of a club that seemed pennant-bound under Steve O'Neill. It has
always been Williams' records first, the team second, and the Sox
non-winning record is proof enough of that.

There are answers to all this, of course. The fatal weakness
of the great Sox slugging teams was not-quite-good-enough
pitching rather than Williams' failure to hit a home run every
time he came to bat. Again, Williams' depressing effect on
his teammates has never been proved. Despite ample coaching
to the contrary, most insisted that they *liked* him. He has
been generous with advice to any player who asked for it. In
an increasingly combative baseball atmosphere, he continued
to duck beanballs docilely. With umpires he was gracious to a
fault. This courtesy itself annoyed his critics, whom there
was no pleasing. And against the ten crucial games (the seven
World Series games with the St. Louis Cardinals, the 1948
playoff with the Cleveland Indians, and the two-game series
with the Yankees at the end of the 1949 season, when one
victory would have given the Red Sox the pennant) that make
up the Achilles' heel of Williams' record, a mass of statistics
can be set showing that day in and day out he was no slouch
in the clutch.* The correspondence columns of the Boston

---

* For example: In 1948, the Sox came from behind to tie the Indians
by winning three straight; in those games Williams went two for two,
two for two; and two for four. In 1949, the Sox overtook the Yankees
by winning nine in a row; in that streak, Williams won four games
with home runs.

papers now and then suffer a sharp flurry of arithmetic on this score; indeed, for Williams to have distributed all his hits so they did nobody else any good would constitute a feat of placement unparalleled in the annals of selfishness.

Whatever residue of truth remains of the Finnegan charge those of us who love Williams must transmute as best we can, in our own personal crucibles. My personal memories of Williams began when I was a boy in Pennsylvania, with two last-place teams in Philadelphia to keep me company. For me, "W'ms, lf" was a figment of the box scores who always seemed to be going 3-for-5. He radiated, from afar, the hard blue glow of high purpose. I remember listening over the radio to the All-Star Game of 1946, in which Williams hit two singles and two home runs, the second one off a Rip Sewell "blooper" pitch; it was like hitting a balloon out of the park. I remember watching one of his home runs from the bleachers of Shibe Park; it went over the first baseman's head and rose methodically along a straight line and was still rising when it cleared the fence. The trajectory seemed qualitatively different from anything anyone else might hit. For me, Williams is the classic ballplayer of the game on a hot August weekday, before a small crowd, when the only thing at stake is the tissue-thin difference between a thing done well and a thing done ill. Baseball is a game of the long season, of relentless and gradual averaging-out. Irrelevance—since the reference point of most individual contests is remote and statistical—always threatens its interest, which can be maintained not by the occasional heroics that sportswriters feed upon but by players who always *care;* who care, that is to say, about themselves and their art. Insofar as the clutch hitter is not a sportswriter's myth, he is a vulgarity, like a writer who writes only for money. It may be that, compared to such managers' dreams as the manifestly classy Joe DiMaggio and the always helpful Stan Musial, Williams was an icy star. But of all team sports, baseball, with its graceful intermittences of action, its immense and tranquil field sparsely settled with poised men in white, its dispassionate mathematics, seems to me best suited to accommodate, and be ornamented by, a loner. It is an essentially lonely game. No other player visible to my generation concentrated within himself so much of the sport's poignance, so assiduously refined his natural skills, so constantly brought to the plate that intensity of competence that crowds the throat with joy.

By the time I went to college, near Boston, the lesser stars Yawkey had assembled around Williams had faded, and his rigorous pride of craftsmanship had become itself a kind of heroism. This brittle and temperamental player developed an unexpected quality of persistence. He was always coming back—back from Korea, back from a broken collarbone, a shattered elbow, a bruised heel, back from drastic bouts of flu and ptomaine poisoning. Hardly a season went by without some enfeebling mishap, yet he always came back, and always looked like himself. The delicate mechanism of timing and power seemed sealed, shockproof, in some case deep within his frame.* In addition to injuries, there was a heavily publicized divorce, and the usual storms with the press, and the

* Two reasons for his durability may be adduced. A non-smoker, non-drinker, habitual walker, and year-round outdoorsman, Williams spared his body the vicissitudes of the seasonal athlete. And his hitting was in large part a mental process; the amount of cerebration he devoted to such details as pitchers' patterns, prevailing winds, and the muscular mechanics of swinging a bat would seem ridiculous, if it had not paid off. His intellectuality, as it were, perhaps explains the quickness with which he adjusted, after the war, to the changed conditions—the night games, the addition of the slider to the standard pitching repertoire, the new cry for the long ball. His reaction to the Williams Shift, then, cannot be dismissed as unconsidered.

Williams Shift—the maneuver, custom-built by Lou Boudreau of the Cleveland Indians, whereby three infielders were concentrated on the right side of the infield.* Williams could easily have learned to punch singles through the vacancy on his left and fattened his average hugely. This was what Ty Cobb, the Einstein of average, told him to do. But the game had changed since Cobb; Williams believed that his value to the club and to the league was as a slugger, so he went on pulling the ball, trying to blast it through three men, and paid the price of perhaps fifteen points of lifetime average. Like Ruth before him, he bought the occasional home run at the cost of many directed singles—a calculated sacrifice certainly not, in the case of a hitter as average-minded as Williams, entirely selfish.

After a prime so harassed and hobbled, Williams was granted by the relenting fates a golden twilight. He became at the end of his career perhaps the best *old* hitter of the century. The dividing line falls between the 1956 and the 1957 seasons. In September of the first year, he and Mickey Mantle were contending for the batting championsʼup. Both were hitting around .350, and there was no one else near them. The season ended with a three-game series between the Yankees and the Sox, and, living in New York then, I went up to the Stadium. Williams was slightly shy of the four hundred at-bats needed to qualify; the fear was expressed that the

---

* Invented, or perpetrated (as a joke?) by Boudreau on July 14, 1946, between games of a doubleheader. In the first game of the doubleheader, Williams had hit three homers and batted in eight runs. The shift was not used when men were on base and, had Williams bunted or hit late against it immediately, it might not have spread, in all its variations, throughout the league. The Cardinals used it in the lamented World Series of that year. Toward the end, in 1959 and 1960, rather sadly, it had faded from use, or degenerated to the mere clockwise twitching of the infield customary against pull hitters.

Yankee pitchers would walk him to protect Mantle. Instead, they pitched to him. It was wise. He looked terrible at the plate, tired and discouraged and unconvincing. He never looked very good to me in the Stadium.* The final outcome in 1956 was Mantle .353, Williams .345.

The next year, I moved from New York to New England, and it made all the difference. For in September of 1957, in the same situation, the story was reversed. Mantle finally hit .365; it was the best season of his career. But Williams, though sick and old, had run away from him. A bout of flu had laid him low in September. He emerged from his cave in the Hotel Somerset haggard but irresistible; he hit four successive pinch-hit home runs. "I feel terrible," he confessed, "but every time I take a swing at the ball it goes out of the park." He ended the season with thirty-eight home runs and an average of .388, the highest in either league since his own .406, and, coming from a decrepit man of thirty-nine, an even more supernal figure. With eight or so of the "leg hits" that a younger man would have beaten out, it would have been .400. And the next year, Williams, who in 1949 and 1953 had lost batting championships by decimal whiskers to George Kell and Mickey Vernon, sneaked in behind his teammate Pete Runnels and filched his sixth title, a bargain at .328.

In 1959, it seemed all over. The dinosaur thrashed around in the .200 swamp for the first half of the season, and was even benched ("rested," Manager Mike Higgins tactfully said). Old foes like the late Bill Cunningham began to offer batting

---

* Shortly after his retirement, Williams, in *Life*, wrote gloomily of the Stadium, "There's the bigness of it. There are those high stands and all those people smoking—and, of course, the shadows. . . . It takes at least one series to get accustomed to the Stadium and even then you're not sure." Yet his lifetime batting average there is .340, only four points under his median average.

tips. Cunningham thought Williams was jiggling his elbows;* in truth, Williams' neck was so stiff he could hardly turn his head to look at the pitcher. When he swung, it looked like a Calder mobile with one thread cut; it reminded you that since 1954 Williams' shoulders had been wired together. A solicitous pall settled over the sports pages. In the two decades since Williams had come to Boston, his status had imperceptibly shifted from that of a naughty prodigy to that of a municipal monument. As his shadow in the record books lengthened, the Red Sox teams around him declined, and the entire American League seemed to be losing life and color to the National. The inconsistency of the new super-stars—Mantle, Colavito, and Kaline—served to make Williams appear all the more singular. And off the field, his private philanthropy—in particular, his zealous chairmanship of the Jimmy Fund, a charity for children with cancer—gave him a civic presence matched only by that of Richard Cardinal Cushing. In religion, Williams appears to be a humanist, and a selective one at that, but he and the abrasive-voiced Cardinal, when their good works intersect and they appear in the public eye together, make a handsome pair of seraphim.

Humiliated by his '59 season, Williams determined, once more, to come back. I, as a specimen Williams partisan, was both glad and fearful. All baseball fans believe in miracles; the question is, how *many* do you believe in? He looked like

---

* It was Cunningham who, when Williams first appeared in a Red Sox uniform at the 1938 spring training camp, wrote with melodious prescience: "The Sox seem to think Williams is just cocky enough and gabby enough to make a great and colorful outfielder, possibly the Babe Herman type. Me? I don't like the way he stands at the plate. He bends his front knee inward and moves his foot just before he takes a swing. That's exactly what I do just before I drive a golf ball and knowing what happens to the golf balls I drive, I don't believe this kid will ever hit half a singer midget's weight in a bathing suit."

a ghost in spring training. Manager Jurges warned us ahead of time that if Williams didn't come through he would be benched, just like anybody else. As it turned out, it was Jurges who was benched. Williams entered the 1960 season needing eight home runs to have a lifetime total of 500; after one time at bat in Washington, he needed seven. For a stretch, he was hitting a home run every second game that he played. He passed Lou Gehrig's lifetime total, and finished with 521, thirteen behind Jimmy Foxx, who alone stands between Williams and Babe Ruth's unapproachable 714. The summer was a statistician's picnic. His two-thousandth walk came and went, his eighteen-hundredth run batted in, his sixteenth All-Star Game. At one point, he hit a home run off a pitcher, Don Lee, off whose father, Thornton Lee, he had hit a home run a generation before. The only comparable season for a forty-two-year-old man was Ty Cobb's in 1928. Cobb batted .323 and hit one homer. Williams batted .316 but hit twenty-nine homers.

In sum, though generally conceded to be the greatest hitter of his era, he did not establish himself as "the greatest hitter who ever lived." Cobb, for average, and Ruth, for power, remain supreme. Cobb, Rogers Hornsby, Joe Jackson, and Lefty O'Doul, among players since 1900, have higher lifetime averages than Williams' .344. Unlike Foxx, Gehrig, Hack Wilson, Hank Greenberg, and Ralph Kiner, Williams never came close to matching Babe Ruth's season home-run total of sixty.* In the list of major-league batting records, not one is held by Williams. He is second in walks drawn, third in home runs, fifth in lifetime average, sixth in runs batted in, eighth in runs scored and in total bases, fourteenth in doubles, and thirtieth in hits.** But if we allow him merely average seasons for the

---

* Written before Roger Maris's fluky, phenomenal sixty-one.

** Again, as of 1960. Since then, Musial may have surpassed him in some statistical areas.

four-plus seasons he lost to two wars, and add another season for the months he lost to injuries, we get a man who in all the power totals would be second, and not a very distant second, to Ruth. And if we further allow that these years would have been not merely average but prime years, if we allow for all the months when Williams was playing in sub-par condition, if we permit his early and later years in baseball to be some sort of index of what the middle years could have been, if we give him a right-field fence that is not, like Fenway's, one of the most distant in the league, and if—the least excusable "if" —we imagine him condescending to outsmart the Williams Shift, we can defensibly assemble, like a colossus induced from the sizable fragments that do remain, a statistical figure not incommensurate with his grandiose ambition. From the statistics that are on the books, a good case can be made that in the *combination* of power and average Williams is first; nobody else ranks so high in both categories. Finally, there is the witness of the eyes; men whose memories go back to Shoeless Joe Jackson—another unlucky natural—rank him and Williams together as the best-looking hitters they have seen. It was for our last look that ten thousand of us had come.

Two girls, one of them with pert buckteeth and eyes as black as vest buttons, the other with white skin and flesh-colored hair, like an underdeveloped photograph of a redhead, came and sat on my right. On my other side was one of those frowning chestless young-old men who can frequently be seen, often wearing sailor hats, attending ball games alone. He did not once open his program but instead tapped it, rolled up, on his knee as he gave the game his disconsolate attention. A young lady, with freckles and a depressed, dainty nose that by an optical illusion seemed to thrust her lips forward for a kiss, sauntered down into the box seat right behind the roof of the

: 139 :

Oriole dugout. She wore a blue coat with a Northeastern University emblem sewed to it. The girls beside me took it into their heads that this was Williams' daughter. She looked too old to me, and why would she be sitting behind the visitors' dugout? On the other hand, from the way she sat there, staring at the sky and French-inhaling, she clearly was *somebody*. Other fans came and eclipsed her from view. The crowd looked less like a weekday ballpark crowd than like the folks you might find in Yellowstone National Park, or emerging from automobiles at the top of scenic Mount Mansfield. There were a lot of competitively well-dressed couples of tourist age, and not a few babes in arms. A row of five seats in front of me was abruptly filled with a woman and four children, the youngest of them two years old, if that. Someday, presumably, he could tell his grandchildren that he saw Williams play. Along with these tots and second-honeymooners, there were Harvard freshmen, giving off that peculiar nervous glow created when a sufficient quantity of insouciance is saturated with enough insecurity; thick-necked Army officers with brass on their shoulders and steel in their stares; pepperings of priests; perfumed bouquets of Roxbury Fabian fans; shiny salesmen from Albany and Fall River; and those gray, hoarse men—taxi drivers, slaughterers, and bartenders—who will continue to click through the turnstiles long after everyone else has deserted to television and tramporamas. Behind me, two young male voices blossomed, cracking a joke about God's five proofs that Thomas Aquinas exists—typical Boston College levity.

The batting cage was trundled away. The Orioles fluttered to the sidelines. Diagonally across the field, by the Red Sox dugout, a cluster of men in overcoats were festering like maggots. I could see a splinter of white uniform, and Williams' head, held at a self-deprecating and evasive tilt. Williams' conversational stance is that of a six-foot-three-inch man under a six-foot ceiling. He moved away to the patter of flash bulbs, and began playing catch with a young Negro outfielder named Willie Tasby. His arm, never very powerful, had grown lax with the years, and his throwing motion was a kind of muscular drawl. To catch the ball, he flicked his glove hand onto his left shoulder (he batted left but threw right, as every schoolboy ought to know) and let the ball plop into it comically. This catch session with Tasby was the only time all afternoon I saw him grin.

A tight little flock of human sparrows who, from the lambent and pampered pink of their faces, could only have been Boston politicians moved toward the plate. The loudspeakers mammothly coughed as someone huffed on the microphone. The ceremonies began. Curt Gowdy, the Red Sox radio and television announcer, who sounds like everybody's brother-in-law, delivered a brief sermon, taking the two words "pride" and "champion" as his text. It began. "Twenty-one years ago, a skinny kid from San Diego, California . . ." and ended, "I don't think we'll ever see another like him." Robert Tibolt, chairman of the board of the Greater Boston Chamber of Commerce, presented Williams with a big Paul Revere silver bowl. Harry Carlson, a member of the sports committee of the Boston Chamber, gave him a plaque, whose inscription he did not read in its entirety, out of deference to Williams' distaste for this sort of fuss. Mayor Collins, seated in a wheelchair, presented the Jimmy Fund with a thousand-dollar check.

Then the occasion himself stooped to the microphone, and his voice sounded, after the others, very Californian; it seemed to be coming, excellently amplified, from a great distance, adolescently young and as smooth as a butternut. His thanks for the gifts had not died from our ears before he glided, as if helplessly, into "In spite of all the terrible things that have been said about me by the knights of the keyboard up there. . . ."

He glanced up at the press rows suspended behind home plate. The crowd tittered, appalled. A frightful vision flashed upon me, of the press gallery pelting Williams with erasers, of Williams clambering up the foul screen to slug journalists, of a riot, of Mayor Collins being crushed. ". . . And they *were* terrible things," Williams insisted, with level melancholy, into the mike. "I'd like to forget them, but I can't." He paused, swallowed his memories, and went on, "I want to say that my years in Boston have been the greatest thing in my life." The crowd, like an immense sail going limp in a change of wind, sighed with relief. Taking all the parts himself, Williams then acted out a vivacious little morality drama in which an imaginary tempter came to him at the beginning of his career and said, "Ted, you can play anywhere you like." Leaping nimbly into the role of his younger self (who in biographical actuality had yearned to be a Yankee), Williams gallantly chose Boston over all the other cities, and told us that Tom Yawkey was the greatest owner in baseball and we were the greatest fans. We applauded ourselves lustily. The umpire came out and dusted the plate. The voice of doom announced over the loudspeakers that after Williams' retirement his uniform number, 9, would be permanently retired—the first time the Red Sox had so honored a player. We cheered. The national anthem was played. We cheered. The game began.

Williams was third in the batting order, so he came up in the bottom of the first inning, and Steve Barber, a young pitcher born two months before Williams began playing in the major leagues, offered him four pitches, at all of which he disdained to swing, since none of them were within the strike zone. This demonstrated simultaneously that Williams' eyes were razor-sharp and that Barber's control wasn't. Shortly, the bases were full, with Williams on second. "Oh, I hope he gets held up at third! That would be wonderful," the girl beside me moaned, and, sure enough, the man at bat walked and Williams was delivered into our foreground. He struck the pose of Donatello's David, the third-base bag being Goliath's head. Fiddling with his cap, swapping small talk with the Oriole third baseman (who seemed delighted to have him drop in), swinging his arms with a sort of prancing nervousness, he looked fine—flexible, hard, and not unbecomingly substantial through the middle. The long neck, the small head, the knickers whose cuffs were worn down near his ankles—all these clichés of sports cartoon iconography were rendered in the flesh.

With each pitch, Williams danced down the baseline, waving his arms and stirring dust, ponderous but menacing, like an attacking goose. It occurred to about a dozen humorists at once to shout "Steal home! Go, go!" Williams' speed afoot was never legendary. Lou Clinton, a young Sox outfielder, hit a fairly deep fly to center field. Williams tagged up and ran home. As he slid across the plate, the ball, thrown with unusual heft by Jackie Brandt, the Oriole center fielder, hit him on the back.

"Boy, he was really loafing, wasn't he?" one of the collegiate voices behind me said.

"It's cold," the other voice explained. "He doesn't play well when it's cold. He likes heat. He's a hedonist."

The run that Williams scored was the second and last of the inning. Gus Triandos, of the Orioles, quickly evened the score by plunking a home run over the handy left-field wall. Williams, who had had this wall at his back for twenty years,* played the ball flawlessly. He didn't budge. He just stood still, in the center of the little patch of grass that his patient foot-

---

* In his second season (1940) he was switched to left field, to protect his eyes from the right-field sun.

steps had worn brown, and, limp with lack of interest, watched the ball pass overhead. It was not a very interesting game. Mike Higgins, the Red Sox manager, with nothing to lose, had restricted his major-league players to the left-field line—along with Williams, Frank Malzone, a first-rate third baseman, played the game—and had peopled the rest of the terrain with unpredictable youngsters fresh, or not so fresh, off the farms. Other than Williams' recurrent appearances at the plate, the *maladresse* of the Sox infield was the sole focus of suspense; the second baseman turned every grounder into a juggling act, while the shortstop did a breathtaking impersonation of an open window. With this sort of assistance, the Orioles wheeled their way into a 4–2 lead. They had early replaced Barber with another young pitcher, Jack Fisher. Fortunately (as it turned out), Fisher is no cutie; he is willing to burn the ball through the strike zone, and inning after inning this tactic punctured Higgins' string of test balloons.

Whenever Williams appeared at the plate—pounding the dirt from his cleats, gouging a pit in the batter's box with his left foot, wringing resin out of the bat handle with his vehement grip, switching the stick at the pitcher with an electric ferocity—it was like having a familiar Leonardo appear in a shuffle of *Saturday Evening Post* covers. This man, you realized—and here, perhaps, was the difference, greater than the difference in gifts—really desired to hit the ball. In the third inning, he hoisted a high fly to deep center. In the fifth, we thought he had it; he smacked the ball hard and high into the heart of his power zone, but the deep right field in Fenway and the heavy air and a casual east wind defeated him. The ball died. Al Pilarcik leaned his back against the big "380" painted on the right-field wall and caught it. On another day, in another park, it would have been gone. (After the game, Williams said, "I didn't think I could hit one any harder than that. The conditions weren't good.")

The afternoon grew so glowering that in the sixth inning the arc lights were turned on—always a wan sight in the daytime, like the burning headlights of a funeral procession. Aided by the gloom, Fisher was slicing through the Sox rookies, and Williams did not come to bat in the seventh. He was second up in the eighth. This was almost certainly his last time to come to the plate in Fenway Park, and instead of merely cheering, as we had at his three previous appearances, we stood, all of us, and applauded. I had never before heard pure applause in a ballpark. No calling, no whistling, just an ocean of handclaps, minute after minute, burst after burst, crowding and running together in continuous succession like the pushes of surf at the edge of the sand. It was a sombre and considered tumult. There was not a boo in it. It seemed to renew itself out of a shifting set of memories as the Kid, the Marine, the veteran of feuds and failures and injuries, the friend of children, and the enduring old pro evolved down the bright tunnel of twenty-two summers toward this moment. At last, the umpire signalled for Fisher to pitch; with the other players, he had been frozen in position. Only Williams had moved during the ovation, switching his bat impatiently, ignoring everything except his cherished task. Fisher wound up, and the applause sank into a hush.

Understand that we were a crowd of rational people. We knew that a home run cannot be produced at will; the right pitch must be perfectly met and luck must ride with the ball. Three innings before, we had seen a brave effort fail. The air was soggy, the season was exhausted. Nevertheless, there will always lurk, around the corner in a pocket of our knowledge of the odds, an indefensible hope, and this was one of the times, which you now and then find in sports, when a density of expectation hangs in the air and plucks an event out of the future.

Fisher, after his unsettling wait, was low with the first pitch.

He put the second one over, and Williams swung mightily and missed. The crowd grunted, seeing that classic swing, so long and smooth and quick, exposed. Fisher threw the third time, Williams swung again, and there it was. The ball climbed on a diagonal line into the vast volume of air over center field. From my angle, behind third base, the ball seemed less an object in flight than the tip of a towering, motionless construct, like the Eiffel Tower or the Tappan Zee Bridge. It was in the books while it was still in the sky. Brandt ran back to the deepest corner of the outfield grass, the ball descended beyond his reach and struck in the crotch where the bullpen met the wall, bounced chunkily, and vanished.

Like a feather caught in a vortex, Williams ran around the square of bases at the center of our beseeching screaming. He ran as he always ran out home runs—hurriedly, unsmiling, head down, as if our praise were a storm of rain to get out of. He didn't tip his cap. Though we thumped, wept, and chanted "We want Ted" for minutes after he hid in the dugout, he did not come back. Our noise for some seconds passed beyond excitement into a kind of immense open anguish, a wailing, a cry to be saved. But immortality is nontransferable. The papers said that the other players, and even the umpires on the field, begged him to come out and acknowledge us in some way, but he refused. Gods do not answer letters.

Every true story has an anticlimax. The men on the field refused to disappear, as would have seemed decent, in the smoke of Williams' miracle. Fisher continued to pitch, and escaped further harm. At the end of the inning, Higgins sent Williams out to his left-field position, then instantly replaced him with Carrol Hardy, so we had a long last look at Williams as he ran out there and then back, his uniform jogging, his eyes steadfast on the ground. It was nice, and we were grateful, but it left a funny taste.

One of the scholasticists behind me said, "Let's go. We've seen everything. I don't want to spoil it." This seemed a sound aesthetic decision. Williams' last word had been so exquisitely chosen, such a perfect fusion of expectation, intention, and execution, that already it felt a little unreal in my head, and I wanted to get out before the castle collapsed. But the game, though played by clumsy midgets under the feeble glow of the arc lights, began to tug at my attention, and I loitered in the runway until it was over. Williams' homer had, quite incidentally, made the score 4–3. In the bottom of the ninth inning, with one out, Marlin Coughtry, the second-base juggler, singled. Vic Wertz, pinch-hitting, doubled off the left-field wall, Coughtry advancing to third. Pumpsie Green walked, to load the bases. Willie Tasby hit a double-play ball to the third baseman, but in making the pivot throw Billy Klaus, an ex-Red Sox infielder, reverted to form and threw the ball past the first baseman and into the Red Sox dugout. The Sox won, 5–4. On the car radio as I drove home I heard that Williams, his own man to the end, had decided not to accompany the team to New York. He had met the little death that awaits athletes. He had quit.

First Person
Singular

THE DOGWOOD TREE

A BOYHOOD

WHEN I WAS BORN, my parents and my mother's parents planted a dogwood tree in the side yard of the large white house in which we lived throughout my boyhood. This tree, I learned quite early, was exactly my age, was, in a sense, me. But I never observed it closely, am not now sure what color its petals were; its presence was no more distinct that that of my shadow. The tree was my shadow, and had it died, had it ceased to occupy, each year with increasing volume and brilliance, its place in the side yard, I would have felt that a blessing like the blessing of light had been withdrawn from my life.

Though I cannot ask you to see it more clearly than I myself saw it, yet mentioning it seems to open the possibility of my boyhood home coming again to life. With a sweet damp rush the grass of our yard seems to breathe again on me. It is just cut. My mother is pushing the mower, to which a canvas catch is attached. My grandmother is raking up the loose grass in thick heaps, small green haystacks impregnated with dew, and my grandfather stands off to one side, smoking a cigar, elegantly holding the elbow of his right arm in the palm of his left hand while the blue smoke twists from under his mustache and dissolves in the heavy evening air—that misted, too-rich Pennsylvania air. My father is off, doing some duty in the town; he is a conscientious man, a school-teacher and deacon, and also, somehow, a man of the streets.

In remembering the dogwood tree I remember the faintly speckled asbestos shingles of the chicken house at the bottom of our yard, fronting on the alley. We had a barn as well, which we rented as a garage, having no car of our own, and between the chicken house and the barn there was a narrow space where my grandfather, with his sly country ways, would urinate. I, a child, did also, passing through this narrow, hidden-feeling passage to the school grounds beyond our property; the fibrous tan-gray of the shingles would leap up dark, silky and almost black, when wetted.

The ground in this little passage seems a mysterious trough of pebbles of all colors and bits of paper and broken glass. A few weeds managed to grow in the perpetual shadow. All the ground at the lower end of the yard had an ungrateful quality; we had an ash heap on which we used to burn, in an extravagant ceremony that the war's thrift ended, the preceding day's newspaper. The earth for yards around the ashpile was colored gray. Chickens clucked in their wire pen. My grand-mother tended them, and when the time came, beheaded them with an archaic efficiency that I don't recall ever witnessing, though I often studied the heavy log whose butt was orna-mented with fine white neck-feathers pasted to the wood with blood.

A cat crosses our lawn, treading hastily on the damp grass, crouching low with distaste. Tommy is the cat's name; he lives in our chicken house but is not a pet. He is perfectly black; a rarity, he has no white dab on his chest. The birds scold out of the walnut tree and the apple and cherry trees. We have a large grape-arbor, and a stone birdbath, and a brick walk, and a privet hedge the height of a child and many bushes behind which my playmates hide. There is a pansy bed that in winter we cover with straw. The air is green, and heavy, and flavored with the smell of turned earth; in our garden grows, among other vegetables, a bland, turniplike cabbage called kohlrabi, which I have never seen, or eaten, since the days when, for a snack, I would tear one from its row with my hands.

History

My boyhood was spent in a world made tranquil by two invisible catastrophes: the Depression and World War II. Between 1932, when I was born, and 1945, when we moved away, the town of Shillington changed, as far as I could see, very little. The vacant lot beside our home on Philadelphia Avenue remained vacant. The houses along the street were neither altered nor replaced. The high-school grounds, season after season, continued to make a placid plain visible from our rear windows. The softball field, with its triptych back-stop, was nearest us. A little beyond, on the left, were the school and its boilerhouse, built in the late 1920s of the same ochre brick. In the middle distance a cinder track circum-scribed the football field. At a greater distance there were the tennis courts and the poor farm fields and the tall double rows of trees marking the Poorhouse Lane. The horizon was the blue cloud, scarred by a gravel pit's orange slash, of Mount Penn, which overlooked the city of Reading.

A little gravel alley, too small to be marked with a street sign but known in the neighborhood as Shilling Alley, wound hazardously around our property and on down, past an untidy sequence of back buildings (chicken houses, barns out of plumb, a gunshop, a small lumber mill, a shack where a blind man lived, and the enchanted grotto of a garage whose cement floors had been waxed to the lustre of ebony by oil drippings and in whose greasy-black depths a silver drinking fountain spurted the coldest water in the world, silver water so cold it made your front teeth throb) on down to Lancaster Avenue, the main street, where the trolley cars ran. All through those years, the trolley cars ran. All through those years Pappy Shilling, the surviving son of the landowner after whom the town was named, walked up and down Philadelphia Avenue with his thin black cane and his snow-white bangs; a vibrating chain of perfect-Sunday-school-attendance pins dangled from his lapel. Each autumn the horse-chestnut trees dropped their useless, treasurable nuts; each spring the dogwood tree put forth a slightly larger spread of blossoms; always the leaning walnut tree in our back yard fretted with the same tracery of branches the view we had.

Within our house, too, there was little change. My grandparents did not die, though they seemed very old. My father continued to teach at the high school; he had secured the job shortly after I was born. No one else was born. I was an only child. A great many only children were born in 1932; I make no apologies. I do not remember ever feeling the space for a competitor within the house. The five of us already there locked into a star that would have shattered like crystal at the admission of a sixth. We had no pets. We fed Tommy on the porch, but he was too wild to set foot in the kitchen, and only my grandmother, in a way wild herself, could touch him. Tommy came to us increasingly battered and once did not come at all. As if he had never existed: that was death. And then there was a squirrel, Tilly, that we fed peanuts to; she became very tame, and under the grape arbor would take them from our hands. The excitement of those tiny brown teeth shivering against my fingertips: that was life. But she, too, came from the outside, and returned to her tree, and did not dare intrude in our house.

The arrangement inside, which seemed to me so absolute, had been achieved, beyond the peripheries of my vision, drastically and accidentally. It may, at first, have been meant to be temporary. My father and grandfather were casualties of the early thirties. My father lost his job as a cable splicer with the telephone company; he and my mother had been living—for how long I have never understood—in boarding-houses and hotels throughout western Pennsylvania, in towns whose names (Hazleton, Altoona) even now make their faces light up with youth, a glow flowing out of the darkness preceding my birth. They lived through this darkness, and the details of the adventure that my mother recalls—her lonely closeted days, the games of solitaire, the novels by Turgenev, the prostitutes downstairs, the men sleeping and starving in the parks of Pittsburgh—seem to waken in her an unjust and unreasonable happiness that used to rouse jealousy in my childish heart. I remember waiting with her by a window for my father to return from weeks on the road. It is in the Shillington living room. My hands are on the radiator ridges, I can see my father striding through the hedge toward the grape arbor, I feel my mother's excitement beside me mingle with mine. But she says this cannot be; he had lost his job before I was born.

My grandfather came from farming people in the south of the county. He prospered, and prematurely retired; the large suburban house he bought to house his good fortune became his fortune's shell, the one fragment of it left him. The two men pooled their diminished resources of strength and prop-erty and, with their women, came to live together. I do not believe they expected this arrangement to last long. For all of them—for all four of my adult guardians—Shillington was a snag, a halt in a journey that had begun elsewhere. Only I belonged to the town. The accidents that had planted me here made uneasy echoes in the house, but, like Tilly and Tommy, their source was beyond my vision.

Geography

As in time, so it was in space. The town was fringed with things that appeared awesome and ominous and fantastic to a boy. At the end of our street there was the County Home—an immense yellow poorhouse, set among the wide orchards and lawns, surrounded by a sandstone wall that was low enough on one side for a child to climb easily, but that on the other side offered a drop of twenty or thirty feet, enough to kill you if you fell. Why this should have been, why the poorhouse grounds should have been so deeply recessed on the Philadelphia Avenue side, puzzles me now. What machinery, then, could have executed such a massive job of grading I don't know. But at the time it seemed perfectly natural, a dreadful pit of space congruent with the pit of time into which the old people (who could be seen circling silently in the shade of the trees whose very tops were below my feet) had been plunged by some mystery that would never touch me. That I too would come to their condition was as unbelievable as that I would really fall and break my neck. Even so, I never acquired the daring that some boys had in racing along the top of the wall. In fact—let it be said now—I was not a very daring boy.

The poorhouse impinged on us in many ways. For one thing, my father, whose favorite nightmare was poverty, often said that he liked living so close to a poorhouse; if worse came to worse, he could walk there. For another, the stench of the poorhouse pigs, when the wind was from the east, drifted well down Philadelphia Avenue. Indeed, early in my life the poorhouse livestock were still herded down the street on their way to the slaughterhouse on the other side of town. Twice, in my childhood, the poorhouse barn burnt, and I remember my father (he loved crowds) rushing out of the house in the middle of one night, and my begging to go and my mother keeping me with her, and the luckier, less sheltered children the next day telling me horrific tales of cooked cows and screaming horses. All I saw were the charred ruins, still smoldering, settling here and there with an unexpected crackle, like the underbrush the morning after an ice storm.

Most whiffs of tragedy came, strangely, from the east end of the street. I remember two, both of them associated with the early morning and with the same house a few doors away in the neighborhood. When I was a baby, a man was run over and crushed by a milk wagon—a horse-drawn milk wagon. It had happened within sight of our windows, and I grew to know the exact patch of asphalt, but could never picture it. I believed all horse-drawn milk wagons were as light as the toy one I had; by the time I understood about this accident they had vanished from the streets. No matter how many times I visited the patch of asphalt, I could not understand how it had happened. And then, the family that succeeded the widow in her house—or it may have been in the other side; it was a brick semi-detached, set back and beclouded by several tall fir or cedar trees—contained a young man who, while being a counsellor at a summer camp, had had one of his boys dive into shallow water and, neck broken, die in his arms. The young counsellor at dawn one day many months later put a bullet through his head. I seem to remember hearing the shot; certainly I remember hearing my parents bumping around in their bedroom, trying to locate what had wakened them.

Beyond the poorhouse, where Philadelphia Avenue became a country lane, and crossed a little brook where water cress grew, there was a path on the right that led to the poorhouse dam. It was a sizable lake, where people fished and swam. Its mud bottom bristled with broken bottles and jagged cans. A little up from one of its shores, the yellow walls and rotten floor of the old pesthouse survived. Beyond the lake was a woods that extended along the south of the town. Here my parents often took me on walks. Every Sunday afternoon that was fair, we would set out. Sun, birds, and treetops rotated above us as we made our way. There were many routes. Farther down the road, toward Grille, another road led off, and went past a gravel cliff and sad little composition-shingled farmhouses whose invisible inhabitants I imagined as gravel-colored skeletons. By way of a lane we could leave this road and walk down toward the dam. Or we could walk up by the dam until we struck this road, and walk on until we came to a road that took us back into the town by way of the cemetery. I disliked these walks. I would lag farther and farther behind, until my father would retrace his steps and mount me on his shoulders. Upon this giddy, swaying perch— I hesitated to grip his ears and hair as tightly as I needed to—I felt as frightened as exultant, and soon confusedly struggled to be put down. In the woods I would hurl myself against dead branches for the pleasure of feeling them shatter and of disturbing whatever peace and solace my parents were managing to gather. If, at moments, I felt what they wanted me to feel— the sweet moist breath of mulching leaves, the delicate scratch of some bird in the living silence, the benevolent intricacy of moss and rocks and roots and ferns all interlocked on some bank torn by an old logging trail—I did not tell them. I was a small-town child. Cracked pavements and packed dirt were my ground.

This broad crescent of woods is threaded with our walks and suffused with images of love. For it was here, on the beds of needles under the canopies of low pine boughs, that our girls—and this is later, not boyhood at all, but the two have become entangled—were rumored to give themselves. Indeed, I was told that one of the girls in our class, when we were in the ninth grade, had boasted that she liked nothing so much as skinny-dipping in the dam and then making love under the pines. As for myself, this was beyond me, and may be myth, but I do remember, when I was seventeen, taking a girl on one of those walks from my childhood so (then) long ago. We had moved from town, but only ten miles, and my father and I drove in to the high school every day. We walked, the girl and I, down the path where I had smashed so many branches, and sat down on a damp broad log—it was early spring, chilly, a timid froth of leaves overhead—and I dared lightly embrace her from behind and cup my hands over her breasts, small and shallow within the stiffness of her coat, and she closed her eyes and tipped her head back, and an adequate apology seemed delivered for the irritable innocence of these almost forgotten hikes with my parents.

The road that came down into Shillington by way of the cemetery led past the Dives estate, another ominous place. It was guarded by a wall topped with spiky stones. The wall must have been a half-mile long. It was so high my father had to hold me up so I could look in. There were so many buildings and greenhouses I couldn't identify the house. All the buildings were locked and boarded up; there was never anybody there. But in the summer the lawns were mowed; it seemed by ghosts. There were tennis courts, and even—can it be?—a few golf flags. In any case there was a great deal of cut lawn, and gray driveway, and ordered bushes; I got the impression of wealth as a vast brooding absence, like God Himself. The road here was especially overshadowed by trees, so a humid, stale, cloistered smell flavored my glimpses over the wall.

The cemetery was on the side of a hill, bare to the sun, which quickly faded the little American flags and killed the potted geraniums. It was a holiday place; on Memorial Day the parade, in which the boys participated mounted on bicycles whose wheels were threaded with tricolor crêpe paper, ended here, in a picnic of speeches and bugle music and leapfrog over the tombstones. From here you had a perfect view of the town, spread out in the valley between this hill and Slate Hill, the chimneys smoking like just-snuffed cigarettes, the cars twinkling down on Lancaster Avenue, the trolleys moving with the dreamlike slow motion distance imposes.

A little to one side of the cemetery, just below the last trees of the love-making woods, was a small gravel pit where, during the war, we played at being guerrillas. Our leader was a sickly and shy boy whose mother made him wear rubbers whenever there was dew on the grass. His parents bought him a helmet and khaki jacket and even leggings, and he brought great enthusiasm to the imitation of war. G.I.'s and Japs, shouting "Geronimo!" and "Banzai!," we leaped and scrambled over boulders and cliffs in one of whose clefts I always imagined, for some reason, I was going to discover a great deal of money, in a tan cloth bag tied with a leather thong. Though I visualized the bag very clearly, I never found it.

Between this pit and the great quarry on the far edge of town, I lose track of Shillington's boundaries. I believe it was just fields, in which a few things were still farmed. The great quarry was immense, and had a cave, and an unused construction covered with fine gray dust and filled with mysterious gears, levers, scoops, and stairs. The quarry was a mile from my home; I seldom went there. It wears in memory a gritty film. The tougher section of town was nearby. Older boys with .22s used the quarry as a rifle range, and occasionally wounded each other, or smaller children. To scale its sides was even more dangerous than walking along the top of the poorhouse wall. The legends of love that scattered condums along its grassy edges seemed to be of a coarser love than that which perfumed the woods. Its cave was short, and stumpy, yet long enough to let you envision a collapse blocking the mouth of light and sealing you in; the walls were of a greasy golden clay that seemed likely to collapse. The one pure, lovely thing about the quarry, beside its grand size, was the frozen water that appeared on its floor in the winter, and where you could skate sheltered from the wind, and without the fear of drowning that haunted the other skating place, the deep dam. Though the area of ice was smaller, the skaters seemed more skillful down at the quarry: girls in red tights and bouncy short skirts that gave their fannies the effect of a pompon turned and swirled and braked backward to a stop on their points, sparkling ice chips sprinkling in twin fans of spray.

Near the quarry was the Shillington Friday Market, where the sight of so many naked vegetables depressed me, and the Wyomissing Creek, a muddy little thing to skip pebbles in, and the hilly terrain where, in those unbuilding years, a few new houses were built. The best section of town, called Lynoak, was farther on, more toward Reading, around the base of Slate Hill, where I sometimes sledded. It was a long walk back through the streets, under the cold street lights, the sled runners rattling on the frozen ruts, my calves aching with the snow that always filtered through my galoshes. This hill in summer was another place my parents hiked to. The homes of the well-off (including an amazingly modern house, of white brick, with a flat roof, and blue trim, like something assembled from the two dimensions of a Hollywood movie) could be seen climbing its sides, but there was still plenty of room for, during the war, Victory gardens, and above that, steep wilderness. The top was a bare, windy, primeval place. Looking north, you saw the roofs of Shillington merge with the roofs of other suburbs in a torn carpet that went right into the bristling center of Reading, under the blue silhouette of

Mount Penn. As Shillington on the south faced the country, northward it faced the city.

Reading: a very powerful and fragrant and obscure city—who has ever heard of it? Wallace Stevens was born there, and John Philip Sousa died there. For a generation it had a Socialist mayor. Its railroad is on the Monopoly Board. It is rumored to be endeared to gangsters, for its citizens make the most tolerant juries in the East. Unexpectedly, a pagoda overlooks it from the top of Mount Penn. This is the meagre list of its singularities as I know them. Larger than Harrisburg and Wilkes-Barre and Lancaster, it is less well known. Yet to me Reading is the master of cities, the one at the center that all others echo. How rich it smelled! Kresge's swimming in milk chocolate and violet-scented toilet water, Grant's barricaded with coconut cookies, the vast velveted movie theatres dusted with popcorn and a cold whiff of leather, the bakeshops exhaling hearty brown drafts of molasses and damp dough and crisp grease and hot sugar, the beauty parlors with their gingerly stink of singeing, the bookstores glistening with fresh paper and bubbles of hardened glue, the shoe-repair nooks blackened by Kiwi Wax and aromatic shavings, the public lavatory with its emphatic veil of soap, the hushed, brick-red side streets spiced with grit and the moist seeds of maples and ginkgos, the goblin stench of the trolley car that made each return to Shillington a race with nausea—Reading's smells were most of what my boyhood knew of the Great World that was suspended, at a small but sufficient distance, beyond my world.

For the city and the woods and the ominous places were peripheral; their glamour and menace did not intrude into the sunny area where I lived, where the seasons arrived like issues of a magazine and I moved upward from grade to grade and birthday to birthday on a notched stick that itself was held perfectly steady. There was the movie house, and the playground, and the schools, and the grocery stores, and our yard, and my friends, and the horse-chestnut trees. My geography went like this: in the center of the world lay our neighborhood of Shillington. Around it there was greater Shillington, and around that, Berks County. Around Berks County there was the State of Pennsylvania, the best, the least eccentric, state in the Union. Around Pennsylvania, there was the United States, with a greater weight of people on the right and a greater weight of land on the left. For clear geometrical reasons, not all children could be born, like me, at the center of the nation. But that some children chose to be born in other countries and even continents seemed sad and fantastic. There was only one possible nation: mine. Above this vast, rectangular, slightly (the schoolteachers insisted) curved field of the blessed, there was the sky, and the flag, and, mixed up with both, Roosevelt.

Democrats

We were Democrats. My grandfather lived for ninety years, and always voted, and always voted straight Democrat. A marvellous chain of votes, as marvellous as the chain of Sunday-school-attendance pins that vibrated from Pappy Shilling's lapel. The political tradition that shaped his so incorruptible prejudice I am not historian enough to understand; it had something to do with Lincoln's determination to drive all the cattle out of this section of Pennsylvania if Lee won the Battle of Gettysburg.

My parents are closer to me. The events that shaped their views are in my bones. At the time when I was conceived and born, they felt in themselves a whole nation stunned, frightened, despairing. With Roosevelt, hope returned. This simple impression of salvation is my political inheritance. That this impression is not universally shared amazes me. It is as if there existed a class of people who deny that the sun is bright. To me as a child Republicans seemed blind dragons; their proto-type was my barber—an artist, a charmer, the only man, my mother insists, who ever cut my hair properly. Nimble and bald, he used to execute little tap-dance figures on the linoleum floor of his shop, and with engaging loyalty he always had the games of Philadelphia's two eighth-place teams tuned in on the radio. But on one subject he was rabid; the last time he cut my hair he positively asserted that our President had died of syphilis. I cannot to this day hear a Republican put forth his philosophy without hearing the snip of scissors above my ears and feeling the little ends of hair crawling across my hot face, reddened by shame and the choking pressure of the paper collar.

Now

Roosevelt was for me the cap on a steadfast world, its emblem and crown. He was always there. Now he is a weakening memory, a semi-legend; it has begun to seem fabulous—like an episode in a medieval chronicle—that the greatest nation in the world was led through the world's greatest war by a man who could not walk. Now, my barber has retired, my hair is a wretched thatch grizzled with gray, and, of the two Philadelphia ball clubs, one has left Philadelphia and one is not always in last place. Now the brick home of my boyhood is owned by a doctor, who has added an annex to the front, to contain his offices. The house was too narrow for its lot and its height; it had a pinched look from the front that used to annoy my mother. But that thin white front with its eyes of green window sash and its mouth of striped awning had been a face to me; it has vanished. My dogwood tree still stands in the side yard, taller than ever, but the walnut tree out back has been cut down. My grandparents are dead. Pappy Shilling is dead. Shilling Alley has been straightened, and hardtopped, and rechristened Brobst Street. The trolley cars no longer run. The vacant lots across the town have been filled with new houses and stores. New homes have been built far out Philadelphia Avenue and all over the poorhouse property. The poorhouse has been demolished. The poorhouse dam and its aphrodisiac groves have been trimmed into a town park and a chlorinated pool where all females must sheathe their hair in prophylactic bathing caps. If I could go again into 117 Philadelphia Avenue and look out the rear windows, I would see, beyond the football field and the cinder track, a new, two-million-dollar high school, and beyond it, where still stands one row of the double line of trees that marked the Poorhouse Lane, a gaudy depth of postwar housing and a Food Fair like a hideous ark breasting an ocean of parked cars. Here, where wheat grew, loudspeakers unremittingly vomit commercials. It has taken me the shocks of many returnings, more and more widely spaced now, to learn, what seems simple enough, that change is the order of things. The immutability, the steadfastness, of the site of my boyhood was an exceptional effect, purchased for me at unimaginable cost by the paralyzing calamity of the Depression and the heroic external effort of the Second World War.

Environment

The difference between a childhood and a boyhood must be this: our childhood is what we alone have had; our boyhood is what any boy in our environment would have had. My environment was a straight street about three city blocks long, with a slight slope that was most noticeable when you were on a bicycle. Though many of its residents commuted to Reading factories and offices, the neighborhood retained a rural flavor. Corn grew in the strip of land between the alley and the school grounds. We ourselves had a large vegetable garden, which we tended not as a hobby but in earnest, to get food to eat. We sold asparagus and eggs to our neighbors. Our peddling things humiliated me, but then I was a new generation. The bulk of the people in the neighborhood were not long off the farm. One old lady down the street, with an immense throat goiter, still wore a bonnet. The most aristocratic people in the block were the full-fashioned knitters; Reading's textile industry prospered in the Depression. I felt neither prosperous nor poor. We kept the food money in a little recipe box on top of the icebox, and there were nearly always a few bills and coins in it. My father's job paid him poorly but me well; it gave me a sense of, not prestige, but *place*. As a schoolteacher's son, I was assigned a role; people knew me. When I walked down the street to school, the houses called, "Chonny." I had a place to be.

Schools

The elementary school was a big brick cube set in a square of black surfacing chalked and painted with the diagrams and runes of children's games. Wire fences guarded the neighboring homes from the playground. Whoever, at soccer, kicked the ball over the fence into Snitzy's yard had to bring it back. It was very terrible to have to go into Snitzy's yard, but there was only one ball for each grade. Snitzy was a large dark old German who might give you the ball or lock you up in his garage, depending upon his mood. He did not move like other men; suddenly the air near your head condensed, and his heavy hands were on you.

On the way to school, walking down Lancaster Avenue, we passed Henry's, a variety store where we bought punch-out licorice belts and tablets with Edward G. Robinson and Hedy Lamarr smiling on the cover. In October, Halloween masks appeared, hung on wire clotheslines. Hanging limp, these faces of Chinamen and pirates and witches were distorted, and, thickly clustered and rustling against each other, they seemed more frightening masking empty air than they did mounted on the heads of my friends—which was frightening enough. It is strange how fear resists the attacks of reason, how you can know with absolute certainty that it is only Mark Wenrich or Jimmy Trexler whose eyes are moving so weirdly in those almond-shaped holes, and yet still be frightened. I abhorred that effect of double eyes a mask gives; it was as bad as seeing a person's mouth move upside down.

I was a Crow. That is my chief memory of what went on inside the elementary school. In music class the singers were divided into three groups: Nightingales, Robins, and Crows. From year to year the names changed. Sometimes the Crows were Parrots. When visitors from the high school, or elsewhere "outside," came to hear us sing, the Crows were taken out of the room and sent upstairs to watch with the fifth grade an educational film about salmon fishing in the Columbia River. Usually there were only two of us, me and a girl from Philadelphia Avenue whose voice was in truth very husky. I never understood why I was a Crow, though it gave me a certain derisive distinction. As I heard it, I sang rather well.

The other Crow was the first girl I kissed. I just did it, one day, walking back from school along the gutter where the water from the ice plant ran down, because somebody dared me to. And I continued to do it every day, when we reached that spot on the pavement, until a neighbor told my mother, and she, with a solemn weight that seemed unrelated to the airy act, forbade it.

I walked to school mostly with girls. It happened that the mothers of Philadelphia Avenue and, a block up, of Second Street had borne females babies in 1932. These babies now teased me, the lone boy in their pack, by singing the new song,

"Oh, Johnny, oh Johnny, how you can love!" and stealing my precious rubber-lined bookbag. The queen of these girls later became the May Queen of our senior class. She had freckles and thick pigtails and green eyes and her mother made her wear high-top shoes long after the rest of us had switched to low ones. She had so much vitality that on the way back from school her nose would start bleeding for no reason. We would be walking along over the wings of the maple seeds and suddenly she would tip her head back and rest it on a wall while someone ran and soaked a handkerchief in the ice-plant water and applied it to her streaming, narrow, crimson-shining nostrils. She was a Nightingale. I loved her deeply, and ineffectually.

My love for that girl carries through all those elementary-school cloakrooms; they always smelled of wet raincoats and rubbers. That tangy, thinly resonant, lonely smell: can love have a better envelope? Everything I did in grammar school was meant to catch her attention. I had a daydream wherein the stars of the music class were asked to pick partners and she, a Nightingale, picked me, a Crow. The teacher was shocked; the class buzzed. To their amazement I sang superbly; my voice, thought to be so ugly, in duet with hers was beautiful. Still singing, we led some sort of parade.

In the world of reality, my triumph was getting her to slap me once, in the third grade. She was always slapping boys in those years; I could not quite figure out what they did. Pull her pigtails, untie her shoes, snatch at her dress, tease her (they called her "Pug")—this much I could see. But somehow there seemed to be under these offensive acts a current running the opposite way; for it was precisely the boys who behaved worst to her that she talked to solemnly at recess, and walked with after school, and whose names she wrote on the sides of her books. Without seeing this current, but deducing its presence,

I tried to jump in; I entered a tussle she was having with a boy in homeroom before the bell. I pulled the bow at the back of her dress, and was slapped so hard that children at the other end of the hall heard the crack. I was overjoyed; the stain and pain on my face seemed a badge of initiation. But it was not. The distance between us remained as it was. I did not really want to tease her, I wanted to rescue her, and to be rescued by her. I lacked—and perhaps here the only child suffers a certain deprivation—that kink in the instincts on which childish courtship turns. He lacks a certain easy roughness with other children.

All the years I was at the elementary school the high school loomed large in my mind. Its students—tall, hairy, smoke-breathing—paced the streets seemingly equal with adults. I could see part of its immensity from our rear windows. It was there that my father performed his mysteries every day, striding off from breakfast, down through the grape arbor, his coat pocket bristling with defective pens. He now and then took me over there; the incorruptible smell of varnish and red sweeping wax, the size of the desks, the height of the drinking fountains, the fantastic dimensions of the combination gymnasium-auditorium made me feel that these were halls in which a race of giants had ages ago labored through lives of colossal bliss. At the end of each summer, usually on Labor Day Monday, he and I went into his classroom, Room 201, and unpacked the books and arranged the tablets and the pencils on the desks of his homeroom puplis. Sharpening forty pencils was a chore, sharing it with him a solemn pleasure. To this day I look up at my father through the cedar smell of pencil shavings. To see his key open the front portals of oak, to share alone with him for an hour the pirate hoard of uncracked books and golden pencils, to switch off the lights and leave the room and walk down the darkly lustrous perspective of the corridor and perhaps halt for a few words by an open door that revealed another teacher, like a sorcerer in his sanctum, inscribing forms beside a huge polished globe of the Earth—such territories of wonder boyhood alone can acquire.

The Playground

The periphery I have traced; the center of my boyhood held a calm collection of kind places that are almost impossible to describe, because they are so fundamental to me, they enclosed so many of my hours, that they have the neutral color of my own soul, which I have always imagined as a pale oblong just under my ribs. In the town where I now live, and where I am writing this, seagulls weep overhead on a rainy day. No seagulls found their way inland to Shillington; there were sparrows, and starlings, and cowbirds, and robins, and occasionally a buzzard floating high overhead on immobile wings like a kite on a string too high to be seen.

The playground: up from the hardball diamond, on a plateau bounded three sides by cornfields, a pavilion contained some tables and a shed for equipment. I spent my summer weekdays there from the age when I was so small that the dust stirred by the feet of roof-ball players got into my eyes. Roof ball was the favorite game. It was played with a red rubber ball smaller than a basketball. The object was to hit it back up on the roof of the pavilion, the whole line of children in succession. Those who failed dropped out. When there was just one person left, a new game began with the cry "*Noo*-oo *gay*-ame," and we lined up in the order in which we had gone out, so that the lines began with the strongest and tallest and ended with the weakest and youngest. But there was never any doubt that everybody could play; it was perfect democracy. Often the line contained as many as thirty pairs of legs, arranged chronologically. By the time we moved away, I had become a regular front-runner; I knew how to flick the ball to give it spin, how to leap up and send the ball skimming the length of the roof edge, how to plump it with my knuckles when there was a high bounce. Somehow the game never palled. The sight of the ball bouncing along the tarpaper of the foreshortened roof was always important. Many days I was at the playground from nine o'clock, when they ran up the American flag, until four, when they called the equipment in, and played nothing else.

If you hit the ball too hard, and it went over the peak of the roof, you were out, and you had to retrieve the ball, going down a steep bank into a field where the poorhouse men had stopped planting corn because it all got mashed down. If the person ahead of you hit the ball into the air without touching the roof, or missed it entirely, you had the option of "saving," by hitting the ball onto the roof before it struck the ground; this created complex opportunities for strategy and gallantry. I would always try to save the Nightingale, for instance, and there was a girl who came from Louisiana with a French name whom everybody wanted to save. At twelve, she seemed already mature, and I can remember standing with a pack of other boys under the swings looking up at the undersides of her long tense dark-skinned legs as she kicked into the air to give herself more height, the tendons on the underside of her smooth knees jumping, her sneakered feet pointing like a ballerina's shoes.

The walls of the pavilion shed were scribbled all over with dirty drawings and words and detailed slanders on the prettier girls. After hours, when the supervisors were gone, if you were tall enough you could grab hold of a crossbeam and get on top of the shed, where there was an intimate wedge of space under the slanting roof; here no adult ever bothered to scrub away the pencillings, and the wood fairly breathed of the forbidden. The very silence of the pavilion, after the day-long click of checkers and *pokabok* of ping-pong, was like a love-choked hush.

Reality seemed more intense at the playground. There was a dust, a daring. It was a children's world; nowhere else did we gather in such numbers with so few adults over us. The playground occupied a platform of earth; we were exposed, it seems now, to the sun and sky. Looking up, one might see a buzzard or witness a portent.

The Enormous Cloud

Strange, that I remember it. One day, playing roof ball—and I could be six, nine, or twelve when it happened—my head was tipped back and there was an enormous cloud. Someone, maybe I, even called, "Look at the cloud!" It was a bright day; out of nowhere had materialized a cloud, roughly circular in shape, as big as a continent, leaden-blue in the mass, radiant silver along the edges. Its size seemed overwhelming; it was more than a portent, it was the fulfillment of one. I had never seen, and never saw again, such a big cloud.

For of course what is strange is that clouds have no size. Moving in an immaterial medium at an indeterminate distance, they offer no hold for measurement, and we do not even judge them relative to each other. Even, as on a rainy day, when the sky is filled from horizon to horizon, we do not think, "What an enormous cloud." It is as if the soul is a camera shutter customarily set at "ordinary"; but now and then, through some inadvertence, it is tripped wide open and the film is flooded with an enigmatic image.

Another time the sky spoke at the playground, telling me that treachery can come from above. It was our Field Day. One of the events was a race in which we put our shoes in a heap, lined up at a distance, ran to the heap, found our shoes, put them on, and raced back. The winner got a ticket to the Shillington movie theatre. I was the first to find my shoes, and was tying my laces when, out of the ring of adults and older children who had collected to watch, a voice urged, "Hurry! Don't tie the laces." I didn't, and ran back, and was disqualified. My world reeled at the treachery of that unseen high voice: I loved the movies.

The Movie House

It was two blocks from my home; I began to go alone from the age of six. My mother, so strict about my kissing girls, was strangely indulgent about this. The theatre ran three shows a week, for two days each, and was closed on Sundays. Many weeks I went three times. I remember a summer evening in our yard. Supper is over, the walnut tree throws a heavy shadow. The fireflies are not out yet. My father is off, my mother and her parents are turning the earth in our garden. Some burning sticks and paper on our ash heap fill the damp air with low smoke; I express a wish to go to the movies, expecting to be told No. Instead, my mother tells me to go into the house and clean up; I come into the yard again in clean shorts, the shadows slightly heavier, the dew a little wetter; I am given eleven cents and run down Philadelphia Avenue in my ironed shorts and fresh shirt, down past the running ice-plant water, the dime and the penny in my hand. I always ran to the movies. If it was not a movie with Adolphe Menjou, it was a horror picture. People turning into cats—fingers going stubby into paws and hair being blurred in with double exposure—and Egyptian tombs and English houses where doors creak and wind disturbs the curtains and dogs refuse to go into certain rooms because they sense something supersensory. I used to crouch down into the seat and hold my coat in front of my face when I sensed a frightening scene coming, peeking through the buttonhole to find out when it was over. Through the buttonhole Frankenstein's monster glowered; lightning flashed; sweat poured over the bolts that held his face together. On the way home, I ran again, in terror now. Darkness had come, the first show was from seven to nine, by nine even the longest summer day was ending. Each porch along the street se   .d to be a tomb crammed with shadows, each shrub seer   to shelter a grasping arm. I ran with a frantic high step, trying to keep my ankles away from the reaching hand. The last and worst terror was our own porch; low brick walls on either side concealed possible cat people. Leaping high, I launched myself at the door and, if no one was in the front of the house, fled through suffocating halls past gaping doorways to the kitchen, where there was always someone working, and a light bulb burning. The icebox. The rickety worn table, oilcloth-covered, where we ate. The windows painted solid black by the interior brightness. But even then I kept my legs away from the furry space beneath the table.

These were Hollywood's comfortable years. The theatre, a shallowly sloped hall too narrow to have a central aisle, was usually crowded. I liked it most on Monday nights, when it was emptiest. It seemed most mine then. I had a favorite seat —rear row, extreme left—and my favorite moment was the instant when the orange side lights, Babylonian in design, were still lit, and the curtain was closed but there was obviously somebody up in the projection room, for the camera had started to whir. In the next instant, I knew, a broad dusty beam of light would fill the air above me, and the titles of the travelogue would appear on the curtains, their projected steadiness undulating as with an unhurried, composed screech the curtains were drawn back, revealing the screen alive with images that then would pass through a few focal adjustments. In that delicate, promissory whir was my favorite moment.

On Saturday afternoons the owner gave us all Hershey bars as we came out of the matinee. On Christmas morning he showed a free hour of cartoons and the superintendent of the Lutheran Sunday school led us in singing carols, gesticulating in front of the high blank screen, no bigger than the shadow of the moth that sometimes landed on the lens. His booming voice would echo curiously on the bare walls, usually so dark and mufflling but that on this one morning, containing a loud sea of Christmas children, had a bare, clean, morning quality that echoed. After this special show we all went down to the Town Hall, where the plumpest borough employee, disguised as Santa Claus, gave us each a green box of chocolates. Shillington was small enough to support such traditions.

Three Boys

A, *B*, and *C*, I'll say, in case they care. *A* lived next door; he *loomed* next door, rather. He seemed immense—a great wallowing fatso stuffed with possessions; he was the son of a full-fashioned knitter. He seemed to have a beer-belly; after several generations beer-bellies may become congenital. Also his face had no features. It was just a blank ball on his shoulders. He used to call me "Ostrich," after Disney's Ollie Ostrich. My neck was not very long; the name seemed horribly unfair; it was its injustice that made me cry. But nothing I could say, or scream, would make him stop. And I still, now and then—in reading, say, a book review by one of the apple-cheeked savants of the quarterlies or one of the pious gremlins who manufacture puns for *Time*—get the old sensations: my ears close up, my eyes go warm, my chest feels thin as an eggshell, my voice churns silently in my stomach. From *A* I received my first impression of the smug, chinkless, irresistible *power* of stupidity; it is the most powerful force on earth. It says "Ostrich" often enough, and the universe crumbles.

A was more than a boy, he was a force-field that could

manifest itself in many forms, that could take the wiry, disconsolate shape of wide-mouthed, tiny-eared boys who would now and then beat me up on the way back from school. I did not greatly mind being beaten up, though I resisted it. For one thing, it firmly involved me, at least during the beating, with the circumambient humanity that so often seemed evasive. Also, the boys who applied the beating were misfits, periodic flunkers, who wore corduroy knickers with threadbare knees and men's shirts with the top button buttoned—this last an infallible sign of deep poverty. So that I felt there was some justice, some condonable revenge, being applied with their fists to this little teacher's son. And then there was the delicious alarm of my mother and grandmother when I returned home bloody, bruised, and torn. My father took the attitude that it was making a boy of me, an attitude I dimly shared. He and I both were afraid of me becoming a sissy —he perhaps more afraid than I.

When I was eleven or so I met *B.* It was summer and I was down at the playground. He was pushing a little tank with moving rubber treads up and down the hills in the sandbox. It was a fine little toy, mottled with camouflage green; patriotic manufacturers produced throughout the war millions of such authentic miniatures which we maneuvered with authentic, if miniature, militance. Attracted by the toy, I spoke to him; though taller and a little older than I, he had my dull straight brown hair and a look of being also alone. We became fast friends. He lived just up the street—toward the poorhouse, the east part of the street, from which the little winds of tragedy blew. He had just moved from the Midwest, and his mother was a widow. Beside wage war, we did many things together. We played marbles for days at a time, until one of us had won the other's entire coffee-canful. With jigsaws we cut out of plywood animals copied from comic books.

We made movies by tearing the pages from Big Little Books and coloring the drawings and pasting them in a strip, and winding them on toilet-paper spools, and making a cardboard carton a theatre. We rigged up telephones, and racing wagons, and cities of the future, using orange crates and cigar boxes and peanut-butter jars and such potent debris. We loved Smokey Stover and were always saying "Foo." We had an intense spell of Monopoly. He called me "Uppy"—the only person who ever did. I remember once, knowing he was coming down that afternoon to my house to play Monopoly, in order to show my joy I set up the board elaborately, with the Chance and Community Chest cards fanned painstakingly, like spiral staircases. He came into the room, groaned, "Uppy, what are you doing?" and impatiently scrabbled the cards together in a sensible pile. The older we got, the more the year between us told, and the more my friendship embarrassed him. We fought. Once, to my horror, I heard myself taunting him with the fact that he had no father. The unmentionable, the unforgivable. I suppose we patched things up, children do, but the fabric had been torn. He had a long, pale, serious face, with buck-teeth, and is probably an electronics engineer somewhere now, doing secret government work.

So through *B* I first experienced the pattern of friendship. There are three stages. First, acquaintance: we are new to each other, make each other laugh in surprise, and demand nothing beyond politeness. The death of the one would startle the other, no more. It is a pleasant stage, a stable stage; on austere rations of exposure it can live a lifetime, and the two parties to it always feel a slight gratification upon meeting, will feel vaguely confirmed in their human state. Then comes intimacy: now we laugh before two words of the joke are out of the other's mouth, because we know what he will say. Our two beings seem marvellously joined, from our toes to our heads, along tingling points of agreement; everything we venture is right, everything we put forth lodges in a corresponding socket in the frame of the other. The death of one would grieve the other. To be together is to enjoy a mounting excitement, a constant echo and amplification. It is an ecstatic and unstable stage, bound of its own agitation to tip into the third: revulsion. One or the other makes a misjudgment; presumes; puts forth that which does not meet agreement. Sometimes there is an explosion; more often the moment is swallowed in silence, and months pass before its nature dawns. Instead of dissolving, it grows. The mind, the throat, are clogged; forgiveness, forgetfulness, that have arrived so often, fail. Now everything jars and is distasteful. The betrayal, perhaps a tiny fraction in itself, has inverted the tingling column of agreement, made all pluses minuses. Everything about the other is hateful, despicable; yet he cannot be dismissed. We have confided in him too many minutes, too many words; he has those minutes and words as hostages, and his confidences are embedded in us where they cannot be scraped away, and even rivers of time cannot erode them completely, for there are indelible stains. Now—though the friends may continue to meet, and smile, as if they had never trespassed beyond acquaintance—the death of the one would please the other.

An unhappy pattern to which C is an exception. He was my friend before kindergarten, he is my friend still. I go to his home now, and he and his wife serve me and my wife with alcoholic drinks and slices of excellent cheese on crisp crackers, just as twenty years ago he served me with treats from his mother's refrigerator. He was a born host, and I a born guest. Also he was intelligent. If my childhood's brain, when I look back at it, seems a primitive mammal, a lemur or shrew, his brain was an angel whose visitation was widely hailed as wonderful. When in school he stood to recite, his cool rectangular forehead glowed. He tucked his right hand into his left armpit and with his left hand mechanically tapped a pencil against his thigh. His answers were always correct. He beat me at spelling bees and, in another sort of competition, when we both collected Big Little Books, he outbid me for my supreme find (in the attic of a third boy), the first Mickey Mouse. I can still see that book, I wanted it so badly, its paper tan with age and its drawings done in Disney's primitive style, when Mickey's black chest is naked like a child's and his eyes are two nicked oblongs. Losing it was perhaps a lucky blow; it helped wean me away from hope of ever having possessions.

C was fearless. He deliberately set fields on fire. He engaged in rock-throwing duels with tough boys. One afternoon he persisted in playing quoits with me although—as the hospital discovered that night—his appendix was nearly bursting. He was enterprising. He peddled magazine subscriptions door-to-door; he mowed neighbors' lawns; he struck financial bargains with his father. He collected stamps so well his collection blossomed into a stamp company that filled his room with steel cabinets and mimeograph machinery. He collected money —every time I went over to his house he would get out a little tin box and count the money in it for me: $27.50 one week, $29.95 the next, $30.90 the next—all changed into new bills nicely folded together. It was a strange ritual, whose meaning for me was: since he was doing it, I didn't have to. His money made me richer. We read Ellery Queen and played chess and invented board games and discussed infinity together. In later adolescence, he collected records. He liked the Goodman quintets but loved Fats Waller. Sitting there in that room so familiar to me, where the machinery of the Shilco Stamp Company still crowded the walls and for that matter the tin box of money might still be stashed, while my thin friend grunted softly along with that dead dark angel on "You're Not the Only Oyster in the Stew," I felt, in the best sense, patronized: the perfect guest of the perfect host. What made it perfect was that we had both spent our entire lives in Shillington.

Concerning the Three Great Secret Things: (1) Sex

In crucial matters, the town was evasive. Sex was an unlikely, though persistent, rumor. My father slapped my mother's bottom and made a throaty noise and I thought it was a petty form of sadism. The major sexual experience of my boyhood was a section of a newsreel showing some women wrestling in a pit of mud. The mud covered their bathing suits so they seemed naked. Thick, interlocking, faceless bodies, they strove and fell. The sight was so disturbingly resonant that afterward, in any movie, two women pulling each other's hair or slapping each other—there was a good deal of this in movies of the early forties; Ida Lupino was usually one of the women —gave me a tense, watery, drawn-out feeling below the belt. Thenceforth my imaginings about girls moved through mud. In one recurrent scene I staged in my bed, the girl and I, dressed in our underpants and wrapped around with ropes, had been plunged from an immense cliff into a secret pond of mud, by a villain who resembled Peg-Leg Pete. I usually got my hands free and rescued her; sometimes she rescued me; in any case there hovered over our spattered, elastic-clad bodies the idea that these were the last minutes of our lives, and all our shames and reservations were put behind us. It turned out that she had loved me all along. We climbed out, into the light. The ropes had hurt our wrists; yet the sweet kernel of the fantasy lay somehow in the sensations of being tightly bound, before we rescued each other.

(2) Religion

Pragmatically, I have become a Congregationalist, but in the translucent and tactful church of my adoption my eyes sting, my throat goes grave, when we sing—what we rarely sang in the Lutheran church of my childhood—Luther's mighty hymn:

> For still our ancient foe
> Doth seek to work us woe;
> His craft and power are great,
> And arm'd with cruel hate,
> On earth is not his equal.

This immense dirge of praise for the Devil and the world, thunderous, slow, opaquely proud, nourishes a seed in me I never knew was planted. How did the patently vapid and drearily businesslike teachings to which I was lightly exposed succeed in branding me with a Cross? And a brand so specifically Lutheran, so distinctly Nordic; an obdurate insistence that at the core of the core there is a right-angled clash to which, of all verbal combinations we can invent, the Apostles' Creed offers the most adequate correspondence and response.

Of my family, only my father attended the church regularly, returning every Sunday with the Sunday Reading *Eagle* and the complaint that the minister prayed too long. My own relations with the church were unsuccessful. In Sunday school, I rarely received the perfect attendance pin, though my attendance seemed to me and my parents as perfect as anybody's. Instead, I was given a pencil stamped KINDT'S FUNERAL HOME. Once, knowing that a lot of racy social activity was going on under its aegis, I tried to join the Luther League; but I had the misfortune to arrive on the night of their Halloween party, and was refused admittance because I was not wearing a costume. And, the worst rebuff, I was once struck by a car on the way to Sunday school. I had the collection nickel in my hand, and held on to it even as I was being dragged fifteen feet on the car's bumper. For this heroic churchmanship I received no palpable credit; the Lutheran Church seemed positively to dislike me.

Yet the crustiness, the inhospitality of the container enhanced the oddly lucid thing contained. I do not recall my first doubts; I doubted perhaps abnormally little. And when they came, they never roosted on the branches of the tree, but attacked the roots; if the first article of the Creed stands, the rest follows as water flows downhill. That God, at a remote place and time, took upon Himself the form of a Syrian carpenter and walked the earth willfully healing and abusing and affirming and grieving, appeared to me quite in the character of the Author of the grass. The mystery that more puzzled me as a child was the incarnation of my ego—that omnivorous and somehow preëxistent "I"—in a speck so specifically situated amid the billions of history. Why was I I? The arbitrariness of it astounded me; in comparison, nothing was too marvellous.

Shillington bred a receptivity to the supernatural unrelated to orthodox religion. This is the land of the hex signs, and in the neighboring town of Grille a "witch doctor" hung out a shingle like a qualified M.D. I was struck recently, on reading Frazer's contemptuous list of superstitions in *The Golden Bough*, by how many of them seemed good sense. My grandmother was always muttering little things; she came from a country world of spilled salt and cracked mirrors and new moons and omens. She convinced me, by contagion, that our house was haunted. I punished her by making her stand guard outside the bathroom when I was in it. If I found she had fallen asleep in the shadowy hallway crawling with ghosts, I would leap up on her back and pummel her with a fury that troubles me now.

Imagine my old neighborhood as an African village; under the pointed roofs tom-toms beat, premonitions prowl, and in the darkness naked superstition in all her plausibility blooms:

The Night-blooming Cereus

It was during the war; early in the war, 1942. *Collier's* had printed a cover showing Hirohito, splendidly costumed and fanged, standing malevolently in front of a bedraggled, bewildered Hitler and an even more decrepit and craven Mussolini. Our troops in the Pacific reeled from island to island; the Japanese seemed a race of demons capable of anything. The night-blooming cereus was the property of a family who lived down the street in a stucco house that on the inside was narrow and dark in the way that houses in the middle of the country sometimes are. The parlor was crowded with obscure furniture decked out with antimacassars and porcelain doodads. At Christmas a splendiferous tree appeared in that parlor, hung with pounds of tinsel and strung popcorn and paper chains and pretzels and balls and intricate, figurative ornaments that must have been rescued from the previous century.

The blooming of the cereus was to be an event in the neighborhood; for days we had been waiting. This night—a clear warm night, in August or September—word came, somehow. My mother and grandmother and I rushed down Philadelphia Avenue in the dark. It was late; I should have been in bed. I remembered the night I was refused permission to go to the poorhouse fire. The plant stood at the side of the house, in a narrow space between the stucco wall and the hedge. A knot of neighborhood women had already gathered; heavy shoulders and hair buns were silhouetted in an indeterminate light. On its twisted, unreal stem the flower had opened its unnaturally brilliant petals. But no one was looking at it. For overhead, in the north of a black sky strewn with stars like thrown salt, the wandering fingers of an aurora borealis gestured, now lengthening and brightening so that shades of blue and green could be distinguished, now ebbing until it seemed there was nothing there at all. It was a rare sight this far south. The women muttered, sighed, and, as if involuntarily, out of the friction of their bodies, moaned. Standing among their legs and skirts, I was slapped by a sudden cold wave of fear. "Is it the end of the world?" one of the women asked. There was no answer. And then a plane went over, its red lights blinking, its motors no louder than the drone of a wasp. Japanese. The Japanese were going to bomb Shillington, the center of the nation. I waited for the bomb, and without words prayed, expecting a miracle, for the appearance of angels and Japanese in the sky was restrained by the same impossibility, an impossibility that the swollen waxy brilliant white of the flower by my knees had sucked from the night.

The plane of course passed; it was one of ours; my prayer was answered with the usual appearance of absence. We went home, and the world reconstituted its veneer of reason, but the moans of the women had rubbed something in me permanently bare.

(3) Art

Leafing through a scrapbook my mother long ago made of my childhood drawings, I was greeted by one I had titled "Mr. Sun talking to Old Man Winter in his Office." Old Man Winter, a cloud with stick legs, and his host, a radiant ball with similar legs, sit at ease, both smiling, on two chairs that are the only furniture of the solar office. That the source of all light should have, somewhere, an office, suited my conception of an artist, who was someone who lived in a small town like Shillington, and who, equipped with pencils and paper, practiced his solitary trade as methodically as the dentist practiced his. And indeed, that is how it is at present with me.

Goethe—probably among others—says to be wary of our youthful wishes, for in maturity we are apt to get them. I go back, now, to Pennsylvania, and on one of the walls of the house in which my parents now live there hangs a photograph of myself as a boy. I am smiling, and staring with clear eyes at something in the corner of the room. I stand before that photograph, and am disappointed to receive no flicker, not the shadow of a flicker, of approval, of gratitude. The boy continues to smile at the corner of the room, beyond me. That boy is not a ghost to me, he is real to me; it is I who am a ghost to him. I, in my present state, was one of the ghosts that haunted his childhood. Like some phantom conjured by this child from a glue bottle, I have executed his commands; acquired pencils, paper, and an office. Now I wait apprehensively for his next command, or at least a nod of appreciation, and he smiles through me, as if I am already transparent with failure.

He saw art—between drawing and writing he ignorantly made no distinction—as a method of riding a thin pencil line out of Shillington, out of time altogether, into an infinity of unseen and even unborn hearts. He pictured this infinity as radiant. How innocent! But his assumption here, like his assumptions on religion and politics, is one for which I have found no certain substitute. He loved blank paper and obedience to this love led me to a difficult artistic attempt. I reasoned thus: just as the paper is the basis for the marks upon it, might not events be contingent upon a never-expressed (because featureless) ground? Is the true marvel of Sunday skaters the pattern of their pirouettes or the fact that they are silently upheld?

Blankness is not emptiness; we may skate upon an intense radiance we do not see because we see nothing else. And in fact there is a color, a quiet but tireless goodness that things at rest, like a brick wall or a small stone, seem to affirm. A wordless reassurance these things are pressing to give. An hallucination? To transcribe middleness with all its grits, bumps, and anonymities, in its fullness of satisfaction and mystery: is it possible or, in view of the suffering that violently colors the periphery and that at all moments threatens to move into the center, worth doing? Possibly not; but the horse-chestnut trees, the telephone poles, the porches, the green hedges recede to a calm point that in my subjective geography is still the center of the world.

End of Boyhood

I was walking down this Philadelphia Avenue one April and was just stepping over the shallow little rain gutter in the pavement that could throw you if you were on roller skates—though it had been years since I had been on roller skates—when from the semidetached house across the street a boy broke and ran. He was the youngest of six sons. All of his brothers were in the armed services, and five blue stars hung in his home's front window. He was several years older than I, and used to annoy my grandparents by walking through our yard, down past the grape arbor, on his way to high school. Long-legged, he was now running diagonally across the high-crowned street. I was the only other person out in the air. "Chonny!" he called. I was flattered to have him, so tall and grown, speak to me. "Did you hear?"

"No. What?"

"On the radio. The President is dead."

That summer the war ended, and that fall, suddenly mobile, we moved away from the big white house. We moved on

Halloween night. As the movers were fitting the last pieces of furniture, furniture that had not moved since I was born, into their truck, little figures dressed as ghosts and cats flitted in and out of the shadows of the street. A few rang our bell, and when my mother opened the door they were frightened by the empty rooms they saw behind her, and went away without begging. When the last things had been packed, and the kitchen light turned off, and the doors locked, the three of us—my grandparents were already at the new house—got into the old Buick my father had bought—in Shillington we had never had a car, for we could walk everywhere—and drove up the street, east, toward the poorhouse and beyond. Somewhat self-consciously and cruelly dramatizing my grief, for I was thirteen and beginning to be cunning, I twisted and watched our house recede through the rear window. Moonlight momentarily caught in an upper pane; then the reflection passed, and the brightest thing was the white brick wall itself. Against the broad blank part where I used to bat a tennis ball for hours at a time, the silhouette of the dogwood tree stood confused with the shapes of the other bushes in our side yard, but taller. I turned away before it would have disappeared from sight; and so it is that my shadow has always remained in one place.

THE LUCID EYE IN SILVER TOWN

THE FIRST TIME I visited New York City, I was thirteen and went with my father. I went to meet my Uncle Quin and to buy a book about Vermeer. The Vermeer book was my idea, and my mother's; meeting Uncle Quin was my father's. A generation ago, my uncle had vanished in the direction of Chicago and become, apparently, rich; in the last week he had come east on business and I had graduated from the eighth grade with high marks. My father claimed that I and his brother were the smartest people he had ever met—"go-getters," he called us, with perhaps more irony than at the time I gave him credit for—and in his visionary way he suddenly, irresistibly felt that now was the time for us to meet. New York in those days was seven dollars away; we measured everything, distance and time, in money then. World War II was over but we were still living in the Depression. My father and I set off with the return tickets and a five-dollar bill in his pocket. The five dollars was for the book.

My mother, on the railway platform, suddenly exclaimed, "I *hate* the Augusts." This surprised me, because we were all Augusts—I was an August, my father was an August, Uncle Quincy was an August, and she, I had thought, was an August.

My father gazed serenely over her head and said, "You have every reason to. I wouldn't blame you if you took a gun and shot us all. Except for Quin and your son. They're the only ones of us ever had any get up and git." Nothing was more infuriating about my father than his way of agreeing.

Uncle Quin didn't meet us at Pennsylvania Station. If my father was disappointed, he didn't reveal it to me. It was after one o'clock and all we had for lunch were two candy bars. By walking what seemed to me a very long way on pavements only a little broader than those of my home town, and not so clean, we reached the hotel, which sprouted somehow from the caramel-colored tunnels under Grand Central Station. The lobby smelled of perfume. After the clerk had phoned Quincy August that a man who said he was his brother was at the desk, an elevator took us to the twentieth floor. Inside the room sat three men, each in a gray or blue suit with freshly pressed pants and garters peeping from under the cuffs when they crossed their legs. The men were not quite interchangeable. One had a caterpillar-shaped mustache, one had tangled blond eyebrows like my father's, and the third had a drink in his hand—the others had drinks, too, but were not gripping them so tightly.

"Gentlemen, I'd like you to meet my brother Marty and his young son," Uncle Quin said.

"The kid's name is Jay," my father added, shaking hands with each of the two men, staring them in the eye. I imitated my father, and the mustached man, not expecting my firm handshake and stare, said, "Why, hello there, Jay!"

"Marty, would you and the boy like to freshen up? The facilities are through the door and to the left."

"Thank you, Quin. I believe we will. Excuse me, gentlemen."

"Certainly."

"Certainly."

My father and I went into the bedroom of the suite. The furniture was square and new and all the same shade of maroon. On the bed was an opened suitcase, also new. The clean, expensive smells of leather and lotion were beautiful to me. Uncle Quin's underwear looked silk and was full of fleurs-de-lis. When I was through in the lavatory, I made for the living room, to rejoin Uncle Quin and his friends.

"Hold it," my father said. "Let's wait in here."

"Won't that look rude?"

"No. It's what Quin wants."

"Now, Daddy, don't be ridiculous. He'll think we've died in here."

"No he won't, not my brother. He's working some deal. He doesn't want to be bothered. I know how my brother works; he got us in here so we'd stay in here."

"*Really*, Pop. You're such a schemer." But I did not want to go in there without him. I looked around the room for something to read. There was nothing, not even a newspaper, except a shiny little phamphlet about the hotel itself. I wondered when we would get a chance to look for the Vermeer book, and what the men in the next room were talking about. I wondered why Uncle Quin was so short, when my father was so tall. By leaning out of the window, I could see taxicabs maneuvering like windup toys.

My father came and stood beside me. "Don't lean out too far."

I edged out inches farther and took a big bite of the high cold air spiced by the distant street noises. "Look at the green cab cut in front of the yellow," I said. "Should they be making U-turns on that street?"

"In New York it's O.K. Survival of the fittest is the only law here."

"Isn't that the Chrysler Building?"

"Yes, isn't it graceful though? It always reminds me of the queen of the chessboard."

"What's the one beside it?"

"I don't know. Some big gravestone. The one deep in back, from this window, is the Woolworth Building. For years it was the tallest building in the world."

As, side by side at the window, we talked, I was surprised that my father could answer so many of my questions. As a young man, before I was born, he had travelled, looking for work; this was not *his* first trip to New York. Excited by my new respect, I longed to say something to remold that calm, beaten face.

"Do you really think he meant for us to stay out here?" I asked.

"Quin is a go-getter," he said, gazing over my head. "I admire him. Anything he wanted, from little on up, he went after it. Slam. Bang. His thinking is miles ahead of mine—just like your mother's. You can feel them pull out ahead of you." He moved his hands, palms down, like two taxis, the left quickly pulling ahead of the right. "You're the same way."

"Sure, sure." My impatience was not merely embarrassment at being praised; I was irritated that he considered Uncle Quin as smart as myself. At that point in my life I was sure that only stupid people took an interest in money.

When Uncle Quin finally entered the bedroom, he said, "Martin, I hoped you and the boy would come out and join us."

"Hell, I didn't want to butt in. You and those men were talking business."

"Lucas and Roebuck and I? Now, Marty, it was nothing that my own brother couldn't hear. Just a minor matter of adjustment. Both those men are fine men. Very important in their own fields. I'm disappointed that you couldn't see more of them. Believe me, I hadn't meant for you to hide in here. Now what kind of drink would you like?"

"I don't care. I drink very little any more."

"Scotch-and-water, Marty?"

"Swell."

"And the boy? What about some ginger ale, young man? Or would you like milk?"

"The ginger ale," I said.

"There was a day, you know, when your father could drink any two men under the table."

As I remember it, a waiter brought the drinks to the room, and while we were drinking them I asked if we were going to spend all afternoon in this room. Uncle Quin didn't seem to hear, but five minutes later he suggested that the boy might like to take a look around the city—Gotham, he called it, Baghdad-on-the-Subway. My father said that that would be a once-in-a-lifetime treat for the kid. He always called me "the kid" when I was sick or had lost at something or was angry—when he felt sorry for me, in short. The three of us went down in the elevator and took a taxi ride down Broadway, or up Broadway—I wasn't sure. "This is what they call the Great White Way," Uncle Quin said several times. Once he apologized, "In daytime it's just another street." The trip didn't seem so much designed for sight-seeing as for getting Uncle Quin to the Pickernut Club, a little restaurant set in a block of similar canopied places. I remember we stepped down into it and it was dark inside. A piano was playing "There's a Small Hotel."

"He shouldn't do that," Uncle Quin said. Then he waved to the man behind the piano. "How are you, Freddie? How are the kids?"

"Fine, Mr. August, fine," Freddie said, bobbing his head and smiling and not missing a note.

"That's Quin's song," my father said to me as we wriggled our way into a slippery curved seat at a round table.

I didn't say anything, but Uncle Quin, overhearing some

disapproval in my silence, said, "Freddie's a first-rate man. He has a boy going to Colgate this autumn."

I asked, "Is that really your song?"

Uncle Quin grinned and put his warm broad hand on my shoulder; I hated, at that age, being touched. "I let them think it is," he said, oddly purring. "To me, songs are like young girls. They're all pretty."

A waiter in a red coat scurried up. "Mr. August! Back from the West? How are you, Mr. August?"

"Getting by, Jerome, getting by. Jerome, I'd like you to meet my kid brother, Martin."

"How do you do, Mr. Martin. Are you paying New York a visit? Or do you live here?"

My father quickly shook hands with Jerome, somewhat to Jerome's surprise. "I'm just up for the afternoon, thank you. I live in a hick town in Pennsylvania you never heard of."

"I see, sir. A quick visit."

"This is the first time in six years that I've had a chance to see my brother."

"Yes, we've seen very little of him these past years. He's a man we can never see too much of, isn't that right?"

Uncle Quin interrupted. "This is my nephew Jay."

"How do you like the big city, Jay?"

"Fine." I didn't duplicate my father's mistake of offering to shake hands.

"Why, Jerome," Uncle Quin said, "my brother and I would like to have a Scotch-on-the-rocks. The boy would like a ginger ale."

"No, wait," I said. "What kinds of ice cream do you have?"

"Vanilla and chocolate, sir."

I hesitated. I could scarcely believe it, when the cheap drugstore at home had fifteen flavors.

"I'm afraid it's not a very big selection," Jerome said.

"I guess vanilla."

"Yes, sir. One plate of vanilla."

When my ice cream came it was a golf ball in a flat silver dish; it kept spinning away as I dug at it with my spoon. Uncle Quin watched me and asked, "Is there anything especially you'd like to do?"

"The kid'd like to get into a bookstore," my father said.

"A bookstore. What sort of book, Jay?"

I said, "I'd like to look for a good book of Vermeer."

"Vermeer," Uncle Quin pronounced slowly, relishing the r's, pretending to give the matter thought. "Dutch school."

"He's Dutch, yes."

"For my own money, Jay, the French are the people to beat. We have four Degas ballet dancers in our living room in Chicago, and I could sit and look at one of them for hours. I think it's wonderful, the feeling for balance the man had."

"Yeah, but don't Degas' paintings always remind you of colored drawings? For actually *looking* at things in terms of paint, for the lucid eye, I think Vermeer makes Degas look sick."

Uncle Quin said nothing, and my father, after an anxious glance across the table, said, "That's the way he and his mother talk all the time. It's all beyond me. I can't understand a thing they say."

"Your mother is encouraging you to be a painter, is she, Jay?" Uncle Quin's smile was very wide and his cheeks were pushed out as if each held a candy.

"Sure, I suppose she is."

"Your mother is a very wonderful woman, Jay," Uncle Quin said.

It was such an embarrassing remark, and so much depended upon your definition of "wonderful," that I dug at my ice cream, and my father asked Uncle Quin about his own wife,

Tessie. When we left, Uncle Quin signed the check with his name and the name of some company. It was close to five o'clock.

My uncle didn't know much about the location of book-stores in New York—his last twenty years had been spent in Chicago—but he thought that if we went to Forty-second Street and Sixth Avenue we should find something. The cab driver let us out beside a park that acted as kind of a backyard for the Public Library. It looked so inviting, so agreeably dusty, with the pigeons and the men nodding on the benches and the office girls in their taut summer dresses, that, without thinking, I led the two men into it. Shimmering buildings arrowed upward and glinted through the treetops. This was New York, I told myself: the silver town. Towers of ambition rose, crystalline, within me. "If you stand here," my father said, "you can see the Empire State." I went and stood beneath my father's arm and followed with my eyes the direction of it. Something sharp and hard fell into my right eye. I ducked my head and blinked; it was painful.

"What's the trouble?" Uncle Quin's voice asked.

My father said, "The poor kid's got something into his eye. He has the worst luck that way of anybody I ever knew."

The thing seemed to have life. It bit. "Ow," I said, angry enough to cry.

"If we can get him out of the wind," my father's voice said, "maybe I can see it."

"No, now, Marty, use your head. Never fool with the eyes or ears. The hotel is within two blocks. Can you walk two blocks, Jay?"

"I'm blind, not lame," I snapped.

"He has a ready wit," Uncle Quin said.

Between the two men, shielding my eye with a hand, I

walked to the hotel. From time to time, one of them would take my other hand, or put one of theirs on my shoulder, but I would walk faster, and the hands would drop away. I hoped our entrance into the hotel lobby would not be too conspicuous; I took my hand from my eye and walked erect, defying the impulse to stoop. Except for the one lid being shut and possibly my face being red, I imagined I looked passably suave. However, my guardians lost no time betraying me. Not only did they walk at my heels, as if I might topple any instant, but my father told one old bum sitting in the lobby, "Poor kid got something in his eye," and Uncle Quin, passing the desk, called, "Send up a doctor to Twenty-eleven."

"You shouldn't have done that, Quin," my father said in the elevator. "I can get it out, now that he's out of the wind. This is happening all the time. The kid's eyes are too far front."

"Never fool with the eyes, Martin. They are your most precious tool in life."

"It'll work out," I said, though I didn't believe it would. It felt like a steel chip, deeply embedded.

Up in the room, Uncle Quin made me lie down on the bed. My father, a handkerchief wadded in his hand so that one corner stuck out, approached me, but it hurt so much to open the eye that I repulsed him. "Don't torment me," I said, twisting my face away. "What good does it do? The doctor'll be up."

Regretfully my father put the handkerchief back into his pocket.

The doctor was a soft-handed man with little to say to anybody; he wasn't pretending to be the family doctor. He rolled my lower eyelid on a thin stick, jabbed with a Q-tip, and showed me, on the end of the Q-tip, an eyelash. He dropped three drops of yellow fluid into the eye to remove any chance of infection. The fluid stung, and I shut my eyes, leaning back into the pillow, glad it was over. When I opened them, my father was passing a bill into the doctor's hand. The doctor thanked him, winked at me, and left. Uncle Quin came out of the bathroom.

"Well, young man, how are you feeling now?" he asked.

"Fine."

"It was just an eyelash," my father said.

"*Just* an eyelash! Well I know how an eyelash can feel like a razor blade in there. But, now that the young invalid is recovered, we can think of dinner."

"No, I really appreciate your kindness, Quin, but we must be getting back to the sticks. I have an eight-o'clock meeting I should be at."

"I'm extremely sorry to hear that. What sort of meeting, Marty?"

"A church council."

"So you're still doing church work. Well, God bless you for it."

"Grace wanted me to ask you if you couldn't possibly come over some day. We'll put you up overnight. It would be a real treat for her to see you again."

Uncle Quin reached up and put his arm around his younger brother's shoulders. "Martin, I'd like that better than anything in the world. But I am solid with appointments, and I must head west this Thursday. They don't let me have a minute's repose. Nothing would please my heart better than to share a quiet day with you and Grace in your home. Please give her my love, and tell her what a wonderful boy she is raising. The two of you are raising."

My father promised, "I'll do that." And, after a little more fuss, we left.

"The child better?" the old man in the lobby called to us on the way out.

"It was just an eyelash, thank you, sir," my father said.

When we got outside, I wondered if there were any book-stores still open.

"We have no money."

"None at all?"

"The doctor charged five dollars. That's how much it costs in New York to get something in your eye."

"I didn't do it on purpose. Do you think I pulled out the eyelash and stuck it in there myself? I didn't tell you to call the doctor."

"I know that."

"Couldn't we just go into a bookstore and look a minute?"

"We haven't time, Jay."

But when we reached Pennsylvania Station, it was over thirty minutes until the next train left. As we sat on a bench, my father smiled reminiscently. "Boy, he's smart, isn't he? His thinking is sixty light-years ahead of mine."

"Whose?"

"My brother. Notice the way he hid in the bathroom until the doctor was gone? That's how to make money. The rich man collects dollar bills like the stamp collector collects stamps. I knew he'd do it. I knew it when he told the clerk to send up a doctor that I'd have to pay for it."

"Well, why *should* he pay for it? *You* were the person to pay for it."

"That's right. Why should he?" My father settled back, his eyes forward, his hands crossed and limp in his lap. The skin beneath his chin was loose; his temples seemed concave. The liquor was probably disagreeing with him. "That's why he's where he is now, and that's why I am where I am."

The seed of my anger seemed to be a desire to recall him to himself, to scold him out of being old and tired. "Well, why'd you bring along only five dollars? You might have known something would happen."

"You're right, Jay. I should have brought more."

"Look. Right over there is an open bookstore. Now if you had brought *ten* dollars—"

"Is it open? I don't think so. They just left the lights in the window on."

"What if it isn't? What does it matter to us? Anyway, what kind of art book can you get for five dollars? Color plates cost money. How much do you think a decent book of Vermeer costs? It'd be cheap at fifteen dollars, even second-hand, with the pages all crummy and full of spilled coffee." I kept on, shrilly flailing the passive and infuriating figure of my father, until we left the city. Once we were on the homeward train, my tantrum ended; it had been a kind of ritual, for both of us, and he had endured my screams complacently, nodding assent, like a midwife assisting at the birth of family pride. Years passed before I needed to go to New York again.

MY UNCLE'S DEATH

He died while shaving; when I was told of this, I pictured him staggering back heavily, stricken, his own amazed face in the mirror the last thing he ever saw. His face flashed there for him, hung there, slipped backward; and then the mirror was full of the blank bathroom wall. I pictured this so sharply I seemed to have been there.

At his funeral I felt, for the first time, my adult height. The Manatees are not a family of breeders, and the number of relatives was small; walking up the aisle to the front pew with my parents, my aunt and my two cousins, I felt tall and prominent. Walking back down the aisle after the service, I caught, from the faces of those still seated, an odd, motionless, intent look, almost an odor, of sympathy and curiosity and reverence for grief. The look, no doubt, was primarily directed at my aunt, the widow, who, on the arm of my father, led our ragged, rustling procession. But we all—all the relatives—shared in it and were for the moment heroes of bereavement: a surviving band, a clan. I carried my role proudly, though doubting that I had felt enough sorrow to earn it. I was just sixteen, still an inch or two short of my eventual height, but walking down that aisle I entered, through that strange odor of respect, pity, and wonder, the company of adulthood. I became a Manatee. Unfairly enough, my two cousins, my uncle's daughters, were a little younger than I and emerged from the church, with all their bewildering weight of loss, still children, though fatherless.

Yet I had loved my uncle, as much as the distance between us permitted. He was famous and rich. Not so famous and rich, I have since discovered, as our branch of the family imagined, but enough for a head shot and a half column on the obituary page of *The New York Times*. Trained as an architect—though he never got his degree—he speculated in real estate, and there are several blocks of Manhattan that would not look quite the same if he had never lived. The phantom presence of his importance hovered about our family table long before I first saw him seated there as a guest, and when I try to remember him as he was, his fame and wealth, which I so obtrusively wanted for myself, inflate and blur his face, making it unreally large and distant—a clown-faced moon hung in the skimpy branches of my family tree.

I cannot reach him. I can remember nothing about him that is quite real except his death; he is like a celestial body which only eclipse renders measurable. He was six feet, four inches tall, but his immensity was narrow-shouldered, small-boned and unmuscular. He was vain of having, for so outsized a man, rather small feet. He usually wore neat black loafers, virtually slippers, of English leather, and, sprawling soddenly in a chair, he generally contrived to thrust his feet forward on the floor, or up on a stool, so they were noticed. I remember my mother —I must have been ten or eleven—teasing him about his dainty feet. I cannot recapture her words, but she was still slim then, and her pose as she spoke—head tilted back, hands half lifted —stuck in my mind; she so seldom struck an unmotherly atti-tude that it was as if a strange spirit had come and for a mo-ment possessed her body. My uncle, presumably, responded with a dry flutter of the sheepish gallantry that he seemed to reserve for my mother and for waitresses in restaurants. My mother seemed exempt from the rather lazy distaste with which my uncle viewed the rest of the world, and perhaps, as her son, I was included in the exemption, for he was kind to me.

He taught me gin rummy. The very name of the game excited me with visions of parlor cars and high hotel rooms full of heavy, expensive men—world-wielders—smoking cigars and playing for a dollar a point. We would play gin rummy for hours on the side porch of our homely little green-shingled house in our once-rural suburb of Providence. My uncle and his wife and daughters would visit us here once a year, always in the summer, and for exactly three days—never more. He would cite the adage about fish and guests stinking after three days, adding, "And we're both." The manatee is, of course, an aquatic mammal, with a flat snout and rounded tail—but my uncle was willing to twist the truth to cinch a joke.

"Leonard, how's your friend Christ?" would be, with each visit, the first and virtually the only question that he would direct at my father. It was a joke, but my father would answer the question seriously; his involvement with church and community affairs was so consuming that he was rarely at home in the evenings. He was older than my uncle by two years but had long ago ceased to be a challenge to him. As my father talked about church feuds and Lions' Club politics, my uncle would sink silently deeper into his chair, a kind of fine powder of resignation would whiten his large face, and the thrust-out, exquisitely shod feet would conspicuously fidget.

Humiliated that my uncle, who manipulated city blocks like a giant, should be bored by the petty details of our timid lives, I scolded my father privately. He said, "No, he's interested. He's my brother. You're an only child, Freddy, so that probably doesn't make any sense to you."

I was an only child, and there was little in my life beyond my uncle's annual visits to broaden my definition of "family." *He's my brother:* this simple assertion plunged me backward into depths I could never understand. By the time I reached my mid-teens, my mind, like a soft surface lightly but repeatedly tapped, had received from these visits some confusing impressions. My father, dismissed by his brother, had turned in his heart toward Thelma, my uncle's wife, a stoic, chain-smoking woman whose face seemed to have suffered so many jolts that certain corners of it would never relax again. She must have found much in her pious, modest brother-in-law that was soothing; she was an amateur gardener in much the same obsessed way that he was a deacon, and the two of them would go for long walks together, she looking at the vegetation, he performing altruistic errands. Sitting side by side on the couch looking at old family photographs, *they* seemed the siblings; there was even a physical resemblance. The skin of both had grown darker with age; their faces were wrinkled as if with the cracks of a tough varnish. Meanwhile my uncle, so fragilely pale and pink, hovering humorously on his pampered feet while my mother, more gracefully than usual, performed the motions of housework, showered upon her a kind of antic indulgence which I supposed was fraternal. These impressions, bafflingly contradicted at the end of each visit when my uncle and aunt got into their gray Cadillac with their girls and, waving, disappeared down the driveway together, suggested to me that in the depths of the mystery called "family" there lay, necessarily, an irrevocable mistake.

"Freddy, who ate the cards?" With this absurd question my uncle would invite me to play rummy. My father would be off at work. My aunt and my mother would be somewhere in the house tugging, with the elaborate and pained tact that lay between them, the housekeeping duties back and forth. My cousins, who lived in a small chaste bivalve world in which they always faced each other, would be engaged underfoot in some conspiratorial girlish game. I would find the cards. My uncle would sit down and deal. We would play for hours on the porch, the side screens sieving the songs of insects, the sounds of traffic swelling from a whisper at noon to a waterfall roar by suppertime. Timidly I would ask if I weren't wasting his time.

He would laugh and shuffle the cards once more. He had a loud, easy way of riffling them together that I could never quite master. "Most of my time, Freddy, is wasted time. I've sat in railroad stations all day long."

"But isn't there something important you should be doing?"

"Because I'm important? You don't understand, Freddy—importance is entirely a matter of belief. The more important you are, the less important what you do is. When you reach my stage, nothing you do matters at all. The most important thing in my life right now is to whump you at this witless game. Your draw."

He played to win, and I loved him for that. So many adults refuse to give a child the compliment of a contest. Now and then, as he deliberated over the upturned pile, and then plunged and took them all into his hand, I felt for an instant the decisive thrust that had carried him so far into the world of money.

I was still groping, trying to discover in him what it was like to be rich and famous. I searched his face; it was an ugly face, a clown's and giant's both. His cheekbones seemed broadened by the extreme closeness of his old-fashioned, centrally parted haircut. His small slanting eyes twitched alertly in their puffy mountings of sleeplessness. His nose, battered by college football, was rose pink, and his teeth were yellowed by tobacco.

"Someday *you'll* be important," he said suddenly.

Startled, I lied, "Oh, I don't think so."

"I think so. You'll do it to please your mother."

"Really? You think she cares?"

He didn't answer, but instead lay down three triplets and went out. As he totted up the points caught in my hand, he said, "Don't do everything to please your mother. It's a mistake."

It was the only advice my uncle ever gave me, and I am not sure I understand it still. I have, in an unimportant way, become important; if I died tomorrow, I might receive three or four inches in the *Times*—about as much, say, as the mother superior of an upstate nunnery. I have taken a slower, more scholarly route than my uncle, and the other day, in reading a treatise on fools, I encountered a certain King Suibhne, of ancient Ireland, who abruptly became a fool in the tumult of battle: "Unsteadiness, restlessness, and unquiet filled him, likewise disgust with every place in which he used to be and desire for every place which he had not reached." I recognized the sensations. They are ours, the Manatees'. I feel now how my father roved the streets, seeking good to do, because he was possessed by "disgust with every place in which he used to be and desire for every place which he had not reached." And my uncle, too, though he sought to escape the curse by remaining in a chair, was an unquiet traveller; the family discontent vibrated in him until he collapsed. Because shuffling cards and striking matches were the most strenuous things I ever saw him do, when I heard of his first heart attack it seemed a mistake. How could a man overwork his heart when he was always sitting with his feet preeningly stretched out before him?

The summer after the winter of his first attack I was invited, alone, to visit his home in Rye, New York. They lived in a big white house on what seemed to my semirural eyes a rather small lawn. My aunt's flower-and-vegetable garden took up most of the land. I was disappointed that the difference between their house and ours was one of degree rather than kind. A maid came in on Mondays and Fridays, and in the living room there was a panelled closet full of liquor bottles, with a faucet for water and a small pine counter like a bar; otherwise it was a house like ours, with rooms (only more) and rugs (only deeper) and chairs and windows and books. Their bookcases smelled like my parents' college yearbooks and held dark brown Modern Library editions from the twenties, with jiggly type and stingy margins, and an English edition of *Ulysses* bearing a longbow on the spine. I opened *Ulysses* and was appalled, in the middle of a blank August afternoon, by the keen scent of death the packed words gave off; my uncle had long ago marked a few passages in the margins, and his pencillings were like the tracks of someone who had preceded me through Hell.

I was fifteen that summer and stayed two weeks, reading books and mowing the lawn and playing badminton with my cousins. Several times my aunt drove me into Manhattan. She became confiding; as an only child I was susceptible to adult confidences. She told me about my uncle's heart. It had been weakened by his work, his weight, his total lack of exercise, his drinking, his smoking, and—her eyes suddenly glittered with tears, making my stomach clench—his lack of will to live. "He doesn't care enough, Freddy, if he lives or dies; he just doesn't see that great a difference." But my attention had snagged on the first thing she had said. His work? But many days he came home from New York on the shoppers' train, and some days he did not go in at all, just loafed around the house in his bathrobe all morning and had lunch by himself at a restaurant in downtown Rye. Though he and Aunt Thelma never quarrelled in my presence, I soon learned to detect, from the atmosphere in the house, when he had returned with liquor on his breath. His doctors had ordered him to stop smoking and drinking.

In the evenings, often, my cousins and my aunt would go to bed while my uncle and I sat up playing gin rummy. As soon as his wife's footsteps hit the stair, he would take a rumpled pack of Camels out of his pocket and begin to smoke. His big, crimped, clownish mouth did not so much smoke the cigarettes as swallow them; one after another they vanished in front of his face, and the light of the bridge lamp over his shoulder turned blue. When it was my turn to shuffle, he would go to the panelled closet; there would be a soft tinkling noise, and he would bring back a glass of ice cubes and amber liquid. I would drink ginger ale to keep him company; many nights I drank a whole quart. We often stayed up past one o'clock, and, though little was said that did not relate to the cards, I felt trusted. My parents kept regular hours, so the region of time beyond midnight still held a romance for me. As the sounds of traffic outside dwindled to an occasional speeder spurting from one horizon of silence to another, my uncle and I seemed to be travelling together like two card players on a perfectly greased train riding absolutely level tracks into a hushed beyond where his harrowed, puffy face was no longer ugly but utterly appropriate, like an angel's in ether. His presence, in the beginning a mere inflated projection on the flat facts of his fame and wealth, was given a shadowy third dimension by what I knew now of his life. His attack had caused my parents to reminisce about him. He had been the precocious, favored baby of my grandmother's house; he had had a double aptitude, for drawing and mathematics, and had resolved it into the ambition to be an architect. He had finished half his training, when his father, in a swift street accident, died, leaving nothing but debts. He had faced the choice of completing his training and beginning his years of apprenticeship, or of quitting and immediately helping my father support their mother; with his slightly brusque decisiveness, he had chosen the latter. Henceforth he lived, as my father put it, "by his wits," and apparently thrived. Their mother lived for twenty more years.

Invariably he kept the score of our games, in precise pencilled numerals, the fours closed at the top, the ones fashioned like small sevens. After several glasses of amber liquid, his architect's printing would become mechanically small and even, and all his motions took on the deliberately slowed efficiency of someone determined to complete a distasteful job. When he finished a pack of Camels, he would crumple it in his hand and stuff the paper ball back into his coat pocket. Once he paused and showed the crumpled pack to me. It lay in his wide white palm like a garish pill, or like a tinfoil-headed beetle with a camel's brown sneer buckled into its back. "You needn't tell Thelma about this," he said mildly, stuffing it into his pocket and drawing out a fresh pack. He took care to return the red cellophane strip to his pocket.

"Should you be doing it?" I asked.

"Oh, sure," he said, huffing through his pink nose with an asthmatic effort I had not noticed before. "I'm an old expert, Freddy, at taking care of myself. In forty-nine years I've never had an accident."

And, anxious to win, I obligingly shuffled another hand, and he heaved to his feet through the blue veil and went to hover, tinkling, at the bar. I suppose I felt that beating him at cards would somehow give me access—if not now, later—to the millions I imagined he had won from the world. In fact, his fortune, inscrutably submerged in loans and options and fractional titles to property, was not so large as my family had thought; his sole bequest to me was a beautiful suitcase of English leather, which I still use.

I never told my aunt how my uncle drank and smoked, though several times an opportunity for telling seemed to have been created. I was fifteen and assumed that adults were their own responsibility. I was flattered by his trust and do not believe now that my betraying it would have significantly added to her knowledge, or helped anyone. Nevertheless, when my mother, one noon in the following autumn, came back from the telephone with a shocked face and told us, "Ed died this morning," I had this sharp sense, for all the intervening distance, of witnessing my uncle's death.

OUTING

A FAMILY ANECDOTE

PRIMITIVE PEOPLE, authorities assert, imagine the word to have power over the thing. Do civilized people believe otherwise? When Harriet Pick, for instance, marries Kenneth Shovel in Oklahoma City, papers in Toronto and Miami carry the news, and *Coronet* and *Time* find space in one of their jocular departments, and Mr. and Mrs. Shovel must begin to wonder if in truth they are, as they seem to each other, flesh and blood, and not a pair of implements.

My own marriage was bothered by a verbal coincidence, one so small I thought it would slip by unnoticed. My wife's maiden name was Pennington, and the Updikes came, two generations back, from Pennington, New Jersey. Our farm there was sold, and fragments of the family settled variously in Connecticut, Kansas, Florida, and Trenton—a typical enough episode in the American dispersal.* My grandfather went to

---

* It is this tireless dispersal, perhaps, this lack of firm family land, that makes names precious to us. They are like tracer bullets branching through the native darkness, and by looking around, and down, we discover ourselves to be not hanging in a vacuum but roosting in an immense ancestral tree; we can even make out, on the moss by the roots, the little Dutch elves tumbling from the boats at Nieuw Amsterdam three centuries ago.

There exists a drab olive volume called *The Op Dyck Genealogy*. The genealogy catalogues up to 1900 all Americans bearing for a name our comic spondee, a stubby arrow of aspiration driven against a deaf seawall. I recall two anecdotes, two glimpses down into the tree. Isaiah T.

Trenton; my father, the year I was born, came to live in Pennsylvania. All Updikes of my father's generation had a special feeling about the town of Pennington: it was the family Paradise out of whose inheritance they had been cheated. Cain and Abel and Seth, as boys, must have had a similar feeling about Eden. Adam and Eve were in this case the many sons and daughters of Samuel Updike, the Creator. On meeting my fiancée, a Connecticut uncle pronounced with religious satisfaction, "At last: the Updikes are returning to Pennington!" The completion of the cycle moved me little. In the scale of the myth I was in the remote position of Seth's son Enos, if not a remoter.

I was alarmed to detect, therefore, the strengthening deter-

Updike, an old man corresponding with the genealogist about the Indiana branch, wrote, *My brothers were celebrated in athletic sports. I have seen one of the family, weighing 185 pounds and measuring 5 feet 9 inches, place himself flat on his back and allow a man 6 feet tall and weighing 190 pounds to lie square across his breast, and after good notice the under-man would throw the upper heels-over-head 12 feet away, and regain his feet before the other and say with a smile, "That is the way the Updike boys do in the West."*

My second glimpse is of Captain James Glenn Updike, leader of Company H of the 4th Virginia Infantry of the Confederate Army, striding the battlefield after the charge of the Stonewall Brigade at the first Battle of Manassas, or Bull Run. In this action Captain Updike had lost of his Company twenty-one men killed and wounded. He came to a wounded Union soldier crying for a drink of water. *The Captain cut the strap of a canteen from a dead soldier and gave water to the wounded man, who seemed in great agony and said he knew he must die. Captain Updike ripped the boot from the foot of the sufferer, tied a handkerchief tightly around the wound, and told him if he would give his name and address, a letter would be sent through the lines to his friends. The soldier said his name was Opdyke (or Updike) from Delaware; the Captain replied that his own name was Updike, but the wounded man looked up incredulously and evidently did not believe this; he did not give his first name or post-office. The Captain had to leave and hurry on, but in about an hour something impelled him to go back there,—probably it was the name,—and he found the poor fellow dead; he was a fine-looking man, with black hair and eyes and rather dark complexion.*

mination of my mother and father to take Mary Pennington to Pennington. There was no one there to visit. The Updikes who had not left had died; the land had swallowed the name. Even Updike Road, along whose length every farm for miles was once owned by the family, had probably been rechristened. But my father had been infected by an idea. The germ may have been my uncle's joyful exclamation; it imposed on the coincidence a clan-sized importance. It gave my father that sensation he sometimes had, of all Updikes, quick and dead, watching him. He must do right, somehow. Then, a mathematically-minded man, he was drawn into the geometry of making tangent the two Penningtons so strangely disposed at the extremities of his life—the one his father's birthplace, the other his son's bride. With these calculations anticipations of pleasure began to mingle. Pennington, throne of earthly goodness, rose before him in all its verdure and birdsong. Memories of boyhood trips assailed him; apple trees and iridescent livestock filled his mind's eye. Siren voices called from across the Delaware.

This is conjecture; when I ask him now about the trip to Pennington, he only says, "I don't know what the hell I was thinking of."

Why my mother helped the idea along is even more obscure. She had been born in Pennsylvania; there was no tug in her blood toward New Jersey. However, she did have a love of words and a vague sense that when Mary came to visit us we should "entertain" her. Judged purely as a verbal concept, "taking Mary Pennington to Pennington, New Jersey," was more entertaining than taking her to the Ephrata Cloisters or the Gettysburg Battlefield, an equivalent distance away. Further, my mother had an educational impulse that she was unable to express directly; it was a grave thing, she felt from her experience, for a woman to marry an Updike, to take upon herself that droll, pointed, yet curiously restless and unresolved name. She felt this gravity, yet had never been able quite to put her finger on its source, and hoped (I surmise) that an entry into Pennington might reveal to Mary's unaided intuition the weight and shape of the burden she had consented to assume. Also, my mother must have expected, as we all did, that something, something magic, *would happen*.

Mary came to visit us for a week early in the June we were to be married late in. She scarcely knew, that overcast morning, why she was being swept into the car, and I was helpless to prevent it. I had always been helpless in regard to my parents' car trips. Again and again in my formative years, carsick and heartsick, I had been transported through endless tracts of Eastern Standard Time to a destination I despised. Like baptism and death, it was a mysterious necessity—the experience, perhaps, with which Americans earn their citizenship.

We sat, my parents in front and Mary and I in back, in attentive and respectful postures, worshipping the mumble of the motor. Inches above our heads stretched the familiar seamed firmament, abysmally neutral in color and ornamented with a celluloid icon of the dead sun. The blank, hairy backs of my parents' disembodied heads seemed idols adored by an unspeakable cult. What with the jiggle, the intertwining cries of motor and tires, the idiot flicker of scenery at the windows, the smell of poisonous gas, and the taste of stirred-up car-seat dust, our senses became dulled. My parents' talk grew wilder. My mother talked about Updikes, searching for the dark thing that was to say about them. One of them had owned Coney Island when it was worthless. The Rhode Island Updikes had played host to Bishop Berkeley and then gone sterile. The oldest one in the *Genealogy* had been discovered on his knees in Cologne Cathedral, doing penance for some—annoyingly—unnamed offense. They were very petty knights. Their arms were a star, a tongs, and a pineapple. Once my mother turned and saw me resting my head in weariness on Mary's shoulder. "Don't *lean*, Johnny!" she cried. "Sit up. That's what they do, Mary. They *lean* on you." My father undertook to recite everyone who had ever hurt his feelings, an expanding list that went back to, but did not include, Samuel Updike, who had given him a penny when he was two. My mother accused him of being suicidal and screamed whenever a truck came down the highway at us.

"Get on your *side*, Wesley."

"It's where you're sitting, Linda. It's an optical illusion. I know what it looks like, it looks like those fenders are in your lap, but I'm way the hell over."

"Don't involve *me* in your suicide," my mother insisted. "I never heard of such a coward that wouldn't commit suicide when he was alone in the car but had to take his whole family with him. Did *you*, Mary?"

Beside me, Mary grew pale and pursed her lips stubbornly. It was not only the discomforts of the back seat; my father, without cracking a smile, *had* begun to twitch the wheel at oncoming vehicles.

"Oh—didn't that girl have a curious expression on her face," my mother said abruptly, determined to "rise above" his teasing.

I asked, "What girl?"

"At the hot-dog place. She's gone now."

Mary, unable to believe the literal sense of what she had been hearing, had deduced that my parents spoke in allegories, and believed that her own expression, glimpsed by my mother in the rear-view mirror, had been meant. Her lips grew grimmer. My father, bouncing with undiminished speed over some road construction, knocked her pocketbook off her lap. The motion of the car, at the start a sign of our life, now seemed as inert and helpless as the fall of a planet through vacant space.

From the height of the Burlington–Bristol Bridge the Delaware resembled a black-shellacked floor nicked by furniture legs. The sun came out as we reached the New Jersey side. In the new state, our mission changed complexion. The sun sparkled on the roadside trees, the Coca-Cola signs, the brilliantined heads of youths in convertibles. Small cities succeeded one another. The American summer reigned on high; its harsh poetry glinted from mica sidewalks and plate-glass windows. Everywhere we looked, as countless as stars in the desert night, were those oblongs of radiance smeared wherever the metal of an automobile curves into an angle reflecting the sun. Concrete and metal dissolved in these highlights. The deepening beauty of the countryside promised to redeem our project. With the insertion of Mary Pennington into Pennington, New Jersey, some illuminating coruscation, some life-enhancing *bang* was bound to occur. As the number of miles to Pennington diminished on the road signs, and my hopes grew higher, I was conscious of being lifted away from my bride-to-be; she, resenting the unity of expectation I enjoyed with my parents, and resenting her demotion to the status of a catalyst, had become sullen.

Pennington was a pleasant enough town, with a more up-to-date air than I had been led to expect. My father parked on the main street near a drugstore. A teen-age girl in shorts walked by, licking an ice-cream cone. Contrasted to our captivity in the car, she had a wonderful freedom and, to my eyes, a tragic inaccessibility. Not only had she blossomed, with an independence almost impudent, a hundred miles from where I could have observed her, but the entire season of life she represented, with her brown legs and her ice-cream cone, my marriage would end for me forever.

My parents, turning their heads minimally, peeked at Mary.

She roused and hunched over to see out the window. *"Isn't it a pretty town,"* she said. "What nice big front yards."

My father took his anticlimax well. He waited long enough to be sure that Mary could think of nothing else to say, then asked me, "Do you want to get some ice-cream cones?"

I said, "I don't, really. It seems a rather odd hour for them." It was noon.

After a little more silence, my mother turned and smiled and said, "Well, this is where they all came from, Mary."

My father said, "Samuel Updike is the only person I ever knew who never hurt my feelings."

My mother asked him, "Do you want to look for Updike Road?"

"No," he said. "It's gone."

Mary offered to get out of the car and walk around, but my parents refused to hear of it. She had done her best, their manner implied. My mother gaily talked of lunch and my father started the car; Mary and I touched hands stiffly, striving to recognize that the hopes that had brought us to our first disappointment in each other had been unreasonable.

MEA CULPA

A TRAVEL NOTE

St. Peter's (San Pietro in Vaticano), the most majestic and the most vast of all the basilicas of Christendom, is a masterpiece of Italian art of the Renaissance and of the early Baroque period. . . . [It] covers about 18,100 sq. yd.; its length is 212 yd.; the breadth of the transept is 150 yd.; the dome is 435 ft. in height and 138 ft. in diameter. . . . The INTERIOR, in spite of its harmonious proportions, often disappoints visitors at first sight; it is only by studying the details that we begin to realise its grandeur and its calm and majestic beauty. — Hachette guide to Italy, page 479.

DISAPPOINTS? Better, "appalls." The vastness struck me as so uniform, so remorseless, as to be self-annihilating, like the vastness of stellar statistics, whose zeros our tiny minds accept so lightly, like necklaces of nothings. What is marvellous about a sky-high ceiling when the walls are remote as horizons? The inflation was insufficiently selective. Gigantic marble popes like vertical gray clouds jutted from niches as high overhead as housetops; church-size side chapels, one after another, slowly rotated into view around the colossal piers; living men walked and talked together as if on the open street. Reverence was not in the air. The ghostly presences of so many commemorated ecclesiastical princes melted together into a faceless, sumptuous ambience that seemed to invite, urbanely, by way of devotion—if any was desired—a kind of secondary pantheism. The most

: **217** :

majestic and most vast basilica in Christendom so successfully aped the scale of Creation that it seemed to me to deliver, like certain dreadful natural landscapes, a crushing comment on human insignificance. *Vanity, vanity*, each overweening vault declared, in polished syllables of porphyry and gilt. If I found space for any holy emotion in this maelstrom of artificial immensity, it was pity for the dizzy workmen who had risked their lives in its construction.

In recent times a Stigler-Otis elevator, manufactured in Milan, has been installed, whereby, for a hundred and fifty lire, one may ascend to the roof. Here, on an uneven terrain of tarred pebbles, rusty octagonal huts house those bits of sunlight and blue mosaic which, seen from within the nave, seem glimpses of the Empyrean. A little low shack with a Coca-Cola sign sells souvenir trinkets and sweetens the air with popular recordings of "Mamma Mia" and "Ave Maria." By walking forward, one can overlook Rome and perceive that the statues crowning the façade have blank backs. By walking the other way one can enter the great central dome which, Hachette explains, *with its simple and majestic lines, forms a canopy above the tomb of St. Peter.* Seen from above, from the balcony rimming the base of the cupola, the interior of the basilica restates its message with a singing urgency. Height sings; it sings to us of annihilation. My legs began to tremble in the wrestle against the angelic urge to push myself over the railing. The very bas-reliefs seemed in danger of letting go. Dots that were tourists like me moved slowly on the symmetrically patterned acres of floor; their footsteps caused the leaning walls of the dome to murmur invitingly. Yes, this was death: to fall through such a space to such a floor, to diminish downward into such a placid flatness. I pulled back from the railing, my palms moist. Yet a perverse aspiration drove me higher still.

It is possible, by means of narrow stairways artfully threaded

between the inner and outer shells, to ascend to the very apex
of the dome. At first, a seemingly endless spiral of stone steps,
which in turning constantly obliterates itself, so that in climbing one seems always to be treading in the same subterranean
place, conducts the tourist straight upward. Other souls caught
in this ancient corkscrew exist as disembodied voices laughing
and panting, but one does not see them. I met only two persons
coming down: a fat Swiss or German with binoculars around
his neck, and a young nun whose face, bare of makeup, seemed
nude. To let the first pass, I hugged the curving wall: for the
second, I pressed myself against the core of the spiral. In both
cases I had a sensation of their passing through me.

The vertical spiral suddenly ended, the curve of the dome
entering the diagonal. I walked up a sharply sloping corridor
whose outer wall gradually pressed inward. The trough worn
in the floor by footsteps moved to one side, and a claustro-
phobic crouch was forced upon me. Then this second episode
of ascent also ended, and I found myself at the foot of a flight
of stairs statelier than those of any palace. Only a Titan or a
monkey could have climbed them comfortably. A zigzag of
wooden steps had been imposed upon them for the use of
human beings. I climbed, saw sky, felt a breeze, and emerged
into the loggia that tops St. Peter's dome.

This island in the sky already supported a tame little population—several phlegmatic guards, one ancient nun, two pairs of
lovers, a family whose father carried a baby in his arms, and a
nudging, snickering quartet of Roman youths. All seemed at
home on this height. Only I, leaning desperately back from the
precipitous parabola of metal that fell away on all sides, seemed
to feel the impossibility of our position. Some birds wheeled
far below my feet. The view was like a map and postcard
mixed, and in the Vatican gardens designs had been executed
in shrubbery apparently for our benefit; my retinas received

these sights mechanically. My mind was too obsessed by fear to see.

But returning into the shelter of the loggia, and heading back down the tortuous path of ascent, I regained my senses, and perceived that the walls enclosing me were covered with names. Pencil, pen, lipstick, and knife had left hardly a square inch uninscribed. There were no irreverent graffiti, merely names and dates solemnly placed wherever hands could reach. Many of the names were Italian, many were English, some were German or Spanish or French, some were impossible to identify nationally, and some—indeed, many—were unmistakably American. A few, soldiers' names, were accompanied by a serial number or the number of a military unit. Not only were names fitted into every interstice between other names, but older names, below these, had been covered up, so that layer upon layer, decade upon decade, of inscription was indicated. There was no indication that any attempt had ever been made to erase the names. It came to me why: these were souls in Heaven. The nave of St. Peter's was the world. At the base of the dome, one died, and entered a purgatory of strait and arduous ways. At the summit, one was, like Dante, blinded. Then one signed the firmament and joined the uncountable host of the blessed that the dome of St. Peter's invisibly poises before the eyes of all Rome. It surprised me that Paradise, which I had pictured, in Sunday school, as being in another dimension, could be a notorious tourist attraction, its construction detailed in guidebooks, its photograph peddled in shops. It shocked my Protestant conscience that the method of salvation should be, strictly, illegal—a matter of defacement. But then, what does the Bible tell us if not that it takes a little daring to enter Heaven? A little daring, and a writing implement. I had a pen. I fingered it in my pocket, and hesitated. I had reached, during my revelation, the spiral stair. In a few minutes I would be down, gone from the dome forever, my opportunity lost. Voices panted and laughed above and below me. Suppose I were discovered? Arrested? Caught in the middle of the leap of faith, is one eternally embarrassed? I paused amid hordes of those who had gone before. If all these, why not I? Taking out my pen, I did, in blue, on a bare patch between two seraphic swirls of lipstick, dare set my name.

ECLIPSE

I WENT OUT INTO THE BACKYARD and the usually roundish spots
of dappled sunlight underneath the trees were all shaped like
feathers, crescent in the same direction, from left to right.
Though it was five o'clock on a summer afternoon, the birds
were singing good-bye to the day, and their merged song
seemed to soak the strange air in an additional strangeness.
A kind of silence prevailed. Few cars were moving on the
streets of the town. Of my children only the baby dared come
into the yard with me. She wore only underpants, and as she
stood beneath a tree, bulging her belly toward me in the
mood of jolly flirtation she has grown into at the age of two,
her bare skin was awash with pale crescents. It crossed my
mind that she might be harmed, but I couldn't think how.
Cancer?

The eclipse was to be over 90 percent in our latitude and
the newspapers and television for days had been warning us
not to look at it. I looked up, a split-second Prometheus, and
looked away. The bitten silhouette of the sun lingered redly
on my retinas. The day was half-cloudy, and my impression
had been of the sun struggling, amid a furious knotted huddle
of black and silver clouds, with an enemy too dreadful to be
seen, with an eater as ghostly and hungry as time. Every
blade of grass cast a long bluish-brown shadow, as at dawn.

My wife shouted from behind the kitchen screen door that

as long as I was out there I might as well burn the waste-paper. She darted from the house, eyes downcast, with the wastebasket, and darted back again, leaving the naked baby and me to wander up through the strained sunlight to the wire trash barrel. After my forbidden peek at the sun, the flames dancing transparently from the blackening paper—yesterday's Boston *Globe*, a milk carton, a Hi-Ho cracker box—seemed dimmer than shadows, and in the teeth of all the warnings I looked up again. The clouds seemed bunched and twirled as if to plug a hole in the sky, and the burning afterimage was the shape of a near-new moon, horns pointed down. It was gigantically unnatural, and I lingered in the yard under the vague apprehension that in some future life I might be called before a cosmic court to testify to this assault. I seemed to be the sole witness. The town around my yard was hushed, all but the singing of the birds, who were invisible. The feathers under the trees had changed direction, and curved from right to left.

Then I saw my neighbor sitting on her porch. My neighbor is a widow, with white hair and brown skin; she has in her yard an aluminum-and-nylon-net chaise longue on which she lies at every opportunity, head back, arms spread, prostrate under the sun. Now she hunched dismally on her porch steps in the shade, which was scarcely darker than the light. I walked toward her and hailed her as a visitor to the moon might salute a survivor of a previous expedition. "How do you like the eclipse?" I called over the fence that distinguished our holdings on this suddenly insubstantial and lunar earth.

"I don't like it," she answered, shading her face with a hand. "They say you shouldn't go out in it."

"I thought it was just you shouldn't look at it."

"There's something in the rays," she explained, in a voice far louder than it needed to be, for silence framed us. "I shut all the windows on that side of the house and had to come out for some air."

"I think it'll pass," I told her.

"Don't let the baby look up," she warned, and turned away from talking to me, as if the open use of her voice exposed her more fatally to the rays.

Superstition, I thought, walking back through my yard, clutching my child's hand as tightly as a good-luck token. There was no question in her touch. Day, night, twilight, noon were all wonders to her, unscheduled, free from all bondage of prediction. The sun was being restored to itself and soon would radiate influence as brazenly as ever—and in this sense my daughter's blind trust was vindicated. Nevertheless, I was glad that the eclipse had passed, as it were, over her head; for in my own life I felt a certain assurance evaporate forever under the reality of the sun's disgrace.

Reviews

Poetry from Downtroddendom

THE LONELINESS OF THE LONG-DISTANCE RUNNER, by Alan Sillitoe.
176 pp. Knopf; 1960.

On a British-owned island in the West Indies recently, I
read through an anthology of "schoolboy" stories—a genre
special to the English, who take their schoolboys with a
singularly high seriousness. Some of the stories were jolly
spoofs, but the most exciting and convincing were those
nakedly concerned with inculcating the social virtues of endeavor, pluck, and fair play. The plot was always the same: a
young lad, named Pip or Snip or Fudge or Pudge, by a mighty
effort succeeded, though half-blinded by the flapping flags of
School and Nation, in kicking the winning goal or bowling
the innings that turned the tide. The title story of Alan Sillitoe's collection, *The Loneliness of the Long-distance Runner*,
is squarely in this tradition, none the less squarely for being an
inversion of it. The school is not Eton or Willows-in-the-Dale
but an Essex Borstal; the hero, Smith, makes his mighty effort
not to win the race but to lose it; the nation for which he
strives is not Green England but the black kingdom of Downtroddendom; and the vision that gives him strength is the
memory of his father's prolonged death of throat cancer.

Now Mr. Sillitoe is a writer of great gifts, and Smith's
inner stream of invective is often very beautiful:

They're training me up fine for the big sports day when all the
pig-faced snotty-nosed dukes and ladies—who can't add two and
two together and would mess themselves like loonies if they

didn't have slaves to beck-and-call—come and make speeches to us about sports being just the thing to get us leading an honest life and keep our itching finger-ends off them shop locks and safe-handles and hairgrips to open gas meters. . . . The pop-eyed potbellied governor said to a pop-eyed potbellied Member of Parliament who sat next to his pop-eyed potbellied whore of a wife. . . .

But it raises the question: Is a literature in which all the Haves are pop-eyed potbellies an improvement over one in which the Have-nots are docile animals in livery or comic grotesques pottering around the street? The question might be irrelevant if the author did not go out of his way, in an unexpectedly awkward bit at the end, to associate himself with his anti-social hero: "And if I don't get caught the bloke I give this story to will never give me away; he's lived in our terrace for as long as I can remember, and he's my pal. That I do know."

It is not for me to doubt the hard lot of the English working class. It was the Industrial Revolution's first child, and took the worst she had to give. A visitor to England, especially to London or Oxford, seems to see two different races of men: the one pink and smooth and gay; the other dwarfish, dark, and sullen. Yet on the evidence of the other stories in this book, one is led to wonder if a sense of alienation as logical and systematic as Smith's is not so exceptional as to be unreal. Elsewhere, there is this glimpse: "On the Sunday morning that my mother and father shook their heads over Chamberlain's melancholy voice issuing from the webbed heart-shaped speaker of our wireless set, I met Frankie in the street." This rings truer; Chamberlain's voice, remote and webbed, still has the power to sadden. For surely the discouraging thing, from the Marxist's point of view, about the English lower class is that they persist in believing they possess a share, if a miserable, bitter share, of the nation. Throughout these stories, for that matter, the revolutionary spirit, where it is articulated, is done so by adolescents, and merges indistinguishably with the revolt against the Grown-ups. And the acquiescent state of old men is portrayed with an insight that cuts through categories of class.

I have taken an uncomfortable amount of space to get this worry off my chest, the worry, that is, that Mr. Sillitoe sometimes plays "tails" to Nancy Mitford's "heads." The comfortable duty remains of praising the author's artistry. It is great. The least of his nine stories is better than fair; the best are splendid. Monologues like "On Saturday Afternoon" and "The Disgrace of Jim Scarfedale" have a rasp, a comedy, a casually callous acceptance of misery that would be remarkable even without the poetic swing, snap, and surprise. They have a wonderful way of going on, of not stopping short (for instance, Mrs. Scarfedale's maternal tirade when her son threatens marriage) that lifts us twice, and shows enviable assurance and abundance in the writer. Now and then he fusses too much with *why* his narrators are telling the story, and occasionally (as in "The Fishing-boat Picture"), seems embarrassed for an ending. To write endings worthy of these beginnings and middles must have been a technical challenge: the "turn" is too complacently bourgeois and the "dying fall" too languidly aristocratic. I liked best those endings in which the boy-narrator stood right up in his shabby shoes and explained what lesson he had learned, as if he were assembling a personal Bible out of scraps blowing in the gutters.

In the third-person stories, the language is not always appropriate to the subject. "Mr. Raynor the School-teacher" is a sequence of words in perfect adjustment. The futile confusion within a classroom and the brutal fate of a pretty girl—*"timide et libertine, et fragile et robuste"*—glimpsed from the window work in effortless parallel to convey the brooding over-presence of a slum. I was grateful, too, for "The Match": a piece of Saturday afternoon fog bottled for keeps. But in "Noah's Ark" the incident is smothered under rather aloof phrase-making, and "Uncle Ernest" is marred by intermittent niceties.

The dust jacket mentions hundreds of poems and a hundred-thousand-word novel that Mr. Sillitoe has destroyed; and in the last story, "The Decline and Fall of Frankie Buller," we discover the author himself, wearing his own name of Alan, glumly contemplating the books he has read (or not read):

And so on and so on, items that have become part of me, foliage that has grown to conceal the bare stem of my real personality, what I was like before I ever saw these books, or any book at all, come to that. Often I would like to rip them away from me one by one, extract their shadows out of my mouth and heart . . .

So would we all. The lack of connection between the experiences, usually accumulated by the age of twenty, that seem worth telling about, and the sophistication needed to render them in writing, is the Unmentionable at the root of the mysterious Fall of so many auspicious beginners. For a moment, the two intersect; the memories are fresh, the new tools are sharp, and a vivid imitation of life is produced. Then the memories recede, and the writer is left holding the tools. It may be merely distance, simplifying distance, that makes the long-distance runner seem a little too pure to be true. But Mr. Sillitoe's achievement is the measure of his shortcomings, and in his battle with his books he is well-armed with intelligence, humor, and (my guess is) stamina.

Snow from a Dead Sky

THE COLLECTED SHORT STORIES OF CONRAD AIKEN. 566 pp. World; 1960.

When I had finished reading this big book, I closed it, and looked at the back, and my tired eyes, without my willing it, went out of focus, placing, to the right of Aiken's face and slightly lower, a dimmer duplicate. Eerily, this secondary image, though less sharp, seemed more *real* than the image it echoed. The shadows around the mouth called into relief muscles potentially expressive of humor and wrath; the cheekbones and eyelids seemed curved and tactile; the hornrim spectacles perched forward dimensionally on the stout, white, pugnacious nose. The photograph was just a photograph, but the photograph's ghost was a man—a man who, when I tried to study him closely, of course vanished. And I wondered if these forty-one stories might best have been viewed, by some hypnotic relaxation of the cerebrum, in the same way; for their truth seems to exist, invisibly, to one side of their vivid surfaces.

Perhaps this author so obsessed with accident and unfulfillment has been himself slightly misplaced. If he had been born a German, his morbidity might have deepened into Kafkaesque prophecy. If he had been born (preferably at the tag end of the Age of Reason) a Frenchman, his aptitude for erotic psychology—his tender, particularizing concern for things female— might have blossomed abundantly. As it is, in our small, ill-tended garden of native Olympians, he seems a somewhat stunted and tenuously elegant growth, putting forth branches in all directions, yet of whose presence—as Mark Schorer tactlessly points out in his introductory appreciation—we need, after more than four productive decades, still to be reminded. He evokes comparison with the very best; and then suffers from the comparison. Just as his poems, compared with, say, Wallace Stevens', seem formless and wan, his short stories, compared with Hemingway's, seem stylistically indecisive, and, compared with Faulkner's, insufficiently material and grasping.

Love and death, those two organic imperatives, are Aiken's all but exclusive subjects. The stories about death—conceived as an ethereal incoherence bombarding our humanity from all sides—are the more strikingly original, and account for his reputation as a teller of sophisticated shudder stories. But he is poles removed from a spook-monger like H. P. Lovecraft; the horror of Aiken's fiction lies not in the possibility that other worlds exist but in the certainty that they do not. The cosmic vacuity, the central *nihil* haunts him; "the great white light of annihilation" illuminates his scenes and to an extent bleaches them. In retrospect many of his stories seem black-and-white film clips from the twenties and thirties. His characters wake from comic dreams and, singing empty little snatches of song to themselves, move through a world crowded with ticking clocks and seething snow and visual details ("dead matches, a rusty horse-chestnut burr, a small concentration of eggshell, a streak of yellow sawdust which had been wet and now was dry and congealed, a brown pebble, and a broken feather") observed with an intensity befitting an insane universe. Aiken's world is so morally insubstantial that hallucinations effortlessly permeate it. In his famous "Silent Snow, Secret Snow," thickening snow becomes the sensible manifestation of an uncaused apathy which closes over a young boy and lures him to death. In "Mr. Arcularis"—a superb fantasy that must be read to be believed—a shipboard romance, rumbling engines, the threat of icebergs, fog, a coffin in the hold, and a sleepwalking exploration of the frozen stars give body and form to a man's progress toward death on an operating table.

"The fair page of the world, thus reset, becomes a brilliant but meaningless jumble of typographical errors"—this from "Gehenna," Aiken's most concentrated and dense explication of a "world of which the only tenable principle is horror." The horror is not Hitlerian but Einsteinian; crime seldom and war never intrude in these stories, but the interstellar gulfs, the chasms in subjectivity, and the atomic near-void are translated into sensual acrophobia. His compulsion to give shapelessness shape does generate, by backwards thrust, a kind of supernaturalism. "The Disciple," more than any other American story I have read, breathes life into Christianity considered as local European folklore; Judas and the Eternal Jew meet and talk in an atmosphere supercharged *à la* Isak Dinesen and Dostoevsky. But in the end, Aiken himself backs away, leaving the reader suspended between realities and doubtful of the author's good faith. Metaphysical fantasy, lacking the conviction of delirium, subsides into allegorical gossip; "Smith and Jones," for instance, reminded me too much of those dental pamphlets in which Irving Incisor and Max Molar debate fluoridation. Perhaps, indeed, Death (as opposed to dying, which is a species of living) is a better subject for meditation than for fiction, since it is, however conceived, unknowable, and emotional effects aimed from one conception of it can too easily, by a slight shift of philosophy, be evaded.

More affecting, on the whole, are Aiken's stories of love. He moves with ease in the swimming minds of women willing to fall in love ("Bring, Bring," "All, All Wasted"); he tastes the uncanny innocence of promiscuity ("Thistledown," "West End"); he conveys, in the tiny interval before the spangled curtain of good taste descends, a strong sexual flavor—"Tom took her gloved hand, inserted his finger in the opening, and stroked her palm. A delicious feeling of weakness, dissolution, came over her." Not that, under the skies of heavenly apathy, seduction is either very difficult or very rewarding. "We came together as naturally as leaf touches leaf or the grass bends to the wind," one adulterer says. In "Hey, Taxi," a cabdriver and a girlish tramp drift into each other's arms like two snowflakes in the universal descent. Such energy as is needed, the women provide; their aggression can be monstrous ("Spider, Spider"). But men are feeble beasts, preoccupied with themselves and their wives, and they send their mistresses alone into howling trolley cars ("The Night Before Prohibition"), betray them to satyrs ("Thistledown"), and begrudge them even the present of a dollar print ("Field of Flowers"). Small wonder, since boredom and abuse invariably follow the scattering of the pollen, that the most moving and ecstatic of these love stories are those in which nothing—physically speaking —happens. The flower opens, the bee hovers, and that is all. In "Farewell! Farewell! Farewell!" an Irish maid and a young architect exchange one kiss. In "Your Obituary, Well Written," nothing is exchanged but some childhood memories about the rain. It *is* well-written; the poet trembles up out of the prose and the page is solid with sensation. Aiken is impressive when he snows, but nutritious when he rains; I wish that somehow the climate had permitted him to rain more.

Franny and Zooey

FRANNY AND ZOOEY, by J. D. Salinger. 201 pp. Little, Brown; 1961.

Quite suddenly, as things go in the middle period of J. D. Salinger, his later, longer stories are descending from the clouds of old *New Yorkers* and assuming incarnations between hard covers. "Raise High the Roof Beam, Carpenters" became available in *Stories from the New Yorker 1950–1960*, and now "Franny" and "Zooey" have a book to themselves. These two stories—the first medium-short, the second novella-length—are contiguous in time, and have as their common subject Franny's spiritual crisis.

In the first story, she arrives by train from a Smithlike college to spend the weekend of the Yale game at what must be Princeton. She and her date, Lane Coutell, go to a restaurant where it develops that she is not only unenthusiastic but downright ill. She attempts to explain herself while her friend brags about a superbly obnoxious term paper and eats frogs' legs. Finally, she faints, and is last seen lying in the manager's office silently praying at the ceiling. In the second story, Franny has returned to her home, a large apartment in the East Seventies. It is the Monday following her unhappy Saturday. Only Franny's mother, Bessie, and her youngest brother, Zooey, are home. While Franny lies sleeplessly on the living-room sofa, her mother communicates, in an interminably rendered conversation, her concern and affection to Zooey, who then, after an even longer conversation with Franny, manages to gather from the haunted atmosphere of the apartment the crucial word of consolation. Franny, "as if all of what little or much wisdom there is in the world were suddenly hers," smiles at the ceiling and falls asleep.

Few writers since Joyce would risk such a wealth of words upon events that are purely internal and deeds that are purely talk. We live in a world, however, where the decisive deed may invite the holocaust, and Salinger's conviction that our inner lives greatly matter peculiarly qualifies him to sing of an America where, for most of us, there seems little to do but to feel. Introversion, perhaps, has been forced upon history; an age of nuance, of ambiguous gestures and psychological jockeying on a national and private scale, is upon us, and Salinger's intense attention to gesture and intonation help make him, among his contemporaries, a uniquely pertinent literary artist. As Hemingway sought the words for things in motion, Salinger seeks the words for things transmuted into human subjectivity. His fiction, in its rather grim bravado, its humor, its privacy, its wry but persistent hopefulness, matches the shape and tint of present American life. It pays the price, however, of becoming dangerously convoluted and static. A sense of composition is not among Salinger's strengths, and even these two stories, so apparently complementary, distinctly jangle as components of one book.

The Franny of "Franny" and the Franny of "Zooey" are not the same person. The heroine of "Franny" is a pretty college girl passing through a plausible moment of disgust. She has discovered—one feels rather recently—a certain ugliness in the hungry human ego and a certain fatuity in her college environment. She is attempting to find her way out with the help of a religious book, *The Way of a Pilgrim*, which was mentioned by a professor. She got the book out of the college library. Her family, glimpsed briefly in the P.S. of a letter she has written, appear to be standard upper-middle gentry. Their name is nowhere given as Glass, though some "brothers" are mentioned—once—in passing. Her boy friend is callow and self-centered but not entirely unsympathetic; he clumsily does try to "get through" to Franny, with a love whose physical bias has become painfully inappropriate. Finally, there is a suggestion, perhaps inadvertent, that the girl may be pregnant.

The Franny of "Zooey," on the other hand, is Franny Glass, the youngest of the seven famous Glass children, all of whom have been in turn wondrously brilliant performers on a radio quiz program, "It's a Wise Child." Their parents, a distinctly unstandard combination of Jewish and Irish, are an old vaudeville team. From infancy on, Franny has been saturated by her two oldest brothers, Seymour and Buddy, in the religious wisdom of the East. *The Way of a Pilgrim*, far from being newly encountered at college, comes from Seymour's desk, where it has been for years. One wonders how a girl raised in a home where Buddhism and crisis theology were table talk could have postponed her own crisis so long and, when it came, be so disarmed by it. At any rate, there is no question of her being pregnant; the very idea seems a violation of the awesome Glass ethereality. Lane Coutell, who for all his faults was at least a considerable man in the first Franny's universe, is now just one of the remote millions coarse and foolish enough to be born outside the Glass family.

The more Salinger writes about them, the more the seven Glass children melt indistinguishably together in an impossible radiance of personal beauty and intelligence. Franny is described thus: "Her skin was lovely, and her features were delicate and most distinctive. Her eyes were very nearly the same quite astonishing shade of blue as Zooey's, but were set farther apart, as a sister's eyes no doubt should be. . . ." Of Zooey, we are assured he has a "somewhat preposterous ability to quote, instantaneously and, usually, verbatim, almost anything he had ever read, or even listened to, with genuine interest." The purpose of such sentences is surely not to particularize imaginary people but to instill in the reader a mood of blind worship, tinged by an envy that the author encourages with a patent leer of indulgence.

In "Raise High the Roof Beam, Carpenters" (the best of the Glass pieces: a magic and hilarious prose-poem with an enchanting end effect of mysterious clarity, like a *koan*), Seymour defines sentimentality as giving "to a thing more tenderness than God gives to it." This seems to me the nub of the trouble. Salinger loves the Glasses more than God loves them. He loves them too exclusively. Their invention has become a hermitage for him. He loves them to the detriment of artistic moderation. "Zooey" is just too long; there are too many cigarettes, too many goddams, too much verbal ado about not quite enough. The author never rests from circling his creations, patting them fondly, slyly applauding. He robs the reader of the initiative upon which love must be given. Even in "Franny," which is, strictly, pre-Glass, the writer seems less an unimpassioned observer than a spying beau vindictively feasting upon every detail of poor Lane Coutell's gaucherie. Indeed, this impression of a second male being present is so strong that it amounts to a social shock when the author accompanies Franny into the ladies' room of the restaurant.

"Franny," nevertheless, takes place in what is recognizably our world; in "Zooey" we move into a dream world whose zealously animated details only emphasize an essential unreality. When Zooey says to Franny, "*Yes*, I have an ulcer for Chrissake. This is Kaliyuga, buddy, the Iron Age," disbelief falls on the "buddy" as much as on "Kaliyuga," and the explanatory "the Iron Age" clinches our suspicion that a lecturer has usurped the writing stand. Not the least dismaying development of the Glass stories is the vehement editorializing on the obvious—television scripts are not generally good, not all section men are geniuses. Of course, the Glasses condemn the world only to condescend to it, to forgive it, in the end. Yet the pettishness of the condemnation diminishes the gallantry of the condescension.

Perhaps these are hard words; they are made hard to write by the extravagant self-consciousness of Salinger's later prose, wherein most of the objections one might raise are already raised. On the flap of this book jacket, he confesses, ". . . there is a real-enough danger, I suppose, that sooner or later I'll bog down, perhaps disappear entirely, in my own methods, locutions, and mannerisms. On the whole, though, I'm very hopeful." Let me say, I am glad he is hopeful. I am one of those—to do some confessing of my own—for whom Salinger's work dawned as something of a revelation. I expect that further revelations are to come. The Glass saga, as he has sketched it out, potentially contains great fiction. When all reservations have been entered, in the correctly unctuous and apprehensive tone, about the direction he has taken, it remains to acknowledge that it *is* a direction, and that the refusal to rest content, the willingness to risk excess on behalf of one's obsessions, is what distinguishes artists from entertainers, and what makes some artists adventurers on behalf of us all.

Credos and Curios

CREDOS AND CURIOS, by James Thurber. 180 pp. Harper and Row; 1962.

The appearance, in the yellow dust jacket that has become traditional, of one more collection of pieces by the late James Thurber is a happy event, even for the reviewer obliged to report that the bulk of the pieces are from his last years and as such tend to be cranky, formless, and lame. "The claw of the sea-puss," Thurber once wrote (quoting F. Hopkinson Smith), "gets us all in the end"; and toward the end Thurber's humor was overwhelmed by puns and dismay.

The puns are understandable. Blindness, in severing language from the seen world of designated things, gives words a tyrannical independence. Milton and Joyce wrung from verbal obsession a special magnificence, and Thurber's late pieces, at their best—for example, "The Tyranny of Trivia," collected in *Lanterns and Lances*—do lead the reader deep into the wonderland of the alphabet and the dictionary. But in such weak rambles as, in this collection, "The Lady from the Land" and "Carpe Noctem, If You Can," logomachic tricks are asked to pass for wit and implausible pun-swapping for human conversation.

As to the dismay: Mrs. Thurber, in her graceful and understated introduction to this posthumous collection, defends her husband against the charge of "bitterness and disillusion." But stories like "The Future, If Any, of Comedy Or, Where Do We Not-Go from Here?" and "Afternoon of a Playwright" do display, by way of monologue in the ungainly disguise of dialogue, an irritation with the present state of things so inclusive as to be pointless. Television, psychoanalysis, the Bomb, the deterioration of grammar, the morbidity of contemporary literature—these were just a few of Thurber's terminal pet peeves. The writer who had produced *Fables for Our Time* and *The Last Flower* out of the thirties had become, by the end of the fifties, one more indignant senior citizen penning complaints about the universal decay of virtue.

The only oasis, in the dreadful world of post-midnight forebodings into which he had been plunged, is the Columbus, Ohio, of his boyhood, which he continued to remember "as fondly and sharply as a man on a sinking ship might remember his prairie home." In *Credos and Curios*, for a few pages entitled "Return of the Native," his prose regains the crisp lucidity and glistening bias of *The Thurber Album*. Then the murky verbosity closes in again.

However, *Credos and Curios* should be cherished by every Thurberite for the seven random tributes he wrote, between 1938 and 1960, to seven artistic colleagues—Mary Petty, Elliott Nugent, and five writers. His acute and sympathetic remarks on Scott Fitzgerald remind us that Thurber, too, was one of the curiously compact literary generation that came to birth in the twenties and whose passing has left the literary stage so strikingly empty. His affectionate memories of John McNulty and E. B. White, two friends who in their different ways achieved the literary tranquility that eluded Thurber, better capture the spirit of *New Yorker* bonhomie than all *The Years With Ross*. His generous appreciation of Robert Benchley is most welcome of all, especially when taken as an antidote to the oddly curt paragraph with which *The New Yorker* noted the death, in 1949, of this remarkable artist. For if Thurber, whose international celebrity made him seem to loom unduly over the other American humorists of his vintage, is to be measured against his peers, the first name we strike is Benchley's. The surprising thing about Benchley is that he remains readable. His writings were so ephemeral they seem to defy being outdated; their utterly casual and innocent surface airily resists corrosion. It is doubtful how much of Thurber will weather so well.

Thurber's cartoons, of course, are incomparable; they dive into the depths of the dilemma that he felt beneath everything. His great subject, springing from his physical disability, was what might be called the enchantment of misapprehension. His masterpieces, I think, are *My Life and Hard Times* and *The White Deer*—two dissimilar books alike in their beautiful evocation of a fluid chaos where communication is limited to wild, flitting gestures and where human beings revolve and collide like planets glowing against a cosmic backdrop of gathering dark. Thurber made of despair a humorous fable. Small wonder that such a gallant feat of equilibrium was not maintained to the end of his life.

Beerbohm and Others

PARODIES: AN ANTHOLOGY FROM CHAUCER TO BEERBOHM—AND AFTER, edited by Dwight Macdonald. 574 pp. Random House; 1960.

This anthology is a book so manifoldly praiseworthy that the reviewer puzzles where to begin. The publishers should be praised for constructing a compact and dignified volume. The dust jacket does not try to cozen us into premature jollity; the necessarily various type does not dance an impudent jig on the page; the paper, without succumbing to translucence, modestly understates the book's considerable bulk. These things matter. What is worth reprinting is worth printing well. Too many lovingly assembled collections emerge from the binderies as fluffed-up jumbles shamelessly aimed at the Christmas trade. Except for a trifling misprint in the parody of Jack Kerouac, this anthology seems to me a physical model of its kind.

The editor should be praised—for his industry, his serious-ness, his taste, his ingenuity. Indeed, Macdonald is rather *too* ingenious. To print the delirious babble of the dying Dutch Schultz as a parody of Gertrude Stein is an excellent joke only if excellent jokes can ever be played upon dying men. "Please mother don't tear don't rip. That is something that shouldn't be spoken about. Please get me up, my friends, please look out, the shooting is a bit wild and that kind of shooting saved a man's life. . . . Police mamma Helen mother please take me out." Who's laughing? There is something vulgar about this editorial prank, and the equally prankish printing of a bit by Samuel Foote (d. 1777) as a parody of Edward Lear (b. 1812). Also, I could have done without all the self-parodies, conscious and unconscious. Authors are in no position to see themselves; conscious self-parodies lack shape and bite. The classic speci-men is "Nephelidia"; Swinburne apparently thought his only sin was alliteration. As for the unconscious self-parodies, where they are not mere boners they demand a rather harsh shift in the gears of our attention. While not too great a sus-pension of sympathy is needed to raise a smile over Poe's beginning a poem, "I dwelt alone / In a world of moan," Dr. Johnson's effusion on glass will probably strike as ludicrous only those already disposed to grow restive under the great man's ornately balanced Latinisms. Myself, I found his noble style no less appropriate to the subject of glass than to the subject of virtue.

But anthologies, if they err, should err on the generous side, and Macdonald's venturesomeness brings in dozens of welcome surprises. The contributions of Jane Austen, Bret Harte, Firman Houghton, Oliver Jensen, and G. K. Chesterton were all new to me, and it was delightful to make their acquaintance. Among old friends, I was glad to greet again Henry Reed's irreproachably deadpan imitation of T. S. Eliot; Edmund Wilson's most unkind treatment of Archibald MacLeish; Wolcott Gibbs' famous tour de force in early timestyle; Maurice Baring's pathetically reasonable letter from Goneril to Regan; C. S. Calverley's immaculate, crackling *reductio* of *The Ring and the Book;* Swift's "A Meditation Upon a Broom-Stick"; Robert Benchley's modernization of a Dickensian Christmas; and J. K. Stephen's resonant and—remarkably—*brief* parody of Whitman. The section of this anthology called "Specialties" is the one that must have given the editor the most pleasure. It makes up half the book and contains, among many diligently unearthed oddments, the originals of the poems travestied by Lewis Carroll in the "Alice" books; twenty-one pages of French; ten pages of Hemingway's obscurely motivated mock-novel *Torrents of Spring;* several political speeches more apt to amuse Democrats than Republicans; and two scientific papers that may not amuse scientists at all. Throughout, Macdonald shepherds his chosen texts with notes, now appreciative, now informative, that in their relaxed pedantry nicely suit the pedantic and exquisite form of humor he has—for some years to come, I should think—definitively anthologized.

And of course the contributors, quick and dead, must be praised. The appointed hero of the collection, quite rightly, is Max Beerbohm. Macdonald considerately resurrects from obscure sources much that is not present in *A Christmas Garland*, as well as much that is. *A Christmas Garland* is surely the *liber aureus* of prose parody. What makes Max, as a parodist, incomparable—more than the calm mounting from felicity to felicity and the perfectly scaled enlargement of every surface quirk of the subject style—is the way he seizes and embraces, with something like love, the total personality of the parodee. He seems to enclose in a transparent omniscience the genius of each star as, in *A Christmas Garland*, he methodically moves across the firmament of Edwardian letters. Anyone who has forgotten the difference between Chesterton and Belloc could have no better refresher than Beerbohm's parodies of them. Chesterton's preposterously nimble good cheer and Belloc's robust and defiant *angoisse* are each crystallized in absurdity, but the amber is so clear we can glimpse even the sombre spots. "Pray for my soul," the puppet-Belloc abruptly concludes, and the reader is touched by a real shadow. Whereas most parodies are distinctly written from beneath their subjects, Beerbohm for the occasion rises to an equality with his great victims; a vintage parody by him is, as the Greek etymology would have it, "a parallel song." In his imitation of a Shavian preface, Beerbohm develops the minuscule plot of a village mummers' play into an allegorical drama of ideas with a fertile virtuosity worthy of Shaw himself. We can *see* the play when he is done; with a hairline difference in gravity, it could be an actual work in the canon, somewhere between *Heartbreak House* and *Saint Joan*. One puts down *A Christmas Garland* wondering why the man who wrote it did not, in his own voice, write great things. Parody this fine is rare perhaps because it requires gifts that usually drive a man to try something more important. When all due homage has been granted to the uniform refinement of Beerbohm's total production—and special tribute paid to those famous radio broadcasts whose impeccably enunciated nostalgia borrows gallantry from the context of blitzed London—there remains something abortive and not entirely pleasing about Beerbohm as a literary figure.

Pure parody is purely parasitic. There is no disgrace in this. We all begin life as parasites within the mother, and writers begin their existence imitatively, within the body of letters. Beerbohm, introducing *A Christmas Garland*, explains his parodies thus:

. . . I was already writing a little on my own account. I had had some sort of aptitude for Latin prose and Latin verse. I wondered often whether those two things, essential though they were (and are) to the making of a decent style in English prose, sufficed for the making of a style more than decent. I felt that I must have other models. And thus I acquired the habit of aping, now and again, quite sedulously, this or that live writer—sometimes, it must be admitted, in the hope of learning rather what to avoid. . . . [*A Christmas Garland*] may be taken as a sign that I think my own style is, at length, more or less formed.

But "decent" is exactly what his style remained. His criticism, so acute and daintily just, is rendered pale by our impression that he himself was never burned. His own efforts at fiction are bounded by a landscape of books. His most extended invention, *Zuleika Dobson*, miscarries, it seems to me, in its climactic holocaust; he treats his paper creations too heartlessly. His essays do show flashes of terrestrial daylight, of felt experience. The most memorable of them, "The Golden Drugget," tells of a strip of light projected across the road through the open doorway of an inn near Rapallo. This sign of human company comforts him as he walks the dark road; he is tempted to enter but, to preserve his illusions, never does. "Don Quixote would have paused here and done something. Not so do I." Art imitates Nature in this: not to dare is to dwindle. S. N. Behrman's fascinating memoir of talks with the octogenarian Max presented, in the kindliest light, a portrait of a miser. Beerbohm's persistent gloating upon his own "little-ness" became somewhat grating, and in the end his delicate belittling of the lack of littleness in others seemed virtually nasty. Magnanimity was reduced in his conversation to a species of conceit, zeal to a form of presumption. Everything withered under the gentle touch of Beerbohm's equanimous depreciation, and his creative energy, which he could never refine quite out of existence, was solipsistically focussed on the ornamentation of his private library with private jokes. As, in his amniotic cave in Rapallo, he continued to play the young man's game of parody, it turned into a childish fiddling with scissors and paste, footnotes and mustaches; in his own drawings of himself, the wispy, ethereal, top-hatted Puck of the London days evolved backward into an elderly fetus with a huge square head, bulging eyes, and a tiny hunched body—an emblem, as ominous as wonderful, of the totally non-quixotic man.

If great parodists are not great writers, great writers, conversely, are not great parodists. Once the spirit has made that harsh emergence, and learned to feed on the sights and sounds of the outer air, there is no returning. Contrast with Beerbohm the contemporaneous young Irishman who set out to forge in the smithy of his soul the uncreated conscience of his race. Macdonald includes in his "Specialties" section excerpts from the "Oxen of the Sun" passage in *Ulysses*, wherein Mrs. Purefoy's son comes to birth through progressive contractions, as it were, of English style. By labelling the excerpts with the names of specific parodees, Macdonald somewhat falsifies the generality and integrity of the passage, and places Joyce in an arena where, at heart, he disdained to compete. *A Christmas Garland* is a program of flawless impersonations by an actor whose own personality is invisible. The "Oxen of the Sun" episode is a boisterous "turn" taken in an antic succession of loosely fitting costumes; behind the bobbing masks we easily recognize the vaudevillian himself, Shem the Penman, the old flabbergaster. There is hardly a sentence of this parodic caper that lacks Joyce's own tone—the compacted incantation, the impelling commaless lilt, the love of rubble that turns history itself into a stream of trash. In reading these excerpts, disconnected as they are, we become caught up in the subterranean momentum of Joyce's earnest obsessions, of a narrative we can hardly see; the glimpses of Bloom and Stephen Dedalus take our eye, and the verbal hurly-burly screening them from clear view becomes something of a nuisance. These paragraphs tell us little about the authors imitated—Dickens was sentimental, Carlyle fulminated, etc.—but they strive to tell us everything about *things*. Their power as fiction mars them as parody—or, rather, they are not parody at all but acts of conquest, a multiple annexation, an assimilation of all previous prose into a "chaffering allincluding most farraginous chronicle" and into Joyce himself. The culminating section, which Macdonald terms "the death of English in the gutter," contains vivid elements of (very possibly) conscious self-parody; that is, as Mrs. Purefoy gives birth to her boy, the English language gives birth to James Joyce.

Passionately creative spirits *use* parody, rather roughly; and if the tool snaps in their hands, what of it? The *Aeneid* is a parody of sorts and is most admirable where it is least Homeric, and we may be grateful that the parodic vestiges in *Madame Bovary* (e.g., the descriptions of Emma's girlhood reading) are all but dissolved by Flaubert's sympathetic immersion in his heroine. Some novels might be fairly described as ruined parodies. The little dolls whittled in fun escape the author's derision and take on life. *Joseph Andrews* and *Northanger Abbey* are examples; *Don Quixote* is the towering instance. Cervantes' masterpiece lives not because it succeeds as parody but because it immensely fails. Setting out to demonstrate the folly of romantic aspirations, Cervantes ends by locating in just this folly, this futility, such aspiration's grandeur, and so provides at the outset of the modern era an adjective and a metaphor for the new human condition.

Parody becomes significant in proportion to the dimensions of the thing parodied. At the bottom of the scale are those burlesques, achieved by crude verbal substitutions, of such specific works as "Excelsior," "Hiawatha," "The Raven," and "The Charge of the Light Brigade." Their humor springs from an instinctive sense of reality that rejects the jingling high-flown; they are parody's folklore. At the middle of the scale—a temperate zone most congenial—are those comprehensive and critical imitations of the manner and style of individual authors that define our modern sense of parody. At the top, reaching into the altitude of (for want of a better word) Literature, are those imaginative creations that, taking certain writings as an excuse, attack the assumptions of an age. If the parodied works present themselves to the parodist as emissaries of a truly formidable threat, the parody may outlive its occasion and become a human, rather than a merely literary, document.

One of Macdonald's most thoughtful strokes is to include the original poems, by Isaac Watts, Robert Southey, G. W. Langford, and assorted female moralists, that Lewis Carroll transmuted into the stuff of Wonderland. To read these verses is to inhale the powerful brown vapors of the Victorian social engine. What is signal about them is not their piety but the utilitarian slant of that piety; behind these homiletic admonitions and consolations looms an explosive national machine steadied by the economic docility of the lower orders and the domestic gentility of the upper. A don and a bachelor, with no great stake, therefore, in the little gliding lies by which society keeps itself in order, and with a perhaps unusually large personal stake in what he called the "divinity in a child's smile," Carroll compulsively substitutes for every smooth piety a bristling absurdity. Southey's unctuously efficient Father William becomes an idiotically adroit curmudgeon, benevolent stars become bats and soup, and Langford's admonition

> Speak gently; it is better far
> To rule by love than fear

becomes

> Speak roughly to your little boy,
> And beat him when he sneezes.

As a scientist, Carroll speaks for the unkind truth; which is truer to nature, Watt's bee or Carroll's crocodile?

> How skillfully she builds her cell!
> How neat she spreads the wax!
> And labors hard to store it well
> With the sweet food she makes.   [*Watts*]

> How cheerfully he seems to grin,
> How neatly spreads his claws,
> And welcomes little fishes in
> With gently smiling jaws!   [*Carroll*]

Nonsense is as a rule subversive. Carroll—and Edward Lear and, in some poems, C. S. Calverley—attempted to strike up, through nonsense, an alliance with children against the heavy oppression of Victorian sense. Macdonald describes the "Alice" books as "systematic parodies of the grown-up world from the viewpoint of a child." Her adventures touch on evolution, Newman, Disraeli, the rise of the newspapers, and many other topical concerns. And their general frame of amiable confusion and obstinate authority derives from the large middle-class Victorian households whose mixed decorums and alarums still echo in the childhood reminiscences of James Thurber and Clarence Day. In his poetic masterpiece "The Hunting of the Snark," Carroll carried parody of his age into its troubled heart. The Snark, W. H. Auden has pointed out, represents the Meaning of Life, which, after being diligently pursued by a posse of respectable Victorian tradesmen, turns out to be a Boojum. Life is meaningless.

Simultaneously, Edward Lear—like Carroll, a solitary, but, unlike him, a wanderer—was populating the geographical vistas opened to British exploitation with persons who amid mad predicaments admirably manifested insular imperturbability and pragmatic resourcefulness. What Carroll did for children's Sunday-school lessons Lear did for their schoolbooks. For both men, cruelty and *non sequitur* were attributes of the perfect freedom that is innocence; they would be appealed to again in the children's verses of Hilaire Belloc, but as the Victorian consensus disintegrated, parody itself went the way of Calverley and J. K. Stephen—subsided, that is, into literary criticism.

The parodist's customary pose is to be more sensible than the parodee. An Age of Sense in literature is, then, a lean time for him. It is no coincidence that modern English parody began, with James and Horace Smith's *Rejected Addresses*, shortly after the onset of romanticism. Between the romantic hallucinations of the dying Middle Ages, whose parodic monument in this collection is Chaucer's *Sir Thopas*, and the appearance of that all-time favorite victim, William Wordsworth, there is precious little English parody—fifty-odd pages in this anthology. And outside of Swift's classic mock meditation and three Shakespearean winks—at euphuism, Marlowe's "mighty line," and Nashe's twittering "wit"—it oscillates between mild imitation and coarse vendetta. There is lacking the right combination of affection and asperity. In truth, the significant neoclassic writers defied parody. Isaac Hawkins Browne apparently had the ideal parodist's temperament; he was a gentleman, wrote little, never finished his Latin masterpiece, and served two terms in Parliament without ever taking the floor. And the samples that Macdonald prints from Browne's slim volume *A Pipe of Tobacco* show meticulous observation and some comic sense. A Popian couplet runs:

> Nor less, the critic owns thy genial aid,
> While supperless he plies the piddling trade.

But the trouble is that a parody of Pope makes no effect qualitatively different from the original; parodied Pope seems second-rate Pope.

Parody is in essence anti-romantic; it is small and hard instead of big and soft, it is selfless instead of self-obsessed. Romanticism presented to parody's gun sights a broad sweep of stylistic excess, a high seriousness, and—most important—an individual distinctness of literary personality. What is inviting about Wordsworth is that his written works behave so humanly. He takes us by the elbow and steers us along on our walk with him, exclaiming, explaining, expecting us to take delight in everything he sees simply because he sees it. When we are not delighted, his innocently wise old eyes seem to widen in astonishment on the face of the page. Milton, equally humorless, equally precipitate in his confident claims on our attention, resists parody, though there are tons of bent burlesque heaped around the base of his monument. The reason lies, perhaps, in the curious impersonality of Milton's poetry; it is unmistakably from a single hand, but the hand might be that of a god or a monster. Milton's *oeuvre* has a consistent identity, and as a man he had a character, but the relationship between the two is, somehow, a deduced one. In Wordsworth the two are inextricable, and his literary face is susceptible of caricature.

Discounting pushovers like Southey and Swinburne, the most-parodied authors in our language are Wordsworth, Browning, Whitman, Henry James, and Hemingway. Why these five? Well, for one thing, these men are all *persons*. We know their faces; they led more or less publicly bardic lives. They are not, like Emily Dickinson and Gerard Manley Hopkins, voices speaking from a hermit's grave. Again, their work presents a constant face; they are not, like Tennyson and Joyce, too protean to catch at one grab. And obviously each carries his style to extremes that verge on the absurd. But extremism is not in itself enough. Shelley and Thomas Wolfe lead parody into extensions of dullness. Involuntary outpour gives parody no foothold; the stylistic eccentricity *must be a willed thing*. The style should contain the visible motions of conscious decision, of choice; to deliberate choices criticism can attach. All five, when they nod, expose the same chink to the arrows of parody: the gap between their literary sophistication and their pretensions to the colloquial. This is perhaps least plain in the case of James, but observe, in Beerbohm's "The Guerdon" and, scarcely diminuendo, in the late James himself, how the scrupulously long sentences tiptoe forward through the demisemiquavers of qualification to offer us, like a dime-store locket on the end of the gold chain, some little cliché, or trinket, mounted proudly in quotes, of contemporary "idiom." A kindred incongruity is present in Wordsworth's and Hemingway's doctrinaire simplicity; Browning's chatty, snorting bookishness; and Whitman's—in Emerson's phrase—"mixture of the *Bhagavad Gita* and the New York *Herald*." All five contain passages in which the style becomes Bergson's encrustation of the mechanical upon the organic—when the author, like the cat in the animated cartoon, continues his stroll over the cliff edge and in serene incognizance pedals the air.

No author is completely invulnerable to parody. Shakespeare has dwarfed his contemporaries out of all comparison, but had one of them (say, that Robert Greene who called him "an upstart crow beautified with our feathers") executed a parody when Shakespeare was still a man among men, we would have a valuable clue to the character of a talent that now seems so uniformly successful as to be characterless.* Like a painting in which each stroke equals a dab of detail or vibration of light, a good parody can be expanded, sentence by sentence, into an analysis of its object. To please us, this analysis should be just. Its malice (and there is always a little) should be cunningly disguised. "Myra Buttle" on Eliot, and Gilbert Highet on Pound—both included in this anthology—are not cunning enough. Highet's imitation of Pound's foul temper is rather too good; his sneers at the poet's Idaho origins are downright painful. Parody perilously floats on the Philistine Sea, and a pinch of invective sinks it. Any overt reaching for gags shatters its illusion. An example, from Felicia Lamport's parody of *By Love Possessed*:

Author Winner went to his desk; he was a man who liked to settle his accounts promptly, his ancestors on both sides having been early settlers.

And I remember a parody of Lawrence Durrell** referring to the "Copt on the beat." The trouble with these puns is that they would not by any stretch of the imagination have occurred in the original. The main comic resource—the pretense

---

* And in fact Beerbohm's "Savonarola," though produced three centuries after the event, is virtually such a clue; at least it declares what seems unreal about Shakespeare's versification and dramaturgy *now*.

** By Roger Angell, who since this was written has established himself, especially with his brilliant three-ply parody of Norman Mailer, Casey Stengel, and Arthur Miller, as the best parodist practicing.

of seriousness—has been dropped to pick up a jimcrack joke. As well as just and pure, a parody should be complex. It should not keep making the same complaint. Since parodies compress critical observations at a fearful rate, they can hardly be too brief. Cyril Connolly's parody of Aldous Huxley keeps up a full head of steam for nine pages of this book—but what a wealth of devices Connolly pours into the boiler! At the other extreme are two very short, and very satisfactory, parodies by Firman Houghton of Emily Dickinson and Robert Frost, two poets somewhat off this particular beaten path.

Finally, a parody is not a piece of patient verbal construction like a crossword puzzle or a palindrome; it must be an inspired thing. It must have a grace, a pleased unfolding, of its own. In this respect, the too few parodies by E. B. White seem to me exceptional. Hemingway as a commuter, Whitman as the comradely afflatus of the Classics Club—White enters into these fancies with a sweet abandon that leaves the finicky problems of imitation far behind, solved as if they had never been posed. This quality, of surrender, seems increasingly rare in American parody, which too brusquely hastens to score points on its subjects. Robert Benchley's parodies are guilty of this, but are redeemed by being, as apparently even Benchley's check endorsements were, implacably funny. His parodies of children's tales, opera plots, and a Spanish folk singer's program notes probably contain the highest density of laughs per square inch attainable without microfilm.

Of the present relative dearth of parody, much might be said. For one thing, there *is* some, written and acted; the comedy team of Nichols and May and the old Sid Caesar television show have presented some delicious, if not strictly literary, parody. The shortage may be not so much of parodists as of parodees. Beerbohm and the American wits of the thirties and forties worked fertile ground; the contemporary men of letters were respectable and prominent. The literary landscape of the fifties, in retrospect (and with exceptions, all of which were hungrily snapped up by parodists), seems a landscape of ruins—of empty temples, jerry-built "developments," exploded timber, and premature collapse. In such a wasteland, even the buzzards starve. Macdonald interestingly relates parody, as a subdivision of satire, to the centralization of civilization—in the English universities of the last century, in the Manhattan of this. It could be that our homogeneous and multitudinous nation no longer possesses a center from which the eccentric can be judged. A Hollywood gossip column recently quoted a young songstress as saying, "I'm strictly a conformist. Nowadays that's the only way to be different."

In any case, the decline of parody is part of the palpable decline in humor as a genre. This decline is generally viewed, by those interested enough to notice it, as a symptom of disease—nuclearphobia, Cold War chilblains, hardening of the emotional arteries, and so forth. With equal reason it might be viewed as a symptom of recovery, and the flowering of humor per se as a sign of unhealth. Laughter is but one of many potential human responses; to isolate humor as a separate literary strain is as unnatural as to extract a genre of pathos or of nobility from the mixed stuff of human existence. Insofar as "serious" literature is indeed exclusively serious, then humor, as in the Victorian age, has a duty, in the Parliament of Man, to act as the loyal opposition. But when, as in this century, the absurd, the comic, the low, the dry, and the witty are reinstated in the imaginative masterworks, then humor as such runs the risk of becoming merely trivial, merely recreational, merely distracting. A skull constantly grins, and in the constant humorist there is a detachment and dandyism of the spirit whose temporary abeyance in this country need not be cause for unmitigated lamenting.

*Rhyming Max**

MAX IN VERSE, rhymes and parodies by Max Beerbohm. 167 pp. Stephen Greene Press; 1963.

Into the present twilight of light verse an oblique ray has entered from the unexpected direction of Vermont, where the Stephen Greene Press, a Brattleboro outfit, has published (handsomely) *Max in Verse*, a collection, painstakingly scavenged from widely scattered sources, of everything from the pen of Max Beerbohm that can be construed, however remotely, as a poem. The construing and scavenging, along with much annotating, have been performed by Professor J. G. Riewald, Beerbohm's bibliographer. His labors have been heroic—in fact, considering the fragility of his subject's claim to the title of poet, mock-heroic. The literary oddments of Shakespeare, were some to turn up, could not be more reverently handled. Eighty-four items by Beerbohm, many of them tiny, are buttressed fore and aft by (1) acknowledgments to forty-eight institutions and individuals for their help; (2) a foreword by S. N. Behrman, one of America's leading "Maximilians," to use a term that apparently has the same relation to Beerbohm that "Mohammedans" does to Mohammed; (3) a preface by Professor Riewald; (4) thirty pages,

---

* After this review appeared, I received a letter from a very old lady who said she had been a personal friend of Beerbohm's and that he had detested being called "Max." I meant no offense; I was misled into impudence by the jaunty title of the collection itself, and by its cozy tone.

in eight-point Baskerville, of sources and annotations; (5) an index of titles and first lines; and (6) another index, of "Persons," ranging from

Alfred, Duke of Edinburgh, 105, 151
Andrea del Sarto, 93

through

James, Henry, 19, 21–4 *passim*, 56, 137, 139
Jerome, Jerome K., 15, 135, 136
Jesus Christ, 126

to

Zeno, 81
Zumpt, Karl, 3, 131

Of the four-score-and-four poems so elaborately enshrined in print, twenty or so were jotted by Max on the flyleaves or in the margins of books, two were scribbled in letters to friends, and one was found in his top hat. Five are in Latin; seven are sonnets of which Beerbohm, playing a game with Edmund Gosse or the William Rothensteins, wrote only alternate or third lines; one is a collection of spurious country saws (e.g., "It isn't the singing kettle that scalds the cook's hand" and "He that hath no teeth hath no toothache" and "A dumb woman sees more things than a blind man hears"); and another is a four-line epitaph for Bernard Shaw recited to two professors at St. Elizabeth's Hospital, in Washington, D.C., by an inmate, Mr. Ezra Pound, who had learned the quatrain at Max's knee when they were neighbors in Rapallo—a remarkable modern instance of the oral poetic tradition, employing none but the most distinguished personnel. The longest items in *Max in Verse* are the pseudo-Shakespearean burlesque "Savonarola," already available in the book *Seven Men*, and "A Sequelula to *The Dynasts*," a blank-verse parody of Hardy that is woven into *A Christmas Garland*. Professor Riewald not only superfluously reprints these staples of Maxiana (as the Maximilians say), he snips from their familiar contexts several parodic snatches of Belloc and Kipling, the decadent poems of the fictional Enoch Soames, and two three-line fragments composed (in Latin and the Oxfordshire dialect) by Zuleika Dobson's unhappy admirer the Duke of Dorset. This accounting leaves to mention a number of elegantly turned ballades, rondeaux, and triolets; some limericks no better than most; a few infallibly deft takeoffs on Kipling, Yeats, and Tom Moore; two relatively heavy and personal ballads; and, here and there, redeemed from quaint corners, delicate as fossils, epigrams marking the flitting imprint of Max's daintily waspish temper.

One might suppose that a collection so curious, a portentously served potpourri of private jokes and *déjà vu*, would add up to a worthless book. But *Max in Verse* is precious in both senses; it is both overrefined and valuable. Its value, which is felt in terms of delight, can perhaps be understood through some consideration of light verse.

Modern light verse, as it was created by Calverley, calls into question the standards of triviality that would judge it. When we open Calverley's *Fly Leaves* to the first page, and read

> 'Tis the hour when white-horsed Day
> Chases Night her mares away;
> When the Gates of Dawn (they say)
>   Phœbus opes:
> And I gather that the Queen
> May be uniformly seen,
> Should the weather be serene,
>   On the slopes,

a universe of importance is pulled down. The conceits and figures by which men have agreed to swear and live are

tripped up by metrics, flattened by the simple inopportuneness
of rhyme.

Language is finite and formal; reality is infinite and formless.
Order is comic; chaos is tragic.* By rhyming, language calls
attention to its own mechanical nature and relieves the represented reality of seriousness. In this sense, rhyme and allied
regularities like alliteration and assonance assert a magical control over things and constitute a spell. When children, in
speaking, accidentally rhyme, they laugh, and add, "I'm a poet /
And don't know it," as if to avert the consequences of a
stumble into the supernatural. The position of rhyme in Western literature is more precarious than is popularly supposed.
The Greeks and Romans were innocent of it, and it appears in
Latin poetry as an adjunct of the Mass, probably as an aid to
the memory of the worshippers. Rhymed sacred poetry, of
which classical examples are the "Stabat Mater" and the "Dies
Irae," dates from the fourth century; for a thousand years
rather pell-mell rhyme and alliteration dominated verse. As
the sea of faith ebbed and consciousness of chaos broke in
again upon civilization, rhymelessness returned—in England,

---

* Perhaps this sibylline sentence should be expanded. I think I meant
that order is comic in the sense that it is deathless. The essence of a
machine is its *idea;* though every part is replaced, the machine persists,
as the (successful) embodiment of certain abstract notions. There is a
something Platonic about machines; we speak, for example, of *the* 1937
Chevrolet as of a reality distinct from all the Chevrolets built in 1937.
Likewise, a poem is a verbal machine infinitely reproducible, whose existence cannot be said to lie anywhere or to depend upon any set of atoms.
Even a poem buried in a dead language can, with scholarship, be dug up
and made to "work" again. Whereas that which is organic is specific and
mortal. Its essence lies in its unique and irreplaceable animation. One says
"He is gone" of a man whose body lies perfectly intact on the deathbed.
Natural beauty is essentially temporary and sad; hence the impression of
obscene mockery which artificial flowers give us, and our aversion—
unlike the ages of faith—from duplicatory realism in painting. Chaos is
tragic because it includes one's individual death, which is to say the waste
and loss of everything.

as both the deliberate revival of quantitative measure sponsored by Gabriel Harvey and the spontaneous ascendance of the pentameter blank verse invented by Surrey and developed by Marlowe and Shakespeare. The bulk of great English poetry, from Shakespeare to Milton, from Wordsworth to Wallace Stevens, is unrhymed. And those poets of the first rank, like Pope, who habitually rhyme do so unobtrusively—that is, Pope's couplets turn on unspectacular monosyllables; there is no glorying in rhyme, as there is in a medieval poet like John Skelton or a modern light-verse writer like Ogden Nash. The last considerable poets who preferred to rhyme are Emily Dickinson, Yeats, and Housman. Emily Dickinson's rhyming is often off-rhyme, Yeats was a magician in pose, and Housman's verse verges on being light. When all the minority reports are in, the trend of our times is overwhelmingly against formal regularity of even the most modest sort; in the *Cantos*, Pound has passed beyond free verse into a poetry totally arhythmic. Our mode is realism, "realistic" is synonymous with "prosaic," and the prose writer's duty is to suppress not only rhyme but any verbal accident that would mar the textural correspondence to the massive, onflowing impersonality that has supplanted the chiming heavens of the saints. In this situation, light verse, an isolated acolyte, tends the thin flame of formal magic and tempers the inhuman darkness of reality with the comedy of human artifice. Light verse precisely lightens; it lessens the gravity of its subject.

Weigh, for example, the opening lines of Swift's "Verses on the Death of Dr. Swift":

> The time is not remote, when I
> Must by the course of nature die;
> When I foresee my special friends,
> Will try to find their private ends:
> Though it is hardly understood,
> Which way my death can do them good . . .

When the same expressions are recast in prose, with the rhymes suppressed, the pert effect turns sombre:

The time is not remote when I must, by the course of nature, die. Then, I foresee, my special friends will try to find their private advantages, though it is hardly understood which way my death can benefit them . . .

The melancholy of the passage survives transposition into blank verse:

> The time is not remote, when by the course
> Of nature I must die: when, I foresee,
> My special friends will seek their private gain,
> Though it is hardly understood which way
> My death can do them good . . .

And even pentameter couplets permit, in their length and variability, a certain speaking seriousness of tone:

> The time, I fear, is not remote when by
> The foreseen course of nature I must die:
> When those that I considered special friends
> Will try to comprehend their private ends;
> Although as yet 'tis hardly understood
> Which way my sorry death can do them good . . .

Pentameter is the natural speaking line in English; hexameter loses track of itself, and tetrameter chops up thoughts comically. Tetrameter is the natural light-verse line.

> So this is Utopia, is it? Well,
> I beg your pardon, I thought it was Hell.

This couplet was written by Beerbohm in a copy of More's *Utopia*, and most of the poems in *Max in Verse* are footnotes, of some sort, to serious literature:

> Milton, my help, my prop, my stay,
> My well of English undefiled,

> It struck me suddenly today
> You must have been an awful child.

On the verso of the title page of a copy of *The Picture of Dorian Gray*, Max, while still at Oxford, wrote a "Ballade de la Vie Joyeuse," beginning:

> Why do men feast upon wormwood and gall
>   When there are roses for every day?
> Let us not leave them to fade on the wall,
>   Knowing of naught but 'la vie limitée.'
>   Is there a heaven? Be that as it may
> Conduct's an image of priest-eaten wood.
>   We are but bits of elaborate clay.
> Let us be happy without being good.

Thus the neo-hedonism of the nineties is wickedly satirized merely by being too neatly put. *Max in Verse* is an enchanted island of a book, and its Ariel is a hovering, invisible, luminous insistence on the comedy (above and beyond the wit of the precious little that is being said) *of versification itself*. Beerbohm, following the lead of his master Calverley, whose parody of Browning abounds in tormented lines, repeatedly frames lines whose scansion is an absurd triumph of pedantry:

> Automata these animalcula
> Are—puppets, pitiable jackaclocks.

> Savonarola will not tempted be
> By face of woman e'en tho' 't be, tho' 'tis,
> Surpassing fair. All hope abandon therefore.
> I charge thee: Vade retro, Satanas!

> Tho' love be sweet, revenge is sweeter far.
> To the Piazza! Ha, ha, ha, ha, har!

Examples abound: one final one. On the copyright page of his first book, *The Works of Max Beerbohm*, Max found the imprint

London: JOHN LANE, *The Bodley Head*
New York: CHARLES SCRIBNER'S SONS

Beneath it, he wrote in pen:

This plain announcement, nicely read,
Iambically runs.

The effortless a-b-a-b rhyming, the balance of "plain" and "nicely," the need for nicety in pronouncing "Iambically" to scan—this is quintessential light verse, a twitting of the starkest prose into perfect form, a marriage of earth with light, and quite magical. Indeed, were I a high priest of literature, I would have this quatrain made into an amulet and wear it about my neck, for luck.

No Use Talking

LETTERS OF JAMES AGEE TO FATHER FLYE. 232 pp. Braziller; 1962.

Of my own writing have been as usual trying this that and the other thing, finishing little or nothing. Most of it has hung somewhere between satire and what I suppose would be called "moral-itsic" writing; I wish I could get both washed out of my system and get anywhere near what the real job of art is: attempt to state things as they seem to be, minus personal opinion of any sort. No use talking: for various reasons of weakness & lack of time I continually fall far short of, i.e. betray, things I know better than to betray.

Had James Agee been more productive of the poetic fiction he seemed destined to write, this book of letters—dispatched over a period of thirty years to his boyhood teacher and lifelong friend the Episcopalian priest James Harold Flye—presumably would not have been published. Both the flap copy and Robert Phelps' introduction invite us to lament over Agee's aborted and distracted career. Phelps quotes an especially precocious early letter, written from Harvard, and asks, "How then did Agee do with his gifts what he did do? Why did he not write a dozen Chekhov–Shakespeare novels [the letter describes such an ambition] instead of a quarter of a million unsigned words for *Time* and *Fortune*?"

Why not indeed? It is a good question; yet to ask it, in the form of a five-dollar book, is to reduce Agee to a question mark. A subtle insult hides in such homage. Phelps explains, "In Europe, works are all that are required of [authors], and they are honored accordingly. Here they must also use their bodies and personal histories and failures (above all, their failures) to make us *emblems*," and goes on to install Agee in the American pantheon "with these letters as his testament, and the image of his scattered vocation as his didactic emblem."

Rather unwittingly, these sentences take the pulse of a very sick literary situation. A fever of self-importance is upon American writing. Popular expectations of what literature should provide have risen so high that failure is the only possible success, and pained incapacity the only acceptable proof of sincerity. When ever in prose has slovenliness been so esteemed, ineptitude so cherished? In the present apocalyptic atmosphere, the loudest sinner is most likely to be saved; Fitzgerald's crack-up is his ticket to Heaven, Salinger's silence his claim on our devotion. The study of literature threatens to become a kind of paleontology of failure, and criticism a supercilious psychoanalysis of authors. I resist Agee's canonization by these unearthly standards. Authors *should* be honored only for their works. If Agee is to be remembered, it should be for his few, uneven, hard-won successes. The author of the best pages of *Let Us Now Praise Famous Men* and *A Death in the Family* owes no apology to posterity. As to "the quarter of a million unsigned words," surely a culture is enhanced, rather than disgraced, when men of talent and passion undertake anonymous and secondary tasks. Excellence in the great things is built upon excellence in the small; Agee's undoing was not his professionalism but his blind, despairing belief in an ideal amateurism.

The truth is that we would not think of Agee as a failure if he did not insist on it himself. "Meanwhile I am thirty and have missed irretrievably all the trains I should have caught." "Or briefly, though the impulse is OK, / I haven't, really, a damned thing to say." "I am depressed because whether I am to live a very short time or relatively longer time depends . . . on whether or not I can learn to be the kind of person I am not and have always detested; and because, knowing my own character pretty well, I know pretty well what my chances are, even though I will try." These letters brim with self-accusations. "I have a fuzzy, very middle-class, and in a bad sense of the word, Christian mind, and a very clouded sensibility." "I knew I had some self-pity; I even defend it, in moderation. But I didn't realize how much I have, and still don't sufficiently." "Another [fault] is the whole habit of physical self-indulgence; the only degree of asceticism or even moderation I've ever given a hoot for, let alone tried briefly to practice, has been whatever might sharpen enjoyment. . . . Another is in some way caring much too little whether I live or die." ". . . I have nothing good to say about myself. . . ."

Of course, in writing to Father Flye, Agee is addressing not only a priest but the embodiment of his boyhood aspirations. Agee was religious in preferring self-disgust and even self-destruction to any downward adjustment of these aspirations.

"I would certainly prefer death to reconciling myself." Among the things he refused to be reconciled to was his own nature as a writer.

Alcohol—which appears in the first Harvard letters ("On the whole, an occasional alcoholic bender satisfies me fairly well") and figures in almost every letter thereafter—was Agee's faithful ally in his "enormously strong drive, on a universally broad front, toward self-destruction." But I think his real vice, as a writer, was talk. "I seem, and regret it and hate myself for it, to be able to say many more things I want to in talking than in writing." He describes his life at Harvard as "an average of 3½ hours sleep per night; 2 or 3 meals per day. Rest of the time: work, or time spent with friends. About 3 nights a week I've talked all night . . ." And near the end of his life, in Hollywood: "I've spent probably 30 or 50 evenings talking alone most of the night with Chaplin, and he has talked very openly and intimately." And what are these letters but a flow of talk that nothing but total fatigue could staunch? "The trouble is, of course, that I'd like to write you a pretty indefinitely long letter, and talk about everything under the sun we *would* talk about, if we could see each other. And we'd probably talk five or six hundred pages. . . ."

He simply preferred conversation to composition. The private game of translating life into language, of fitting words to things, did not sufficiently fascinate him. His eloquence naturally dispersed itself in spurts of interest and jets of opinion. In these letters, the extended, "serious" projects he wishes he could get to—narrative poems in an "amphibious style," "impressionistic" histories of the United States, an intricately parodic life of Jesus, a symphony of interchangeable slang, a novel on the atom bomb—have about them the grandiose, gassy quality of talk. They are the kind of books, rife with Great Ideas, that a *Time* reviewer would judge "important." The poignant fact about Agee is that he was not badly suited to working for Henry Luce.

He half knew it. "The only writing I do which approaches decency is on this job [for *Fortune*]—and on other stuff I seem to be pretty well congealed." Twelve years later, Agee *wants* "to write a weekly column for some newspaper or magazine—very miscellaneous but in general, detailed topical analysis of the very swift and sinister decline and perversion of all that might be meant by individualism . . . etc., etc." In praising Kafka, he observes with curiosity that Kafka appears "in a way totally uninterested in 'literature' or 'art' except in so far as they are his particular instrument for studying, questioning and suggesting more sharply than he otherwise could." Whereas Agee was far *too* "much moved and excited by Ideas —related with general existence and with art." Ideas—particularly the American idea of the Great Novel, literature as a Puritan Absolute—obsessed Agee, and hounded him out of contentment with his genius, which was for spontaneous, gregarious commentary rather than patient, eremitical invention.

In the last of these letters, mostly written from the hospital bed where his overstrained heart had taken him, there are hints of reconciliation. His work with the movies—the coöperative art *par excellence*—affects him rather cheerfully. His prose takes on crispness. The tortuous, grinding note of self-reproach diminishes. Looking back on his career, he is pleasantly "surprised I have gotten done even the little that I have." He coherently and masterfully sketches several script ideas—a scene from *Candide*, a moral (*and* satiric) film fantasy about elephants. His versatility, his ardent interest in "this that and the other thing," were beginning to find channels; perhaps there *was* some use in talking. But his body was ruined, and abruptly his magnanimous spirit and eager intelligence vanished from the world of American letters, to whose Manichaean stresses he had been so sensitive, and whose opportunities he had been so ingeniously reluctant to seize.

Stuffed Fox

THE FOX IN THE ATTIC, by Richard Hughes. 352 pp. Harper; 1961.

Described in a prefatory note as the first installment of a long opus entitled *The Human Predicament* and concerned with Europe between the World Wars, this novel suffers from its condition as a curtain-raiser. The author is so busy setting the stage that the actors can scarcely be heard above the noise of carpentry. The prose, though occasionally brilliant and rarely careless, is generally wooden; the characterization, though it gives evidence of a broad experience of life and a genial, humane world view, is badly cramped by the exigencies of panoramism. The action shuttles back and forth between the England and the Germany of 1923, between the rich and the poor, between historical figures and fictional characters. Mr. Hughes has taken Tolstoy and Stendhal to heart; his rendering of the frustrated Munich *Putsch* pays an open debt to the Waterloo of *The Charterhouse of Parma*. But the overriding message of his masters—the essential *idiocy* of history—has eluded him, with the result that his personae seldom break free of the points they were created to illustrate. In its intervals of straight essay and speculation, the book is interesting, and it contains a daring attempt to make a "character" out of Hitler. The shocking fact is that, reduced to the intimate dimensions of fiction, this Chaplinesque, tormented outcast engages our sympathy and steals the show.

Honest Horn

THE GATES OF HORN: A Study of Five French Realists, by Harry Levin. 554 pp. Oxford University Press; 1963.

Among the formulae of faint praise, none is more galling, and in a sense more futile, than the assertion that a book has the faults of its virtues. Yet Professor Levin's massive and intensely meditated critical study does seem to me limited by the very elegance, balance, and scholarly scrupulosity that make it, within limits, wonderful. *The Gates of Horn,* the product of twenty-five years' intermittent labor, is concerned, at its narrowest, with the novels of Stendhal, Balzac, Flaubert, Zola, and Proust. More broadly, it surveys, through the windows of nineteenth-century French fiction, the social history of France itself. And its broadest subject, announced in the first sentence, is "the relation between literature and life." As the exposition advances outward through these spheres from the specific to the general, its encyclopedic apparatus of quotation, allusion, and paraphrase explodes into a kind of wildly detailed vagueness. Nowhere, in these half-thousand packed pages, is there any statement about the relation between art and reality as incisive and memorable as, say, T. E. Hulme's famous metaphor of the architect's curves:

You know what I call architect's curves—flat pieces of wood with all different kinds of curvature. By a suitable selection from these you can draw approximately any curve you like. The artist I take to be the man who simply can't bear the idea of that "approximately." He will get the exact curve of what he sees whether it be an object or an idea in the mind. . . . Suppose that instead of your curved pieces of wood you have a springy piece of steel of the same types of curvature as the wood. Now the state of tension or concentration of mind, if he is doing anything really good in this struggle against the ingrained habit of the technique, may be represented by a man employing all his fingers to bend the steel out of its own curve and into the exact curve which you want.

Ungrammatical, undocumented, and dogmatic, Hulme hits the mark. Professor Levin, with his eye on the same target ("the movement of realism, technically considered, is an endeavor to emancipate literature from the sway of conventions") eschews the intuitive rifle in favor of the scholarly shotgun. Having mentioned Stendhal's crucial definition of the novel as "a mirror riding along a highway," he not quite relevantly busies himself with a brisk survey of the mirror/art image from Plato, through Cicero and Shakespeare, to Wilde and Joyce. The reader too frequently overhears the rustle of index cards. At times the exposition takes on the texture of a *Saturday Review* literary quiz:

By reducing power politics to a Lilliputian scale, by observing the strict protocol of comic opera, Stendhal secures for Parma the hegemony among imaginary kingdoms—Nephelococcygia, Illyria, Gerolstein, Erewhon, Ruritania, Zembla, Poictesme, and the various islands and territories of Cockaigne.

(Ten points for each imaginary kingdom identified by work and author, with a bonus ten for pouncing on "Zembla," still warm from last year's Nabokov novel.)

While Professor Levin's allusiveness is occasionally trivial[1] and his prose overburnished,[2] he compresses worlds of reading

---

[1] "Writing day and night, from twelve to eighteen hours out of every twenty-four, [Balzac] might well have sighed, with Eliot's Prufrock, 'I have measured out my life with coffee spoons.'" P. 162.

[2] "The names Proust dropped now glitter in a glamour reflected on them from his name and fame." Pp. 375–6.

into virtual epigrams[3] and on every page chisels some dimly felt facet of literature into the brilliance of exact expression.[4] Levin's criticism perhaps marks the highest reach criticism can attain while remaining academic. As a theorist, he is tame and fussy. As a reader, he is unsurpassably discriminating, patient, and sympathetic. Although the introductory and epilogic matter concerned with reality and romance, realism and anti-realism never quite grips the great urgencies of death and sex that make unreality, as it were, so real, the heart of the book, the essays on the five classic French novelists, is solidly alive. The five chapters, in retrospect, each seem empathetically tinted with the qualities of the author discussed: the chapter on Stendhal rather easy and improvised, the one on Flaubert slightly slow and laborious, the one on Proust meandering and ornate, the ones on Balzac and Zola miniature engines of con-structive energy. I was struck especially by the enthusiasm with which Levin synopsizes and appraises the accomplish-ment of these last two authors, whose uniformly bound *oeuvres* certainly need a vigorous dusting. The classics stand in need of constant inventory; as an inventory, and as an in-citement to reread, *The Gates of Horn* is very valuable.

The title comes from Homer: "Two gates for ghostly dreams there are: one gateway / of honest horn, and one of ivory." Through the gates of ivory pass fantasies and illusions; through the gates of horn pass dreams that "may be borne out," that is, realistic dreams. Levin's presiding assertion,

---

[3] "But, where religious irony had viewed life as a dance of death, humanistic irony praised folly and popular irony glorified roguery." P. 41.

[4] "The airplane, the automobile, the telephone, the electric light, and other such mechanical inventions have become the merest routine of our daily lives; but they were the astonishing innovations of Proust's day; and his sense of wonder has estranged them anew and quickened them into tutelary divinities." Pp. 428–9.

"realism presupposes an idealism to be corrected," aligns the masterpieces of the novel behind the premier exemplar, *Don Quixote*, and relates them, in France, more or less intimately to the many political disillusions between the Revolution and the First World War. By way of emphasis, a chronology at the back of the book intermingles events like "Third Republic proclaimed, after defeat of Napoleon III in Franco-Prussian War" (1870) with events like "Proust experiences his first asthmatic attack" (1880). Such an approach has more in it of honest horn than of ivory, although as horn it is beautifully polished and painstakingly wrought. If the novel is in essence realistic, and if "the realistic movement and the bourgeois life-style" are linked in a necessary "cohabitation," then indeed the novel may be as dead as the epic and the romance, for at least in the West social entropy has melted away the aristocrat and the peasant whose flanking contrast gave the term *bourgeois* pungency and shape. M. Homais reigns unchallenged; social distinctions no longer exist, only degrees of wealth and poverty. There does remain, revealed all the more sharply in the present lull that has settled over Western society, the great aboriginal distinction between inner and outer, between *anima* and *res*; and Professor Levin's survey, which like anything monumental has a touch of the tombstone, would seem to leave us—to his regret—with nowhere to turn but toward the gate of ivory. Prose narrative needs to refresh itself at the springs of myth and dream. Is this to be deplored? The contemporary attempts to shake off the heavy spell of realism, however seemingly formless and irresponsible, are a worthy phase of man's attempt to educate himself through literature.

Faith in Search of Understanding

ANSELM: FIDES QUAERENS INTELLECTUM, by Karl Barth, translated from the German by Ian W. Robertson. 173 pp. World; 1962.

"There is no way from us to God—not even a *via negativa*— not even a *via dialectica* nor *paradoxa*. The god who stood at the end of some human way . . . would not be God."* This assertion, which would seem to discourage all theology, is by Karl Barth, the most prominent, prolific, and (it seems to me) persuasive of twentieth-century theologians. His theology has two faces—the No and the Yes. The No, which first resounded in 1919, when the original edition of Barth's impassioned commentary on Romans was published, is addressed to all that is naturalistic, humanistic, demythologized, and merely ethical in the Christianity that German Protestantism had inherited from the nineteenth century. The liberal churches, as Barth saw them, were dedicated to "the god to whom in our pride and despair we have erected the tower of Babel; to the great personal or impersonal, mystical, philosophical, or naive Background and Patron Saint of our human righteousness, morality, state, civilization, or religion. . . . This god is really an unrighteous god, and it is high time for us to declare ourselves thoroughgoing doubters, skeptics, scoffers, and atheists in regard to him." The real God, the God men do not invent, is *totaliter aliter*—Wholly Other. We cannot reach Him; only

---

* Most of the quotations not specifically assigned are from the collection of addresses titled *The Word of God and the Word of Man*, available as a Harper Torchbook and quite the best introduction to Barth's work. A brief life and full bibliography is provided by Georges Casalis in *Portrait of Karl Barth* (tr. Robert McAfee Brown. Doubleday; 1963).

He can reach us. This He has done as the Christ of Biblical revelation, and the Yes of Barth's theology is the reaffirmation, sometimes in radically original terms (for instance, his virtually antinomian doctrine of all-inclusive Grace),* of the traditional Christian message. As a critical theologian, Barth ranks with Kierkegaard; as a constructive one, with Aquinas and Calvin. His elaboration of the Yes may be dated from 1932, when he began to publish the huge series of *Church Dogmatics*, which, after twelve volumes totalling nearly seven thousand pages, still engages him.

Between, as it were, the No and the Yes, Barth published, in 1931, a small book, *Anselm: Fides Quaerens Intellectum*, devoted to a detailed explication of the so-called "ontological" proof of God's existence definitely formulated by St. Anselm (1033–1109) in his treatise the *Proslogion*. Not until 1958 was it reprinted in German, and not until recently was it published in this country. Barth, in introducing the second German edition, expresses "sorrow and surprise" that "this book, on which at the time I expended special care and devotion, has remained until now in its first edition and has long been out of print." No doubt the Nazi interregnum is partly to blame for this neglect, but this essay on Anselm is, even for a piece of theology, uncommonly tedious and difficult, replete with untranslated passages of Latin, English words like "ontic," "noetic," and "aseity," and non-stop sentences of granitic opacity. Yet it is, for the author, a pivotal work; in his preface Barth writes, "In this book on Anselm I am working with a vital key, if not the key, to an understanding of that whole process of thought that has impressed me more and more . . . as the only one proper to theology."

This is surprising, because Barth's theology is intrinsically

---

* See *Christ and Adam* (Harper; 1957).

scornful of proofs and the kind of metaphysics that admits them. "Metaphysical absolutes," he has written, "are an abomination unto the Lord and abolished in Christ." In Volume II, Book 1, of *Church Dogmatics* he goes to some lengths to unmask the Catholic doctrine of *analogia entis* (the analogy of being, which argues toward the existence of God from the reality of created beings) as disguised natural theology, and as such non-Biblical, unrevealed, and worse than worthless. Even less stringent varieties of Christian thought have learned to do without proofs. The Very Reverend Walter Robert Matthews, Dean of St. Paul's, concludes his discussion of the traditional proofs in the Encyclopaedia Britannica with the mild claim that "in spite of their failure as demonstrative arguments they have great value as indicating lines of thought, suggested by experience, which tend to substantiate the Theistic theory." Certainly the traditional proofs, in the light of modern science, are no more than suggestive. The cosmological argument, which survived the shift from the Ptolemaic to the Newtonian cosmos, is hopelessly strained between the unimaginable macrocosm of super-stellar astronomy and the inscrutable microcosm of particle physics. And the teleological argument (i.e., many things—e.g., the human eye—are intricately designed for purposive ends; *ergo*, a directing Intelligence exists) was administered a mortal blow when Darwin demonstrated how the organic world, for all its seemingly engineered complexity, might be a self-winnowing chaos. Anselm's proof, unlike these, makes no appeal to the natural world; with peculiar elegance it sidesteps external phenomena entirely. It gives God a name, and seeks to demonstrate that the name excludes the possibility of non-existence.

Anselm's proof, as customarily expressed, is: "Something beyond which it is impossible to conceive anything greater" must exist in reality as well as in the mind, for if it existed only in the mind, it would not be "something beyond which it is impossible to conceive anything greater." The customary criticism, expressed by the Benedictine monk Gaunilo in Anselm's lifetime and since then by many others, including Aquinas and Kant, is that existence is not a quality but the precondition of all qualities. Gaunilo applied to the proof the *reductio ad absurdum* of the "perfect island," which, though undiscovered in a far-off sea, must, by Anselm's principle, exist because of its supposed perfection. Anselm's rebuttal was that God is conceived of as greater absolutely rather than as the greatest of a class of objects; though in all other instances essence and existence are separable, and a being may be conceived of as not existing, this is not possible in the single case of God. This reasoning was to be echoed by Descartes, one of the several post-medieval thinkers—Leibniz and Hegel are others—who have found in the ontological argument something more than an absurd transposition of fact and fancy. Indeed, the ontological argument is a kind of logical prism that, depending on how it is tipped, looks shallow as a mirror or profound as a well.

Anselm: Fides Quaerens Intellectum begins with Barth's analysis of how Anselm conceived of theology and what, specifically, he meant by "prove." The terms *"probare"* and *"probatio"* were first used, in connection with Anselm's proof in *Proslogion*, by Gaunilo in his counter-work *Liber pro Insipiente* ("Book on Behalf of the Fool"). Though Anselm accepted these terms and employed them in his refutation, *Contra Gaunilonem*, his initial description of what he is doing is not *probare* but *intelligere*. To Anselm, as Barth reads him, theology is the attempt to understand what has already been given by faith; proof, far from being the aim of this attempt, is the rather incidental "polemical-apologetic result of *intelligere*." In establishing this precedence—understanding subsumed under faith, and proof under understanding—Barth contradicts the common impression of theology as the justification *a nihilo* of the articles of faith. This, he says in a footnote, "would be like trying to support Mount Olympus with pegs and ropes." His conception of theology's role may strike the non-Christian as scandalously modest: "The aim of theology cannot be to lead men to faith, nor to confirm them in the faith, nor even to deliver their faith from doubt. Neither does the man who asks theological questions ask them for the sake of the existence of his faith; his theological answers, however complete they may be, can have no bearing on the existence of his faith." While the words are Barth's, ample footnotes root them to Anselm; Barth's exposition follows the Latin so closely that even an apparently spontaneous metaphor, "bats and owls squabbling with eagles about the reality of the beams of the midday sun," turns out to be a translation of *"vespertiliones et noctuae non nisi in nocte caelum videntes de meridianis solis radiis disceptent contra aquilas."*

The unbeliever, the bat or owl blind to the sun, the "fool [*insipiens*] who has said in his heart, 'There is no God,' " may well question the relevance to him of this theology, this utterly secure exploration—Barth observes a "characteristic absence of crisis in Anselm's theologizing"—of the terrain enclosed between the subjective *credo* of personal belief and the objective Credo of the Church. In a sense, to the faithless theology can have no relevance. Its announced purpose is "to give the faithful joy in believing by a demonstration of the *ratio* of their faith." Anselm writes, *"Credo ut intelligam"* ("I believe in order to understand"). And Barth insists that Anselm insists on the impossibility of the *intelligere* shifting itself to the alien ground of *non credo.* Yet Anselm, as aware as any medieval Christian of heathens and heretics, not to mention contentious Benedictine monks, is distinguished by an exceptional polemical mildness. "Perhaps Anselm did not know any other way of speaking of the Christian *Credo* except by addressing the sinner as one who has not sinned, the non-Christian as a Christian, the unbeliever as believer, on the basis of the great 'as if' which is really not an 'as if' at all, but which at all times has been the final and decisive means whereby the believer could speak to the unbeliever."

What Barth here describes is, of course, his own evangelical stance. In recent years he has rarely preached to any congregation except those of the prison of Basel. His sermons (collected as *Deliverance to the Captives*) repeatedly assure the inmates that he, "a professor of theology and as such presumably a convinced Christian if not a half-saint," is in fact as great a sinner and as much of a captive as they. In 1946, when the University of Bonn was half in ruins, Barth returned from Switzerland to Germany to deliver the series of lectures eventually published as *Dogmatics in Outline*.* Midway through this uncompromisingly supernaturalist exposition of the Apostles' Creed, he interrupted himself: "At this point I should

---

* Barth was an early and vigorous enemy of Nazism—"pure unreason, the product of madness and crime." Teaching theology at Bonn in 1933, Barth (with Martin Niemöller and others) transformed the Evangelical Church in Germany into the "Confessing Church"—confessing, that is, the Barmen Confession, which Barth wrote and which begins with a condemnation of the Hitler-supported "German Christians." In 1935 the Gestapo expelled Barth from Germany; he returned to his native city of Basel, on the German border, where he could oversee and with volumes of exhortation encourage the spiritual struggle against Nazism. In his foreword to *Dogmatics in Outline*, Barth describes his 1946 audience: "The audience consisted partly of theologians, but the larger part was of students from the other faculties. Most people in the Germany of to-day have in their own way and in their own place endured and survived much, almost beyond all measure. I noted the same in my Bonn lads. With their grave faces, which had still to learn how to smile again, they no less impressed me than I them, I who was an alien, the center of all sorts of gossip from old times. For me the situation will remain unforgettable. By a mere coincidence it was my fiftieth semester. And when it was past, my impression was that for me it was the best ever."

like, in passing, to answer a question which has been put to me several times during these weeks: 'Are you not aware that many are sitting in this class who are not Christians?' I have always laughed and said, 'That makes no difference to me.' "

Having defined and restricted the meaning of *probatio*, Barth examines Anselm's proof step by step. *Aliquid quo maius cogitari nequit* ("something beyond which it is impossible to conceive anything greater") is given as a name of God. Barth admires the designation as one purely negative, "designed to exclude just this conceivability of the non-existence or imperfection of God which lurks in the background of every ontic conception of God." That, so designated, God can exist as an idea in the mind of even non-believers is at some length established. With Barth's copious commentary solicitously ushering Anselm's terse Latin every inch of the way, the two theologians proceed side by side, and a certain suspense builds up as the reader anticipates the gigantic leap that lies ahead, from existence as a concept to existence as a fact—from *esse in intellectu* to *esse in re*. Then a strange thing happens. Anselm takes the leap, and Barth does not, yet he goes on talking as if he had never left Anselm's side. The medieval philosopher, having satisfied himself that to exist *in solo intellectu* is a limitation incompatible with the total superiority of God as conceived, writes:

Existit ergo procul dubio aliquid quo maius cogitari non valet, et in intellectu et in re.

Literally translated: "There exists, therefore, without doubt, 'something beyond which it is impossible to conceive anything greater,' both in knowledge and objectively (in thing)." The three tiny words "*et in re*" carry an immense freight; indeed, it would be difficult to conceive of any words carrying more.

For on their backs God rides from the realm of ideas into the realm of objective existence.

Barth glosses this crucial sentence as "Thus as God he cannot exist in knowledge as the one who merely exists in knowledge." Now, this is a typical Barthian remark, of a piece with "one cannot speak of God simply by speaking of man in a loud voice." It is also a fairly unexceptionable assertion, except perhaps to Unitarians, pragmatists, and lunatics. That is, we cannot pray to or believe in a God whom we recognize as a figment of our own imaginations. But can this be all Anselm meant? Barth firmly says so: "All that is proved is just this negative. The positive statement about the genuine and extramental existence of God (in the general sense of the concept 'existence') does not stem from the proof and is in no sense derived from it but is proved by the proof only in so far as the opposite statement about God's merely intramental existence is shown to be absurd. Where then does this positive statement come from? . . . The positive statement cannot be traced back as it originates in revelation." To Barth, then, faith and faith alone, faith in the Christian revelation, has supplied the "*et in re.*" Anselm's proof is merely the scouring of a cup that is then filled from above.

Barth devotes the remainder of the book to arguing that his conception of Anselm's proof and Anselm's own conception are identical. Gaunilo is taken to task because "quite obstinately and in actual fact very shortsightedly all he demanded was proof that God exists in the manner of created things." Such, we must weakly confess, is the proof that we had hoped for. And such—it is our obstinate impression—was the kind of proof that Anselm thought he had supplied. Barth's enthusiastic recommendation of Anselm's proof differs only in emphasis from the traditional criticisms: "The fact that God is infinite does not prove that he exists. Rather the fact that God is infinite proves that (if he exists) he exists differently from beings who are not infinite." But, granted that Anselm built from faith and granted that he conceived of God's existence as extending into dimensions beyond those of creaturely existence, surely he also believed that he had rendered forever unnecessary the parenthetic "if he exists" so conspicuous in Barth's paraphrase. The section of the *Proslogion* containing the *probatio* concludes with a prayer thanking God that now *"si te esse nolim credere, non possim non intelligere"* ("even if I did not wish to believe Thine existence, I could not but know it").

Whereas Barth admits that "By the miracle of foolishness it is possible to think of God as not existing. But only by this miracle. Anselm had certainly not reckoned with this." There is, then, a difference between the modern and the medieval theologian—the theologian of crisis and the theologian without a sense of crisis. They are separated by nine centuries in which the miracle of disbelief has so often recurred that to call it a miracle seems an irony. The gap between *credere* and *intelligere* across which Anselm slung his syllogism has grown so broad that only Jahweh's unappealable imperatives can span it: "God," Barth says, "shatters every syllogism." Several times Barth speaks of Anselm's formula *quo maius cogitari nequit* as an "embargo," as a Divine prohibition in the style of the First Commandment: "God is the One who manifests himself in the command not to imagine a greater than he." This "embargo" is in fact on freedom of thought, "the most inward and most intimate area of freedom. *Bene intelligere* means: to know once and for all, as a real ox knows its master or a true ass its master's stall." Here Barth's vocabulary and theology seem more Biblical than the Bible itself. The Christian believer, awaking from the medieval dream wherein Church and State, faith and science, thoughts and things seemed to merge, has been restored with a vengeance to his primitive desperation.

The understanding that faith seeks is, for Barth, fundamentally an understanding of what man and religion are *not*. Anselm's proof—"a model piece of good, penetrating, and neat theology"—interests him in its rigorous negativity, its perfect independence of natural phenomena, and the "key" it holds for him is, possibly, that it proves nothing—probes, that is, the nothingness from which rises the cry for God. In "The Task of the Ministry," Barth preached:

We cannot speak of God. The mystics, and we all in so far as we are mystics, have been wont to *assert* that what annihilates and enters into man, the Abyss into which he falls, the Darkness to which he surrenders himself, the No before which he stands is *God;* but this we are incapable of *proving*. The only part of our assertion of which we are *certain*, the only part we can *prove*, is that man is negatived, negated.

Tillich

MORALITY AND BEYOND, by Paul Tillich. 95 pp. Harper & Row; 1963.

This slim but dense entry in the Religious Perspective series consists of three lectures delivered by Professor Tillich at Dartmouth and two chapters lifted from an earlier book. Morality is defined as obedience to an unconditional imperative —"the demand to become actually what one is essentially and therefore potentially." Our "essential nature" is equated with our "created nature," though Divine Creation seems to be understood as little more than a metaphor. The myth of the Fall, by which traditional Christianity explained Man's estrangement from his created nature, Tillich rather individually reads to mean that Adam had lost innocence *before* the temptation of Jehovah's prohibition, and already stood on a boundary of "desire" between guilt and innocence. Moral law, though valuable as cumulative wisdom and as an inculcator of moral habit, is inferior to love, "the urge for participation in the other one," which is "the ultimate principle of moral demands." Only love, particularly in the form of self-transcending *agape*, "can transform itself according to the concrete demands of every individual and social situation without losing its eternity and dignity." Tillich carries forward this somewhat diagrammatic exposition with admirable intelligence. The last two chapters, which discuss ethical systems in the context of history, are especially brilliant. Yet the net effect is one of ambiguity, even futility—as if the theologian were trying to revivify the Christian corpse with transfusions of Greek humanism, German metaphysics, and psychoanalytical theory. Terms like "grace" and "Will of God" walk through these pages as bloodless ghosts, transparent against the milky background of "beyond" and "being" that Tillich, God forbid, would confuse with the Christian faith.

More Love in the Western World

LOVE DECLARED, by Denis de Rougemont, translated from the French by Richard Howard. 235 pp. Pantheon; 1963.

Denis de Rougemont, the Swiss theologian and essayist who is presently director of the Centre Européen de la Culture, in Geneva, is best known in this country as the author of *Love in the Western World*, which was first published in France in 1939 and, considerably revised and augmented, again in 1954; a translation of the revised edition was published by Pantheon in 1956. The self-announced purpose of this famous book is "to describe the inescapable conflict in the West between passion and marriage." It begins with a detailed examination of the legend of Tristan and Iseult, and in the inconsistencies of the narrative discovers a furtive conflict between two religions: an exoteric creed of feudal honor and fealty, and an esoteric creed of unlimited passion. Tristan and Iseult are, de Rougemont concludes, in love not with one another but with love itself, with their own *being* in love; "their unhappiness thus originates in a false reciprocity, which disguises a twin narcissism." Hence their passion secretly wills its own frustrations and irresistibly seeks the bodily death that forever removes it from the qualifications of life, the disappointments and diminishments of actual possession. "Passionate love, the longing for what sears us and annihilates us in its triumph—there is the secret which Europe has never allowed to be given away; a secret it has always repressed—and preserved!"

This analysis—indeed, psychoanalysis—of the legend is but the center of an interwoven sequence of theses that in sum boldly blame the modern Occidental obsession with romantic love directly on Catharism, a neo-Manichaean heresy that, before being crushed by the Albigensian crusade, flourished in twelfth-century Provence. Manichaeanism, denying the Christian doctrines of the Divine Creation and the Incarnation, radically opposes the realms of spirit and matter. The material world is evil. Man is a spirit imprisoned in the darkness of the flesh. His only escape is through asceticism and mystical "knowing." Women are Devil's lures designed to draw souls down into bodies; on the other hand, each man aspires toward a female Form of Light who is *his own true spirit*, resident in Heaven, aloof from the Hell of matter. Moreover, in some permutations of Dualist mythology the Mother of Christ becomes Maria Sophia, *sophia aeterna*, an Eternal Feminine that preëxisted material creation. "Bernard Gui, in his *Manuel de l'Inquisiteur*, shows that although the Cathars venerated the Blessed Virgin, she was not, in their belief, a woman of flesh and blood, the Mother of Jesus, *but their Church*." From such doctrines, de Rougemont maintains in his most strenuously and carefully argued chapters, it is a very short step to the erotic rhetoric of the troubadours of Languedoc, and from there to courtly love, epithalamian mysticism, Héloïse and Abelard, Tristan and Iseult, and all the romances, medieval and modern, that torment Western man with Gnostic longings.

De Rougemont personifies the ramifying influence of the troubadors as a love-myth, a Venus born of the foam of Eastern religions and imported into Europe, like Cleopatra smuggled in rugs, wrapped in a cult of chastity. The love-myth, simply, is the daughter of a creed that holds Creation in contempt. She stands in the same relation to fruitful marriage as does Dualism to the Christian Monism precariously hinged on the dogma of the God-man. Her essence is *passion itself;* her concern is not with the possession, through love, of another person but with the prolongation of the lover's state of mind. Eros is allied with Thanatos rather than Agape; love becomes not a way of accepting and entering the world but a way of defying and escaping it. Iseult is the mythical prototype of the Unattainable Lady to whom the love-myth directs our adoration, diverting it from the attainable lady (in legal terms, our "wife"; in Christian terms, our "neighbor") who is at our side. Passion-love feeds upon denial; hence Tristan and Iseult, alone together in the woods of Morois, place the "sword of chastity" between them, foreshadowing the equally artificial devices of the countless playwrights, novelists, and scenarists who so wearilessly have obstructed the natural union of lovers and whose pathetic inventions continue to propagate, all unwittingly, a heresy inimicable to marriage, social stability, and international peace.

Such a summary of *Love in the Western World* cannot do justice to the elegance and interest of the original. For over three hundred pages the book sustains an aphoristic crackle. The section wherein de Rougemont traces the love-myth's progress through Western literature from Dante to Baudelaire is literary high adventure pursued with unflagging energy and assurance. The section discussing passion in politics and war opens with an insight—"inasmuch as our notion of love enfolds our notion of woman, it is linked with a theory of the *fruitfulness of suffering* which encourages or obscurely justifies in the recesses of the Western mind a liking for war"—that is worth a volume in itself. Unlike most accretions of learning and intelligence, *Love in the Western World* has the unity of an *idea*, an idea carried through a thousand details but ultimately single and simple, and an idea that, however surprising its route of arrival, strikes home. Love as we experience it *is* love for the Unattainable Lady, the Iseult who is "ever a stranger, the very essence of what is strange in woman and of all that is eternally fugitive, vanishing, and almost hostile in a fellow-being, that which indeed incites to pursuit, and rouses in the heart of a man who has fallen a prey to the myth an avidity for possession so much more delightful than possession itself. She is the woman-from-whom-one-is-parted; to possess her is to lose her." There is even a weird congruence between our romantic dispositions and the strict terms of the Manichaean myth: a man in love, confronting his beloved, seems to be in the presence of *his own spirit,* his self translated into another mode of being, a Form of Light greeting him at the gate of salvation. A man in love ceases to fear death. In the chapter titled "Marrying Iseult?"—the question mark is intentional and may be taken as the capstone of M. de Rougemont's entire discourse—a phrase identifies a man's Iseult as "the woman . . . of his most intimate nostalgia." The hint is provocative. While nostalgia does not create women, perhaps it does create Iseults. What is it that shines at us from Iseult's face but our own past, with its strange innocence and its strange need to be redeemed? What is nostalgia but love for that part of ourselves which is in Heaven, forever removed from change and corruption? A woman, loved, momentarily eases the pain of time by localizing nostalgia; the vague and irrecoverable objects of nostalgic longing are assimilated, under the pressure of libidinous desire, into the details of her person. Freud says she is our mother. But the images we hoard in wait for the woman who will seem to body them forth include the inhuman—a certain slant of sunshine, a delicate flavor of dust, a kind of rasping tune that is reborn in her voice; they are nameless, these elusive glints of original goodness that a man's memory stores toward an erotic commitment. Perhaps it is to the degree that the beloved crystallizes the lover's past that she presents herself to him, alpha and omega, as his Fate.

However suggestive, *Love in the Western World* is imperfectly convincing. Its exposition of "mysteries" in the Tristan legend seems at times farfetched—nowhere more so than in the incident of the "sword of chastity" laid between the lovers, which de Rougement takes as the exemplar of those obstacles that passion-love, lacking external obstructions, imposes on itself. In the synoptic text collated by Joseph Bédier (translated into English by Hilaire Belloc), the relevant passage occurs after Tristan, who is living in the wood of Morois with Iseult and his servant Gorvenal, has returned from hunting:

When Tristan came back, broken by the heat, he embraced the Queen.
"Friend, where have you been?"
"Hunting a hart," he said, "that wearied me. I would lie down and sleep."

So she lay down, and he, and between them Tristan put his naked sword. To their good fortune they had kept on their clothes. On the Queen's finger was that ring of gold with emeralds set therein, which Mark had given her on her bridal day; but her hand was so wasted that the ring hardly held. Thus they slept, one of Tristan's arms beneath the neck of his friend, the other stretched over her fair body, close together; only their lips did not touch.

King Mark, seeking to kill the lovers, enters the hut and finds them thus asleep.

Then he said to himself: "My God, I may not kill them. For all the time they have lived together in this wood, had it been with a mad love that they loved each other, would they have placed this sword between them? Does not all the world know that a naked sword separating two bodies is the proof and the guardian of chastity? If they loved each other with mad love, would they lie here so purely?"

A sunbeam falls on the white face of Iseult. Mark inserts his ermined gloves, which she lately gave him, into the crevice admitting the sunlight. He withdraws his ring from her finger, replaces it with one she gave him, replaces Tristan's sword with his own, and leaves.

Then in her sleep a vision came to Iseult. She seemed to be in a great wood and two lions near her fought for her, and she gave a cry and woke, and the gloves fell upon her breast; and at the cry Tristan woke, and made to seize his sword, and saw by the golden hilt that it was the King's.

De Rougemont appears to accept King Mark's reasoning that the sword between them proves chastity. Yet the chapter makes abundantly clear that they are not living chastely: "No lovers ever loved so much." On this occasion, the heat of the day and Tristan's weariness are emphasized. They keep on their clothes *implicitly as an exception.* They sleep so that "only their lips did not touch." Iseult's wedding ring is, symbolically, about to slip from her hand. Why the sword? The answer is given when Iseult's cry wakens Tristan; he seizes it to defend them. The passage, read without presuppositions, describes a *fortuitous* escape from the King's revenge. His interpretation of the sword is obviously mistaken. The proper focus of psychological explication is not the sword but the King's mind; honor-bound to kill his wife, he seizes on a flimsy appearance of innocence to excuse himself from this dreadful duty. Superficially an anecdote of The Cuckold Deceived Again, the episode under the surface subtly portrays a triumph of merciful instinct over brutal custom. Neither level supports de Rougemont's interpretation. The telling detail is the beam of sunlight that Mark shades from Iseult's sleeping face, not the sword, which has been placed between the lovers not so much by Tristan as by the anonymous bard, as an excuse for the King to relent and as an excuse for the story to continue. Indeed, de Rougemont's frequent complaint that in Western literature "happy love has no history" seems willfully naïve in regard to the necessities of narrative. The essence of a story is conflict—obstruction, in his term. Happy love, unobstructed love, is the possibility that animates all romances; their plots turn on obstruction because they are plots. One might as well complain that "easy success has no history." Too frequently de Rougemont seems to sight his metaphysical conclusions by gazing over the heads, as it were, of explanations closer to hand.

Again, the charge of narcissism that de Rougemont levels against lovers of the Tristan-and-Iseult type seems dubiously fair, for, as Freud in his essay on narcissism points out, "the human being has originally two sexual objects: himself and the woman who tends him." That is, in feeling or making love, the lover shares in the glorification—the "overestimation"—of the beloved; his own person becomes itself lovely. The selfish and altruistic threads in these emotions are surely inseparable.

And the book creaks at its central joint—the connection between Catharism and courtly love. The evidence, however persuasively reinforced by analogy, remains circumstantial: courtly love and Catharism flourished side by side in southern France in the twelfth century. But no troubadour ever confessed to being a Cathar. In his search for "Manichaean esotericism" in later literature, de Rougemont verges on a kind of Rosicrucian absurdity. For example:

So long as the life and even the identity of Shakespeare remain matters of speculation, it is futile to inquire whether or not he was privy to the secret traditions of the troubadours. But it may be noted that Verona [the site of *Romeo and Juliet*] was a main center of Catharism in Italy. According to the monk Ranieri Saccone—for seventeen years a heretic—Verona contained nearly five hundred Perfect, not to mention the far more numerous Believers.

After such a titillating piece of scholarly gossip, de Rougemont unhesitatingly caps Romeo's tomb soliloquy with this triumphant gloss—"Death's *consolamentum* has sealed the one kind of marriage that Eros was ever able to wish for." *Consolamentum*, it should be explained, is the specific term for a Gnostic sacrament.

To be fair, post-medieval writers breathed an atmosphere still saturated with notions now dispelled, and de Rougemont, in the revised edition, meets manfully the scholarly objections to his principal hypothesis. The nagging implausibility of the book has less to do with its details of evidence than with its ground of assumptions. De Rougemont seems captivated by a rather Thomistic faith in the apparatus of cause-and-effect, and he religiously insists on the supremacy of mind over matter:

The time has come for us to be arbitrary in this way and to decide the question in favor of the mental—that is to say, in favor of the primacy of the mind. Whether arbitrary *ante* or *post rem*—and in this case there is no real difference—the decision can nevertheless be justified by arguments. In the first place, it seems to me that the language of passion can be accounted for on the view that mind comes before matter because it expresses, not the triumph of nature over mind, but an encroachment of mind over instinct.

But might not this "encroachment of mind over instinct" be an instinctive response to the encroachments of matter, in the form of practical social law, upon the lawless libido? In relating, as cause to effect, the *sophia aeterna* of Dualist mysticism to the idealized woman to whom the troubadours addressed their songs, and in deriving modern man's romantic malaise from the ubiquitous popularizations of the love-myth stemming from these songs, the author has possibly confused the fruit with the branch. Of course, literature and life interact, but de Rougemont, in his zeal to equate the doctrines of Rome with the decrees of Nature, seems to mislocate the *point de départ* of the interaction. In the French fashion, he claims too much for literature. His thesis at bottom grants "myths" a ghostly vitality independent of the men who create them, and ascribes to the mirror a magical shaping power.

Love Declared: Essays on the Myths of Love is a somewhat unified collection of essays in which de Rougemont elaborates and clarifies his theory of "myths." The book, titled in French *Comme Toi-Même*, begins with a long introductory chapter reframing the argument of *Love in the Western World*. Gnosticism is an attempt to make the "transition from Eros to the Spirit" without passing through the paradox of the Incarnation. Eroticism is "a lyrical or reflective transcendence of biological sexuality." Love is "linked more than any other behavior, impulse, sentiment, or ambition to its literary, musical, or plastic expression; that is, to *language* in general, but in those forms most richly endowed with popular and suggestive turns, clichés, metaphors, and accepted symbols." There exists an "eternal debate between a passionate Gnosticism and the moderating wisdom of the Church, between the personal adventure and the collective orthodoxy, which the rising tide of Eros is now renewing among us." The theatre of this debate is neither the mind nor the body but the third human constituent, which animates them both and which de Rougemont calls "the soul." "The soul is the realm of the impulses that transcend the demands of instinct and conflict with the decrees of society . . . which counteract the 'programs' of physiological life recorded by our chains of chromosomes, which contradict the anticipations of economy and disturb our systems of rational and spiritual communications, in the manner of solar explosions." These solar storms that ravage the hypothetical ether between mind and body are, of course, myths. "Between the sciences of the body and of the mind, between biology and theology, beyond the necessities of the species but this side of good and evil, without laws or dogmas, but not without symbols governing our emotive life, mythology performs its function—which is a function of the soul." De Rougemont proposes to himself, then, a "mythanalysis of culture," which will "make explicit religious elements generally repressed or quite simply unrealized." The method, he states, is "exactly the inverse of Freud's, but thereby comparable to his"; the myths are compared to the forces of Nature, which man can control only by understanding.

After handing the reader so grand a menu, de Rougemont serves up seven consecutive snacks: (1) An examination of three modern novels—Nabokov's *Lolita*, Musil's *The Man Without Qualities*, and Pasternak's *Doctor Zhivago*—as latter-day variants on the Tristan myth in which the necessary complication of passion has been intensified beyond mere adultery, (2) an ingenious comparison of Hamlet and Kierkegaard in which the two Danes are described as struggling with the cruel demands of "vocation," (3) an abrupt indictment of Don Juan and Nietzsche as "cheats," (4) a four-cornered "meditation" on Kierkegaard, Don Juan, Tristan, and Nietzsche, (5) a memoir of André Gide, who schizophrenically disassociated the Tristan and Don Juan within him, (6) a contrasting of Western and Eastern mysticism and eroticism, centering upon a somewhat elusive concept of "the person," (7) five beautiful pages of natural theology lyrically evoking Man's cosmic position in a Void that is "colorful, accessible, dense, and stable" and made actual by Love.

The fare is delicious but not filling. Freud extracted from the testimony of anonymous patients psychic principles of general application; it is not clear what application to our lives the "mythanalysis" of a few singular thinkers and artists possesses. Further, in de Rougemont's culture-laden mind, myths and men seem to have whimsically equal status: Shakespeare's Hamlet and Denmark's Kierkegaard are put on the same plane, and Casanova and Don Giovanni appear interchangeable. The effect is less to make myths real than to make men unreal. While Kierkegaard's rejection of Regine Olsen is aptly described as a form of Tristanian "possession by loss" and while this characterization can be extended to Kierkegaard's religious thought, the fact remains that in all his voluminous work, which includes hundreds of pages on Don Juan, Tristan is never mentioned. Conversely, to make of Nietzsche a "Don Juan of knowledge" who "wanted to *violate* the secret of each idea, of each belief, of each value" is to confuse a metaphor with an influence.

These essays, for all their cunning, do not make "myths" palpable; we remember chiefly, after this excursion through so many intellectual terrains, the incidents of wit and insight. In a hilarious footnote, General de Gaulle is revealed as the Tristanian politician:

His Iseult is France. , . . For years he loved her from afar, in his exile. He restored her to her legitimate Husband, represented by the Legality of the State, after having delivered her in battle from the giant who held her captive and who demanded his tribute of young men (Minotaur-Morholt-Hitler). Then he was obliged to withdraw again, disgusted by the plotting of the felonious barons.

And on the same page, discussing Don Juan's "nomadism," de Rougemont suddenly plunges into the European subconscious:

To the question of a woman whom he is trying to seduce: "Ah, Heaven! Man, who art thou?" Tirso de Molina's Don Juan answers "Who am I? A man without a name." This *man without a name*, without a past, without a future, is one of the riders from the times when the nomad hordes suddenly appeared on the lands of the first settlers, pillaged, raped their women, taught them pleasure in the keenness of dread, and galloped back to their wasteland. And he is also the priest or the divine hero in the ancient primitive religions: the man who is holy or strong enough to dare to assume the supposed dangers of the act of defloration—perils of the soul, loss of *mana*.

Such an aside (the one phrase "taught them pleasure in the keenness of dread" compresses volumes of female psychology) has the kind of concreteness and resonance that the book as a whole lacks. Since *Love in the Western World*, the theory of "myths," in being expanded, has lost seriousness. Tristan is spoken of rather indulgently, as the personification of a possible erotic style, whereas in the earlier book he was given the dignity of a Luciferian heretic, guilty of the supreme blasphemy of preferring death to life. Don Juan, originally considered an inverse illusion projected by the momentary eclipse (in the eighteenth century) of Tristan, now emerges as a full-fledged rival entitled to equal time on the airways of myth. Both are degraded from active thought forms to passive name tags. Oedipus does not become a myth by having a complex named after him. Tristan and Don Juan, as their semblances are sought in this philosophy and that life history, become mere *descriptive terms,* puppets in the play of ingenuity.

De Rougemont reminds me of another international European, the Spaniard Salvador de Madariaga, who has written with such suspect brilliance and fluency (in *Englishmen, Frenchmen, Spaniards* and *Portrait of Europe*) about national characters.* The two men have the same debonairly borne learning, the same acute worldly wisdom, the same poetic weakness for heightened parallels, the same agility at painting their way out of awkward corners. I can envision a collaboration between them that would enchantingly show Tristan and Don Juan, Faust and Don Quixote to be the national myths of, respectively, France, Italy, Germany, and Spain. I can even glimpse the possibility that each myth represents the *bad conscience* of its nation, the defect of the national psyche magnified and propelled forward into a logical doom—Spain confessing its insanity and passing into apathy, Germany industriously draining swamps after its holiday on the Witches' Mountain, Italy operatically descending into a Hell in which it does not believe, France repining to its death in love of an Ideal from which it

---

* Another internationally minded Latin sensitive to the poetry of national character is the noble Argentine writer Jorge Luis Borges. On page 142 of *Labyrinths* (New Directions; 1964) one finds, in a footnote: "Other nations live innocently, in themselves and for themselves, like minerals or meteors; Germany is the universal mirror which receives all, the consciousness of the world (*das Weltbewusstsein*). Goethe is the prototype of that ecumenic comprehension." And, a few pages further on: ". . . the Spanish land, where there are few things, but where each seems to exist in a substantive and eternal way."

is perpetually exiled. England has no comparable myth because England does not have a bad conscience—unless Hamlet is taken to personify that historical moment when medieval Albion wavered before embarking upon the course of dynamic pragmatism that has ever since determined its national character.

Certainly Tristan is more specifically French than de Rougemont seems to realize. Not only the legend itself but the parent troubadours and the preponderant majority of the literary descendants that de Rougemont cites—*Le Roman de la Rose, L'Évangile des femmes, L'Astrée, La Princesse de Clèves, La Place royale, Phèdre, La Nouvelle Héloïse, Le Lys dans la vallée, Les Fleurs du mal, Madame Bovary, La Porte étroite, Un Amour de Swann*—are French; de Rougemont's analysis of Western culture is virtually a supplemented discussion of French literature. Might it not be that the French are especially prone to Tristanian renunciation? Nancy Mitford, an Englishwoman who has long lived in Paris, states in the introduction to her translation of *La Princesse de Clèves*:

Indeed the whole book is intensely French, in atmosphere, in point of view, and in the virtues and vices of the characters. *Specially so is the curious shrinking from happiness of Madame de Clèves herself.* [Italics mine.]

The reasons Mme. de Clèves gives, at the end of this classic tale of obstructed love, for not marrying the man she loves and who loves her are twofold. On the one hand, there is a scruple of honor: the Duc de Nemours has unwittingly caused the death of her husband. But, she confesses, "the duty I owe to M. de Clèves's memory would, in itself, be too weak, were it not reinforced by considerations of my own peace of mind." These considerations steal strength from her very love of the man she renounces:

It is quite possible that the reasons for what seems to be my duty would not be so insuperable were it not that I do so distinguish you. That is what makes me feel that loving you can only end in unhappiness for me. . . . The fact is that I dare not expose myself to the misery of seeing your love grow cold. It is sure to happen, it seems to me the most terrible of fates, and, since it is not my duty to risk it, I feel that I cannot do so. . . . In these eternal relationships does any man preserve his original passion? Can I expect a miracle in my case? And dare I put myself in a position whence I shall be obliged to witness the death of a love in which lies all my joy? There was perhaps one man and one man only capable of being in love with his wife, and that was M. de Clèves. It was my bad luck that this brought me no happiness—possibly this passion of his would not have continued so strong if I had requited it, but I cannot use that means for keeping yours. Then I have an idea that it was the obstacles which kept you so true to me; there were enough of them to rouse your mettle, while my involuntary actions and the various things you found out by chance gave you the necessary amount of hope to sustain you.*

No italics are needed to emphasize how perfectly this *practical* reasoning illustrates the mystical motifs de Rougemont discovers in the legend of Tristan and Iseult. Though the Duc de Nemours cries out, "You have put yourself between me and my happiness, inventing a law which neither virtue nor sense would have imposed upon you," the Princesse enters a nunnery, and as for the Duc: "At last, after the passage of whole years, his love and his grief became less acute."

It fell to the French—that strange race neither northern nor southern, both sensual and ascetic, the epitome in turn of chivalry and the bourgeoisie—it fell to the French to invent what "neither virtue nor sense would have imposed," the Tristanian technique of containing Man's biological rage. The body's chronic appetites can be satisfied by repetition, but, merged with the mind's quest for new knowledge, they become

---

* Translated by Nancy Mitford.

insatiable. Fickleness is the price we pay for individualizing one another. Don Juan and Tristan are alternate answers to the question the Princesse de Clèves poses: "In these eternal relationships does any man preserve his original passion?" Don Juan loves Woman under the guise of many women, exhaustingly. To seduce a thousand and three women in Spain alone!—this is not a diversion but a consuming career, a career, furthermore, for which Society does not thank him, because its effects are all disruptive. Whereas to love Woman under the guise of one woman who repeatedly escapes leaves the social fabric intact, conserves physical energy, and induces a possibly creative private pain.

De Rougemont, in his haste to deplore a heresy, does not sufficiently admire the practical advantages of Tristanism—though he does notice the tormented West's unique material accomplishments as against the technological torpor of the sexually sane East. Tristanism is in effect an economy of the person, an economy prodigal Nature compels. A Tristan (*the* Tristan, of course, is an impure case, as athletic on occasion as Don Juan) enjoys the exquisite and fructifying sensations of love without external inconvenience. On the most meagre diet of echoes and glimpses he nourishes his passion. In the image of Iseult he has supplied himself with a focus for the efforts of his sublimated energy. In addition, he has obtained an honorable exemption from the distracting claims of accessible women. Clinchingly, Don Juans are born and not made, whereas any man can elect to be a Tristan. The puzzling quality—a basic indifference?—that makes a few men inexhaustibly seductive is a gift as arbitrary in its bestowal as an artistic talent. And, as with a possessed artist, Don Juan is as much to be pitied as envied. It is his heroic fate to project into the treacherous realm of the actual the fantasies that most of us suffer in safety. The sanctioned joys of commerce and domesticity, work and play are forbidden him. Envy, rather, the busy bourgeois Tristan who inwardly nurtures a chivalrous secret—he eats of this world while tasting the next.

Yes, but . . . But what of that thunderous congestion in the chest, that suffusion of emotion as harsh as a blow, which Tristan endures at the sight of the Unattainable Lady, or even at the mention of her name? It would seem that, however arguable the construction he has put upon it, de Rougemont is dreadfully right in asserting that love in the Western world has by some means acquired a force far out of proportion to its presumed procreative aim. Do we need a heresy, or even a myth, to explain it? Might it not simply be that sex has become involved in the Promethean protest forced upon Man by his paradoxical position in the Universe as a self-conscious animal? Our fundamental anxiety is that we do not exist—or will cease to exist. Only in being loved do we find external corroboration of the supremely high valuation each ego secretly assigns itself. This exalted arena, then, is above all others the one where men and women will insist upon their freedom to choose—to choose that other being in whose existence their own existence is confirmed and amplified. Against the claims of this mighty self-assertion, the arguments embodied in law and stricture for self-preservation appear trivial and base. The *virtus* of the choice is diminished if others would also have chosen it for us. The heart *prefers* to move against the grain of circumstance; perversity is the soul's very life. Therefore the enforced and approved bonds of marriage, restricting freedom, weaken love. Since de Rougemont derives our erotic attitudes from the religion of courtly love, it is just to let a Court of Love have the last word. The favorite question proposed in those courts was "Can true love exist between married people?" ("*Utrum inter conjugatos amor possit habere locum?*") Here is the verdict delivered by the Comtesse de Champagne in 1174:

We state and affirm, by the tenor of these presents, that love cannot extend its rights over two married persons. For indeed lovers grant each other all, mutually and freely, without being constrained by any motive of necessity, whereas husband and wife are holden, by their duty, to submit their wills to each other and to refuse each other nothing.

May this judgment, which we have delivered with extreme caution, and after consulting with a great number of other ladies, be for you a constant and unassailable truth.

A Foreword for Young Readers

Introducing three fairy tales by Oscar Wilde: "The Young King," "The Devoted Friend," and "The Happy Prince." 42 pp. Macmillan; 1962.

These are called fairy stories. Why? The word "fairy" comes from the Latin word *fata*, which means "one of the Fates." The Fates were the supreme gods of the Roman world whose architecture survives in post offices and railroad stations, whose language lingers in mottoes, and whose soldiers and officials may be glimpsed in the background of the New Testament. In fact, fairies and all such spirits and tiny forest presences are what is left of the gods who were worshipped before Christ.

Imagine a forest, and imagine the forest overswept by an ocean. The forest is drowned; but along the shore twigs and sticks, dwindled and worn and soaked with salty water, are washed up. These bits are fairy stories, and the ocean is the Christian faith that in a thousand years swept over Europe, and the forest is the world of pagan belief that existed before it. So, when you pick up a fairy story, the substance is pagan wood, but the taste and glisten is of Christian salt.

Understand that once upon a time there really *were* palaces, and young princes and princesses, and deep dark forests where it seemed very possible that elves lived and animals talked. This time is called the Middle Ages. When the Middle Ages were over, writers like Charles Perrault, a Frenchman, and Hans Christian Andersen, a Dane, collected the fairy stories that people remembered, and even made up some of their own. The three stories in this book were made up by an Irishman, Oscar Fingal O'Flahertie Wills Wilde, less than a hundred years ago. Yet they are true fairy stories and not just imitations; they are serious.

They are serious for two reasons. One is that Ireland, where Oscar Wilde was a child, remained a magical country long after magic had fled other countries. People believe in fairies there, or half believe in them, to this day. When, in "The Happy Prince," a swallow and a statue talk, they talk naturally, without fuss, as birds sing.

The second reason for this seriousness is that Oscar Wilde wrote in a time when grown men wrote very seriously for young readers. For instance, Hawthorne and Longfellow in America, and in England Lewis Carroll, Robert Louis Stevenson, and Rudyard Kipling all wrote stories and poems for children to read. They did not do it offhand, or with a sly smile, but in earnest, with all the skill and wisdom they had, as if their lives depended upon it, which in a way they did. For if men do not keep on speaking terms with children, they cease to be men, and become merely machines for eating and for earning money. This danger was not so clear until machines entered the world in force and began to make men resemble them.

In "The Young King" you can read a description of a factory where the people and the machines have become horribly intertwined. It is not "made up"; many factories were like this, and some still are. It was when factories appeared, at the beginning of the nineteenth century, that adult writers like William Blake and William Wordsworth began to address children not as miniature persons to be shaped into grown-ups but as the possessors of a secret that grown-ups had lost. This secret might be called faith or trust or the capacity for wonder or the belief that wishing matters.

The world of fairy stories is one where wishing matters, where the motions of the heart move the "real" world. Beauty in her heart at last crosses the bridge of love, and Beast becomes a handsome prince. And it is not to some extent so, that things become what we wish them to be? But only "to some extent," for the resistance of the "real" world is very real. To win from Beauty the magic word of acceptance, Beast must travel through pain to the edge of death. Do not think that, like so many modern books for children, fairy tales skip the subject of suffering. On the contrary: suffering is exactly what they are about.

"Dear little Swallow," said the Prince, "you tell me of marvellous things, but more marvellous than anything is the suffering of men and of women. There is no mystery so great as Misery. Fly over my city, little Swallow, and tell me what you see there."

So the Swallow flew over the great city, and saw the rich making merry in their beautiful houses, while the beggars were sitting at the gates. He flew into dark lanes, and saw the white faces of starving children looking out listlessly at the black streets.

You will find this passage in the last story, and in the middle story you will read how a good-natured man was cruelly abused by a hypocritical friend, and in the first story you will learn how all beautiful things are "fashioned by Grief." I do not want to spoil the stories by telling you more than this. Perhaps you should take these hints as a warning, and turn to something safer; for, as I said, the author was writing in earnest, as if his own life depended upon it, and he did not seek to spare the feelings of his readers, however young. The sadness of a man and the sadness of a century are in these tales.

But if you dare read them, you will enter a rich and precious world. You do not need me to tell you that the account of the Swallow courting the Reed is witty, or that the Miller is very comic in his smug wickedness, or that the words used to describe the Young King's jewels are themselves polished and set in place like jewels. You *do* need me, perhaps, to tell you that Oscar Wilde, that nineteenth-century Irishman, was in his own life, like the Young King, "one who was seeking to find in beauty an anodyne from pain, a sort of restoration from sickness"; and that a criticism,[1] or indictment,[2] of beauty lies like a thorn at the heart of these stories.

Two palaces are named in the following pages: *Sans-Souci,* which means Without Sorrow, and *Joyeuse,* whose meaning you can guess. Such palaces are built not to live in but to leave; our lives from their first cry are a leaving. Can we ever return? These stories say so. Beauty is overwhelmed by Evil, but her sister Goodness conquers everything. If wishing matters, however little, it offers a lever whereby the world can be moved and indeed, turned upside-down. Through these stories you will enter a world where a king properly wears a beggar's rags and where a cracked heart of lead and a dead bird are the most precious things in the city. Is this too strange? Or have you, in fact, always known it to be true?

---

[1] & [2] You can look up these words in the dictionary, along with "anodyne."

Creatures of the Air

THE BACHELORS, by Muriel Spark. 219 pp. Lippincott; 1961.

The dust jacket of Muriel Spark's fifth novel in five years displays a new picture of the authoress. The broad-faced young sphinx, one hand clapped over an apparent earache, who rather fiercely frowned out from the previous jacket flaps has yielded to a pert and, indeed, bonny lass who studies her potential reader with a relaxed acuteness and a fraction of a smile. The graceful chins-up pose is so strongly reminiscent of a college yearbook that I take this photograph to signify Mrs. Spark's graduation to the title of master. Not that *The Bachelors* is her best novel. Her masterpiece, for the moment, remains *Memento Mori*; the clairvoyance is easier, the humor keener, the compassion less embarrassed. But *The Bachelors* does seem her second-best, and a distinct improvement over its predecessor, *The Ballad of Peckham Rye*, wherein her most obvious singularities—a swift complication of plot and a curt diffidence of style—reached, perhaps, the threshold of diminishing returns; the camera was so speeded up that the flicker fatigued the eye. I have no such complaint about *The Bachelors*; it is packed but alive in every detail, and convinces me, at least, that Mrs. Spark is one of the few writers of the language on either side of the Atlantic with enough resources, daring, and stamina to be altering, as well as feeding, the fiction machine.

The theme of *The Bachelors* is bachelordom considered as a territory of damnation. Its plot concerns the ripples stirred in a set of unmarried London men and women by the legal prosecution of a villainous, but genuine, spiritualist medium. Among the principals, I count ten bachelors and, on the female side, three maidens, two widows, and one divorcée. That in the space of a work little more than two hundred pages long all these persons are set in motion and made not merely distinct from one another but individually memorable illustrates Mrs. Spark's remarkable gifts of draftsmanship. Her psychology is penetrating but unassuming; her descriptive strokes are few but they cut deep. Once in a while, she offers a sentence that indicates the power of elaboration she keeps in reserve:

She was crying, and it satisfied him to see her cry and to think that he had brought about this drooping of her stately neck, the leaning of her head on her hand, the tremor of her jade earrings, the resigned dabbing of her eyes with her handkerchief, and the final offended sniff.

In general, she writes the prose of a poet who has decided that prose is something else again. Her determinedly declarative sentences at moments feel, in their very tautness, close to exhaustion and exasperation. The sentences of Henry Green reach, with an eagerness that blurs grammar and punctuation out of them, to touch the surface of the thing described. Mrs. Spark's simplicity is diagrammatic rather than sensual; her hard, unflecked prose seems laid on from a calculated distance that this admirer, sometimes, would be relieved to see reduced.

But detachment is the genius of her fiction. We are lifted above her characters, and though they are reduced in size and cryptically foreshortened, they are all seen at once, and their busy interactions are as plain and pleasing as a solved puzzle. The use by a serious author of fun-house plots, full of trapdoors, abrupt apparitions, and smartly clicking secret panels, may strike American readers as incongruous. We are accustomed to honest autobiographical shapelessness. Ishmael and Huck Finn are alike adrift on vessels whose course they cannot control, through waters whose depths are revealed with a shudder. We remain somewhat aghast at a world that has never been tamed, by either a consecrated social order or an exhaustive natural theology. Our novels tend to be about education rather than products of it; they are soul-searching rather than worldly-wise. English fiction, for all the social and philosophical earthquakes since Chaucer, continues to aspire, with the serenity of a treatise, to a certain dispassionate elevation above the human scene. Hence its greater gaiety and ease of contrivance, its (on the whole) superior finish, and its flattering air of speaking to the reader who, himself presumably educated, may be spared the obvious. But in the last analysis human experience is mired in a solipsism to which America's strenuous confessional exercises are faithful, and authors who rise above the accidents of autobiography are at the mercy of the accidents of knowledgeability.

Mrs. Spark knows a great deal. She knows how people act and talk. She has a surprising fund of specific information; her medical, legal, and otherwise technical terms are employed with an air of being authentic without having been "worked up." How she gathered the fascinating material on séances in modern London, I can't imagine. She knows her London as Defoe knew his and Dickens his. She ranges with aplomb through all varieties of social modes, from teashop waitresses to convolutely neurotic intellectuals; she knows how epileptics feel as the fit approaches, what women say when they put on lawyers' wigs (they say, "The quality of mercy is not strained"), how the London underworld does its drab business, how a would-be murderer can rationalize his crime into a vision of tenderness. Jane Austen, that angel, never trod into a scene where men were talking without a lady present; *The Bachelors* consists almost entirely of such conversations, and though an Englishman might detect more false notes than I, there seem uncannily few. With maximum terseness, ten bachelors are given a spectrum of motives for their lonely state; not even the shades of homosexuality, from shadowy latency to painted blatancy, are safe from Mrs. Spark's remorseless insight. She seems able to derive artistic nourishment from the homogenized sophistication of the urban intelligentsia. One surmises that her sombre tapestry of "London, the great city of bachelors," is woven from the conversational lint of parties and casual meetings.

Since Hawthorne praised Trollope's novels as "solid, substantial . . . as real as if some giant had hewn a great lump out of the earth and put it under a glass case," American writers have coveted the assurance that enables their British counterparts to build persuasively and at length upon the overheard, the glimpsed, and the guessed. When, however, like Henry James, they boldly attempt to appropriate to themselves this ability, strange things result; James' novels, for all their lovely furniture, remain pilgrim's progresses whose substance thins gaseously beyond the edges of the moral issue. There is intrinsic in the novel of knowledgeability a crisis that no refinement of form can avoid: How does all this information add up? The crisis is not acute if the author believes that life adds up to nothing. But Mrs. Spark surely does not believe this. She writes as a Roman Catholic—very much so. Catholic converts dot her casts of characters, and theological questions nag on all sides. Yet the effect of all this evident concern is to form a shell of hints around a hollow center; our sense of Mrs. Spark, for all she tells, not telling all she knows, becomes unnerving. Her God seems neither the dreadful *deus absconditus* of Pascal and Greene nor the sunny *lux mundi* who illumines the broad optimism of Aquinas and Chesterton. As in a photograph of a solar eclipse, a corona of heresy and anxiety surrounds a perfectly black, blank disc. To be fair, this probably is, through Mrs. Spark's eyes, an accurate photograph. Then why does she bother to shock our materialist credulity with so much casual, trivial supernaturalism? In this book Patrick Seton indubitably *does* make contact with the dead; in *Memento Mori* it apparently really *is* Death itself on the telephone; in *The Ballad of Peckham Rye* Dougal Douglas may or may not be a devil; in *The Comforters* the heroine hears the author's typewriter clacking as it writes the book. In one short story, "The Seraph and the Zambesi," Mrs. Spark entirely drops the reins on her otherworldliness. A heavenly seraph inexplicably interrupts the performance of an African Christmas pageant, and the marvel is described in an intense flight of what I can only call comic mysticism:

This was a living body. The most noticeable thing was its constancy; it seemed not to conform to the law of perspective, but remained the same size when I approached as when I withdrew. And altogether unlike other forms of life, it had a completed look. No part was undergoing a process; the outline lacked the signs of confusion and ferment which are commonly the signs of living things, and this was also the principle of its beauty. The eyes took up nearly the whole of the head, extending far over the cheekbones. From the back of the head came two muscular wings which from time to time folded themselves over the eyes, making a draught of scorching air. There was hardly any neck. Another pair of wings, tough and supple, spread from below the shoulders, and a third pair extended from the calves of the legs, appearing to sustain the body. The feet looked too fragile to bear up such a concentrated degree of being.

This is gorgeous medieval illumination, but the text it adorns remains dreary and unimpressed. A little later, this astonishing creature is prosaically observed skimming along the highway "at about seventy miles an hour." Perhaps this is the way it would be. The spiritual fatigue of the West has proceeded so far that the distinction between reality and unreality is no longer one to which much passion can attach. Miracles are now and again reported in the middle pages of newspapers, and no one bothers to disprove them.

Mrs. Spark, following Firbank and Waugh, carries on that traditional bemusement with which English converts to Catholicism seem to regard the church of their choice. A character in her first novel remarks that "the True Church was awful, though unfortunately, one couldn't deny, true." Our impression is less that the Church has an overpowering case than that the world is too flimsy and foolish to offer much resistance to the leap of faith. Nor is it very heartily suggested that being a Christian improves or comforts one; Mrs. Spark's Catholic characters differ from the others only in having the articles of an ancient creed built into their grids of reflexes, predispositions, and quirks. The possibility of redemption hovers over Sparkland rather bleakly. The people have neither much body nor much soul; they are bundles of nerves. The unimpeachable triumph of *Memento Mori* may spring from the fact that old people actually have, by and large, shrivelled to such neural skeletons, which twitch uninhibited by the claims of flesh, sense, or the future. But her young people seem thin; perhaps, more materially realized, they would repel the incursions of her impudent witchcraft. I do not mean to complain; it is just the metaphysical *ambiance*, vaguely earnest and wryly grim, that gives Mrs. Spark's fiction its final fillip of interest. Her books narrow, through the lucid complications of incident, toward a culminating focus, in a sentence or two, of virtually total obscurity. In *The Bachelors*, the sentences are:

It is all demonology and to do with creatures of the air, and there are others beside ourselves, he thought, who lie in their beds like happy countries that have no history. Others ferment in prison; some rot, maimed; some lean over the banisters of presbyteries to see if anyone is going to answer the telephone.

Thus Mrs. Spark adds it all up; and such irrational numbers, which can never be carried to their final terms, perhaps do compose the true sum. If I, for my part, resist consignment to the ranks of demons, it is because a convincing depiction of evil needs somewhere in it a glimmer of the good. This Mrs. Spark does not provide; her moral cosmos is limited by a certain personal impatience. But her sharp invention and austere style have in them something of Dante, and there are signs in *The Bachelors* that she is preparing to leave the sulphuric and antic scene she has mastered for the more familiar terraces of purgatory.

Between a Wedding and a Funeral

THE GIRLS OF SLENDER MEANS, by Muriel Spark. 176 pp. Knopf; 1963.

The fiction of Muriel Spark, which burst upon English literature as something supernaturally impersonal and coolly fantastic, has taken a turn toward autobiography and history. Her last novel, *The Prime of Miss Jean Brodie*, concerned the female students of an inwardly Fascistic Scots schoolmarm in the middle nineteen-thirties—the era when Mrs. Spark herself was a schoolgirl in Edinburgh. Her new novel, *The Girls of Slender Means*, again concerns a group of young women, this time ten years older and resident, like the authoress herself, in London in 1945. The historical and physical context is firmly set in the first, characteristically beautiful paragraph:

Long ago in 1945 all the nice people in England were poor, allowing for exceptions. The streets of the cities were lined with buildings in bad repair or in no repair at all, bomb-sites piled with stony rubble, houses like giant teeth in which decay had been drilled out, leaving only the cavity. Some bomb-ripped buildings looked like the ruins of ancient castles until, at a closer view, the wallpapers of various quite normal rooms would be visible, room above room, exposed, as on a stage, with one wall missing; sometimes a lavatory chain would dangle over nothing from a fourth- or fifth-floor ceiling; most of all the staircases survived, like a new art-form, leading up and up to an unspecified destination that made unusual demands on the mind's eye.

Those familiar with Mrs. Spark's severe economy of method will not be surprised to know that, at the unspecified destination the reader reaches on page 176 of this short novel, unusual demands are made on the mind's eye, and almost every phrase in these first sentences can be seen in retrospect as an omen. "Ominous," indeed, is the adjective at the heart of Mrs. Spark's witchcraft, though she rarely deigns to use it. The undercurrents of destruction, cruelty, madness, and—ever more insistently—sexual repression are allowed to run unspoken, welling up here and there, as they do in life, with an unexpectedness that would be comic if we could laugh. An unfettered laugh implies release, however fleeting, from reality, and Mrs. Spark, for all her surface prankishness and verbal shrugging, never quite relinquishes her claim that the farcical world of her portrayal is the *real* world, contingent on an actual doom. The catastrophe that climaxes *The Girls of Slender Means* is all the more vivid and believable for being rather casually rendered.

I will refrain from revealing the catastrophe. Though the lax manners that currently obtain in book reviews condone plot-blabbing, the discourtesy seems double in the case of a writer whose plots are so pure. There is little in Mrs. Spark's books that is *not* plot. Virtually fanatic is her adherence to Chekhov's dictum that a gun mentioned on the first page must be discharged by the last. But she is less interested in the shot than in the subtler action of the recoil. Her plots are as luxuriant and mysterious as her style is spare and clear; her deliberate clarity, like Kafka's, ironically underlines the mysteriousness of what is being said. She is mysterious as both Agatha Christie and Isak Dinesen are mysterious; like the former, she is utterly at home in the many-roomed mansion of English society, and, like the latter, she has nourished her vision on the inhuman landscape of Africa. Her people suggest tropical flora and fauna in their grotesque specialization; like giraffes and flower-imitating insects, they have no second thoughts. The palpable darkness that lurks behind her social friezes, truncating a figure here and swallowing one whole there, is an African darkness—that is, the darkness of what is not known in the universe; this merges with the social darkness, what is not known in people, the darkness wherein murders are planned, legacies coveted, and love affairs and religious conversions hatched. Like detective stories, her novels pose puzzles temporarily; like parables, they pose puzzles finally.

In general, *The Girls of Slender Means* is about being young and female and poor in London in 1945, that supremely eventful year when the Hitlerian holocaust ended and the Balance of Terror began. In England, Churchill was defeated by Labour, and in London undetonated bombs sometimes tardily exploded in the rubble. On V-E Day, and on again on V-J Day, the Royal Family, "four small straight digits," punctually appeared upon the floodlit balcony of Buckingham Palace every half hour and dutifully waved to the monstrous crowd below, whose "huge organic murmur" was "different from anything like the voice of animate matter but rather more a cataract or a geological disturbance"—"something," as one character observes, "between a wedding and a funeral on a world scale." In this historical hesitation between a wedding and a funeral, amid the precarious ruins of London, live and thrive the girls of the May of Teck Club, a tall brick house in Kensington devoted, since "some remote and innocent Edwardian date," to "the Pecuniary Convenience and Social Protection of Ladies of Slender Means below the age of Thirty Years, who are obliged to reside apart from their Families in order to follow an Occupation in London."

As they realized themselves in varying degrees, few people alive at the time were more delightful, more ingenious, more movingly lovely, and, as it might happen, more savage, than the girls of slender means.

The innocent savagery of youth would appear to be the theme; the girls "were not greatly given to scruples and consideration for others, by virtue of their unblighted spirits." The loveliest of these unblighted spirits, Selina Redwood ("Selina's long unsurpassable legs arranged themselves diagonally from the deep chair where she lolled in the distinct attitude of being the only woman present who could afford to loll"), undertakes an affair with a young anarchist, Nicholas Farringdon: "In the meantime she looked at Nicholas . . . and thought she could use him." Nicholas, who eventually will die as a Christian martyr in Haiti, delightedly agrees to be used, while keeping his spiritual eye on Joanna Childe, "large, with light shiny hair, blue eyes and deep-pink cheeks." Joanna, a minister's daughter, having loved a curate in vain, has "decided to enter maimed into the Kingdom of Heaven," and, rather than defile her first love by falling in love again, has declined to respond to another curate, a clerical gallant who loves her and who is immortalized in a sentence:

His wide mouth suggested to Joanna generosity and humour, that type of generosity and humour special to the bishop sprouting within him.

Having denied herself this vegetable treat, Joanna diverts her sexual energy into elocution lessons, which involve the declamation aloud of much anthology poetry, skillfully chosen by Mrs. Spark to give her dormitory halls a weird and ominous clangor.

The triangle of Selina, Nicholas, and Joanna is the book's center, around which Mrs. Spark circumscribes other designs, using as her drawing implement one Jane Wright, a plump girl of slender means connected with "the world of books" and probably, like Sandy Stranger in *The Prime of Miss Jean Brodie*, the writer's modestly disguised stand-in. The rest is plot. The girls—a dozen or so are named—do and say this and that, often hilariously: Dorothy Markham, who talks like a debutante, opens Jane's door and announces, "Filthy luck. I'm preggers. Come to the wedding." Naked and slippery with rationed soap, the girls test their slenderness against a tiny bathroom window, seven inches by fourteen, which leads onto a roof whose uses are various. In the end, this window becomes a vital escape hatch, and the degrees of slenderness— But here I am, at the catastrophe again. Read the book in confidence that there is one, and in confidence that Mrs. Spark's darkling imagination, playing across the concrete details of a remembered historical moment, is as phosphorescent as ever.

How How It Is Was

How It Is, by Samuel Beckett, translated from the French by the author. 147 pp. Grove Press; 1964.

how it is I quote and unquote by Samuel Beckett published by Grove Press translated from the French by the author Samuel Beckett

in French how it is is comment c'est which is a pun id est commencez which means begin in English no pun simply how it is otherwise not much probably lost in translation

begin beginning not so easy book is written how it is I quote unquote in words like this unpunctuated clumps of words with spaces white between the I guess you'd call them paragraphs I write it as I read it

word clumps no punctuation commas no periods colons no semi colons none of them ampersands and asterisks or even arse yes arsterisks not one but now and then in caps I said in ARE YOU LISTENING capitals to make it quite clear CAPI-TALS and there it is how how it is is written technically considered

aesthetically considered

something wrong here

aesthetically considered quote how it is unquote can hardly be considered as it is deliberately antiaesthetic like graphic art of Dubuffet like plastic art of Giacometti whose figures cosmic vastness whittles to such a painful smallness

style if style it is conveys effect of panting more or less for hero who is crawling face down in the mud and dragging sack of jute containing cans of food also something incantatory also makes of language something viscous which images push through with effort awful effort blue sky there was one blue did you see it sky

plot faceless nameless hero crawling through the mud as mentioned dragging sack of cans as mentioned can opener not mentioned there is one nameless hero murmuring in the mud and dark alone

when something other in the dark and mud called Pim the name is PIM comes lies beside or under difficult to gather precisely which and suffers being stabbed in many places inducing speech or yells when stabbed with the can opener just mentioned

then departs or fades or sinks or was entirely imagined by hero faceless nameless who retrospectively divides his crawl through mud into three stages before Pim with Pim after Pim and that is plot of how it is

delightfully retold and thank you

welcome surely clearly hero faceless voice is us mankind you me brother and mud the earth or hell or both and sack the body dragged along and Pim is Christ name in Greek begins chi rho iota looks XPI take away X add M which is Sam SAM Beckett's favorite letter and you have PIM whose name is also BOM to come the second coming of PIM is BOM mob spelled arsyversy also bomb also KRIM a scribe a tribe of scribes to follow PIM must be the Christian church apostles popes so that before Pim with Pim after Pim is human history how it is demarcated Christianly surely not sure not clear you're welcome

hero everyman not only Christianly but biologically for as with elementary organisms mouth and cloaca are confused and tongue and penis mud and merde and words the same somehow the panting wriggling struggle evokes the fish who out of water gasped to breathe evolving manwards

incarnation felt as animal encounter analogy a worm encounters a pebble nibbles then must crawl around it

Pim and hero cruelly copulate with graphic inexpertness a blasphemous analogy with buggery that Beckett LOUDLY underlines also analogy with any love affair I quote there wherewith to beguile a moment of this vast season end of quote

the period after Pim full of numbers analogy with modern science the empty universe proliferates with the explicit mathematicism in which the author so boringly delights OKAY

attempt to take the novel into bowels beneath society and circumstance COMMENDABLE obstinacy in producing novels each one of which is smaller than the one before ADMIRABLE with less furniture VERY WORTHY kind of fierce poetry YOU BET out of rancid Platonism WHY NOT but BUT

something wrong here

something undergraduate inert a neoclassicism in which one's early works are taken as the classics a laziness in which young urgencies become old rhetoric hermetic avantgardism unviolated by the outer word the world beyond the skin except the customary almost automatic glimpse of rural maybe Irish bliss which bothers Beckett like a mote of blue sky in his eye

this proud priest perfecting his forlorn ritual

the plays OKAY very the stage an altar anyway the radio plays EVEN BETTER the ear rebuilds the actors foist existence on the words I remember the wonderful lavender sandals of the messenger boy in a certain production of Godot and his mystical haircut BUT

in how it is where Joyce and Kafka intersect one misses now the one and now the other compare The Burrow compare

Nighttown compare The Penal Colony and deplore the relative thinness the sterile stridency

question is the novel no longer a fit vessel for Beckett's noble sorrow and quote comedy of incapacity unquote Hugh Kenner

unanswered but good the end of review the END of meditating upon this mud and subprimate sadism NO MORE no more thinking upon it few books have I read I will not reread sooner SORRY but that is how it is

Grandmaster Nabokov

THE DEFENSE, by Vladimir Nabokov, translated by Michael Scammell in collaboration with the author. 256 pp. Putnam; 1964.

One hesitates to call him an "American writer"; the phrase fetches to mind Norman Mailer and James Jones and other homegrown cabbages loyally mistaken for roses. Say, rather, that Vladimir Nabokov distinctly seems to be the best writer of English prose at present holding American citizenship, the only writer, with the possible exception of the long-silent Thornton Wilder, whose books, considered as a whole, give the happy impression of an *oeuvre*, of a continuous task carried forward variously, of a solid personality, of a plenitude of gifts exploited knowingly. His works are an edifice whose every corner rewards inspection. Each book, including the super-slim *Poems* and the uproariously pedantic and copious commentaries to his translation of *Eugene Onegin*, yields delight and presents to the aesthetic sense the peculiar hardness of a finished, fully meant thing. His sentences are beautiful out of context and doubly beautiful in it. He writes prose the only way it should be written—that is, ecstatically. In the intensity of its intelligence and reflective joy, his fiction is unique in this decade and scarcely precedented in American literature. Melville and James do not, oddly, offer themselves for comparison. Yet our literature, that scraggly association of hermits, cranks, and exiles, is strange enough to include this arrogant immigrant; as an expatriate Nabokov is squarely in the native tradition.

Very curiously, his *oeuvre* is growing at both ends. At one end, the end pointed toward the future, are the works composed in English, beginning with the gentlest of his novels, *The Real Life of Sebastian Knight*, and terminating, for the time being, in his—the word must be—monumental translation of *Onegin*, a physically gorgeous, sumptuously erudite gift from one language to another; it is pleasant to think of Nabokov laboring in the libraries of his adopted land, the libraries fondly described in *Pnin*, laboring with Janus-faced patriotism on the filigreed guy-wires and piled buttresses of this bridge whereby the genius of Pushkin is to cross after him into America. The translation itself, so laconic compared to the footnotes, with its breathtaking gaps, pages long, of omitted stanzas whose lines are eerily numbered as if they were there, ranks with Horace Gregory's Catullus and Richmond Lattimore's *Iliad* as superb, quirky, and definitive: a permanent contribution to the demiart of "Englishing" and a final refutation, let's hope, of the fallacy of equivalent rhyme. In retrospect, Nabokov's more recent novels—obviously *Pale Fire* but there are also Humbert Humbert's mysterious "scholarly exertions" on a "manual of French literature for English-speaking students"—transparently reveal glimpses of the Pushkinian travail begun in 1950.

At the other end (an end, as in earthworms, not immediately distinguishable), Nabokov's *oeuvre* is growing backwards, into

the past, as English versions appear of those novels he wrote
in Russian, for a post-Revolutionary émigré audience concentrated in Paris and Berlin, during his twenty years of European
residence (1919–40), under the pen name of "V. Sirin." *The
Defense*, originally *Zashchita Luzhina*, is the latest of these to
be translated.* In the chronology of his eight Russian novels,
The Luzhin Defense (this literal title was used by *The New
Yorker* and seems better, in clearly suggesting a chess ploy,
though the ghosts of "illusion" and "losin'" fluttering around
the proper name perhaps were worth exorcising) comes third,
after two untranslated ones and just before *Laughter in the
Dark*. It is thus the earliest Nabokov work now available in
English. An author's foreword states that it was written in
1929—that is, when Nabokov was thirty, which is the age of
Luzhin, an ex-chess prodigy and international grandmaster.
Like his hero, the author seems older; few Americans so young
could write a novel wherein the autobiographical elements are
so cunningly rearranged and transmuted by a fictional design,
and the emotional content is so obedient to such cruelly ingenious commands, and the characterization shows so little of
indignation or the shock of discovery. On this last point, it needs
to be said—so much has been pointlessly said about Nabokov's
"virtuosity," as if he is a verbal magician working with stuffed
rabbits and hats nobody could wear—that Nabokov's characters live. They "read" as art students say; their frames are
loaded with bright color and twisted to fit abstract schemes

---

* It is a matter for some gratitude, I think, that Nabokov (by way of
Lolita, which other publishers gutlessly declined to print) has fallen
into the hands of a publisher, G. P. Putnam's Sons, willing to issue his
fiction, both new and resurrected, in a sensible uniform format. The
Nabokov bibliography is still untidy: Doubleday, characteristically, has
allowed all of the titles it controlled to go out print; *Bend Sinister* and
Poems can be bought new only in England; and *Three Russian Poets*
(verse translations) and a mysterious novel listed as *Despair* are, in the
midst of the present paperback plethora, nowhere to be found.

but remain anatomically credible. The humanity that has come within Nabokov's rather narrow field of vision has been illuminated by a guarded but genuine compassion. Two characters occur to me, randomly and vividly: Charlotte Haze of *Lolita*, with her blatant bourgeois Bohemianism, her cigarettes, her Mexican doodads, her touchingly clumsy sexuality, her utterly savage and believable war with her daughter; and Albinus Kretschmar of *Laughter in the Dark*, with his doll-like dignity, his bestial softness, his hobbies, his family feelings, his abject romanticism, his quaint competence. An American housewife and a German businessman, both observed, certainly, from well on the outside, yet animated from well within. How much more, then, can Nabokov do with characters who are Russian, and whose concerns circle close to his own aloof passions!

His foreword, shameless and disdainful in his usual first-person style, specifies, for "hack reviewers" and "persons who move their lips when reading," the forked appeal of "this attractive novel"—the intricate immanence in plot and imagery of chess as a prevailing metaphor, and the weird lovableness of the virtually inert hero.

Of all my Russian books, *The Defense* contains and diffuses the greatest "warmth"—which may seem odd seeing how supremely abstract chess is supposed to be. In point of fact, Luzhin has been found lovable even by those who understand nothing about chess and/or detest all my other books. He is uncouth, unwashed, uncomely—but as my gentle young lady (a dear girl in her own right) so quickly notices, there is something in him that transcends both the coarseness of his gray flesh and the sterility of his recondite genius.

What makes characters endearing does not admit of such analysis: I would divide Luzhin's charm into (a) the delineation of his childhood (b) the evocation of his chess prowess. As to (a), Nabokov has always warmed to the subject of children, precocious children—David Krug, Victor Wind, the all-seeing "I" of *Conclusive Evidence*, and, most precocious and achingly childlike of all, Dolores Haze. The four chapters devoted to little Luzhin are pure gold, a fascinating extraction of the thread of genius from the tangle of a lonely boy's existence. The child's ominous lethargy; his father's brooding ambitiousness for him; the hints of talent in his heredity; the first gropings, through mathematical and jigsaw puzzles, of his peculiar aptitude toward the light; the bizarre introduction, at the hands of a nameless violinist who tinges the game forever with a somehow cursed musicality, to the bare pieces; his instruction in the rules, ironically counterpointed against an amorous intrigue of which he is oblivious; his rapid climb through a hierarchy of adult opponents*—all this is witty, tender, delicate, resonant. By abruptly switching to Luzhin as a chess-sodden adult, Nabokov islands the childhood, frames its naïve brightness so that, superimposed upon the grown

---

* In the course of the novel Luzhin plays, in order:
  (1) his red-haired aunt, whose "pieces would conglomerate in an unseemly jumble, out of which there would suddenly dash an exposed helpless King"
  (2) her suitor, an old gentleman always fragrant of the flowers he brings her and who "played divinely"
  (3) Luzhin Sr., a poor player the child beats easily
  (4) "the gloomy country doctor," a better player
  (5) his geography teacher, "a well-known amateur"
  (6) "a gray-haired Jew"—"a senile chess genius who had been victorious in all the cities of the world but now lived in idleness and poverty, purblind, with a sick heart, having lost forever his fire, his grip, his luck..."
  (7) "the most respectable German players"
  (8) "the decrepit champion of England," who after two days forces a draw
  (9) a Hungarian ⎤
  (10) a Russian ⎟
  (11) "a grizzled Englishman who played with invariable sangfroid and invariably lost" ⎬ the Berlin tournament
  (12) Moser ⎟
  (13) Turati ⎦

figure, it operates as a kind of heart, as an abruptly doused light reddens the subsequent darkness.

As to (b), Nabokov has never shied from characters who excel. In *Pale Fire* he presumed to give us a long poem by an American poet second only to Frost; Adam Krug in *Bend Sinister* is the leading intellectual of his nation; no doubt is left that Fyodor Godunov-Cherdyntsev of *The Gift* is truly gifted. Luzhin's "recondite genius" is delineated as if by one who knows—though we know, from Chapter XIV of his autobiography, that Nabokov's *forte* was not tournament play but the "beautiful, complex, and sterile art" of composing chess problems of a "poetico-mathematical type." On its level as a work-epic of chess (as *Moby Dick* is a work-epic of whaling) *The Defense* is splendidly shaped toward Luzhin's match with Turati,* the dashing Italian grandmaster against whose unorthodox attack, "leaving the middle of the board unoccupied by Pawns but exercising a most dangerous influence on the center from the sides," Luzhin's defense is devised. Of Turati physically we are given the briefest glimpses, "rubbing his hands and deeply clearing his throat like a bass singer," but his chess presence is surpassingly vivid, and during the tournament in which Luzhin thinks himself into a nervous breakdown keen suspense mounts as to whether "the limpidity and lightness of Luzhin's thought would prevail over the Italian's tumultuous fantasy." Their game, a potential draw which is

---

* A letter to me from Mr. Hugh E. Myers, of Decatur, Illinois, states: "The character of Turati clearly was modelled after the famous Czech grandmaster Richard Réti. . . . The description of Turati's opening . . . describes Réti's own favorite opening, still known as the Réti System." Curiously, Réti also somewhat resembled Luzhin; he died in 1929, at the age of forty, and in 1926 had married a Russian girl much younger than himself. There were many Russian émigré masters during this period, the greatest of them Alexander Alekhine (1892–1946), world's champion from 1927 to 1935. Mr. Myers' helpful letter goes on to differ with my reservations about the novel's end: "Luzhin's suicide seemed inevitable and natural. A good chessplayer resigns a lost game."

never completed, draws forth a display of metaphorical brilliance that turns pure thought heroic. Beneath the singing, quivering, trumpeting, humming battlefield of the chessboard, Turati and Luzhin become fabulous monsters groping through unthinkable tunnels:

Luzhin's thought roamed through entrancing and terrible labyrinths, meeting there now and then the anxious thought of Turati, who sought the same thing as he. . . . Luzhin, preparing an attack for which it was first necessary to explore a maze of variations, where his every step aroused a perilous echo, began a long meditation: he needed, it seemed, to make one last prodigious effort and he would find the secret move leading to victory. Suddenly, something occurred outside his being, a scorching pain—and he let out a loud cry, shaking his hand stung by the flame of a match, which he had lit and forgotten to apply to his cigarette. The pain immediately passed, but in the fiery gap he had seen something unbearably awesome, the full horror of the abysmal depths of chess.

The game is adjourned, and after such an evocation we have no difficulty in feeling with Luzhin how the chess images that have haunted the fringes of his existence now move into the center and render the real world phantasmal. The metaphors have reversed the terms.

Chess imagery has infiltrated the book from all sides. Nabokov in his foreword preens perhaps unduly on the tiled and parqueted floors, the Knight-like leaps of the plot. His hero's monomania plays tricks with the objective world: "The urns that stood on stone pedestals at the four corners of the terrace threatened one another across their diagonals." "He sat thinking . . . that with a Knight's move of this lime tree standing on a sunlit slope one could take that telegraph pole over there . . ." ". . . Luzhin involuntarily put out a hand to remove shadow's King from the threat of light's Pawn." He warily watches the floor, "where a slight movement was taking place perceptible to him alone, an evil differentiation of shadows." Throughout the book, glimpses of black and white abound—tuxedos, raspberries and milk, "the white boat on the lake, black with the reflected conifers." Many lamps are lit against the night; Luzhin's father thinks it "strange and awesome . . . to sit on this bright veranda amid the black summer night, across from this boy whose tensed forehead seemed to expand and swell as soon as he bent over the pieces," this boy for whom "the whole world suddenly went dark" when he learned chess and who is to glide, across the alternation of many nights and days, from the oblivion of breakdown into the whiteness of a hospital where the psychiatrist wears "a black Assyrian beard."

The squares on the board can also be construed as chess vs. sex. The child maneuvers his own initiation on the blind board of an illicit affair. His father, while he is poring over chess diagrams in the attic, fears that "his son might have been looking for pictures of naked women." Valentinov (!), his sinister "chess father," part manager and part pimp, "fearing lest Luzhin should squander his precious power in releasing by natural means the beneficial inner tension . . . kept him at a distance from women and rejoiced over his chaste moroseness." His marriage, then, is a kind of defensive castling undertaken too late, for the black forces that have put him in check press on irresistibly, past his impotent Queen, toward certain mate. The Luzhin defense becomes abandonment of play—suicide. Such a design eminently satisfies Nabokov's exacting criteria of artistic performance, which, in a memorable section in *Conclusive Evidence* concerning butterflies, he relates to the "mysteries of mimicry": "I discovered in nature the non-utilitarian delights that I sought in art. Both were a form of magic, both were a game of intricate enchantment and deception."

However, I am not sure it perfectly works, this chess puzzle pieced out with human characters. In the last third of the book, the author's youth may begin to show; émigré parties, arranged by Mrs. Luzhin, are introduced for no apparent better reason (not a *bad* reason) than that Nabokov was going to such parties at this time. A "mercilessly stupid" Leningrad visitor pops up irrelevantly, as a naked index of editorial distaste for the Soviet regime. It is as if pawns were proliferating to plug a leaky problem. The reintroduction of Valentinov, though well-prepared, does not function smoothly; if the plot were scored like a game, this move would receive a (?). One becomes conscious of rather aimless intricacies: the chronic mention of a one-armed schoolmate (Nabokov's teasing of cripples, not the most sympathetic of his fads, deserves a monograph to itself),* and the somewhat mannered withholding of the hero's first name and patronymic until the last sentences, which then link up with the first. In short, the novel loses inevitability as it needs it most. Suicide, being one experience no writer or reader has undergone, requires extra credentials

---

* Consider deaf Dick Schiller and his one-armed pal Bill in *Lolita;* the moving Siamese twins of "Scenes from the Life of a Double Monster"; and this couplet from "The Ballad of Longwood Glen":
  Pauline had asthma, Paul used a crutch.
  They were cute little rascals but could not run much.
Uncomfortably often we seem to be invited to share a lordly impatience with the unfortunate. In *Bend Sinister*, Paduk's schoolboy disciples are described: "Every one of his followers had some little defect or 'background of insecurity' as an educationist after a fruit cocktail might put it: one boy suffered from permanent boils, another was morbidly shy, a third had by accident beheaded his baby sister, a fourth stuttered so badly that you could go out and buy yourself a chocolate bar while he was wrestling with an initial *p* or *b*. . . " Paduk himself has a shaved "gray-blue cranium with bumps," and Krug, the novel's hero, is portrayed as somehow *right* in tormenting him by sitting on his face. This identical mode of abuse, incidentally, turned up recently in the newly translated story "Lik," only now the hero is the victim, and the bully is the loathsome Koldunov. In the autobiography appended to his study of Gogol, Nabokov says, "I am good at games, especially at tennis."

to pass into belief. I can believe in the suicides of Anna Karenina and Emma Bovary as terrible but just—in the sense of fitting—events within the worlds the authors have evolved. I am even more willing to believe in Kirillov's suicide in *The Possessed* as the outcome of a philosophic-psychotic mental state explored with frightening empathy. But I am unable to feel Luzhin's descent into an eternity of "dark and pale squares" as anything but the foreordained outcome of an abstract scheme that, however pretty, is less weighty than the human fictions it has conjured up.

Early in *The Defense* Nabokov describes an obtuse chess spectator who, exasperated by what seems to him a premature concession, itches to pick up the pieces and play the game out. So too, I cannot see why, now that Luzhin is equipped with a willing if not enthusiastic female caretaker and, what's more, a wealthy father-in-law, the grandmaster is hopelessly blocked from pursuing, this side of madness, his vocation. He is lovable, this child within a monster, this "chess moron," and we *want* him to go on, to finish his classic game with Turati, and, win or lose, to play other games, to warm and dazzle the exquisite twilit world of his preoccupation with the "limpidity and lightness" of his thought. He seems blocked by something outside the novel, perhaps by the lepidopterist's habit of killing what it loves; how remarkably few, after all, of Nabokov's characters do evade the mounting pin. But in asking (irrationally, he has been dead for over thirty years) that Luzhin survive and be fruitful, we are asking no more than his creator, no pet of fate, has asked of himself and has, to his great honor, done.

A Note about the Author

JOHN UPDIKE was born in 1932, in Shillington, Pennsylvania. He graduated *summa cum laude* from Harvard in 1954, and spent a year in England on the Knox Fellowship, at the Ruskin School of Drawing and Fine Art in Oxford. From 1955 to 1957 he was a member of the staff of *The New Yorker*, to which he has contributed short stories, essays, and poems. His last novel, *The Centaur*, received the National Book Award for Fiction in 1964, and in the same year Updike was elected to the National Institute of Arts and Letters. He presently lives in Ipswich, Massachusetts, with his wife and four children.

April 1965

A Note on the Type

The text of this book was set on the Linotype in Janson, a recutting made direct from type cast from matrices long thought to have been made by the Dutchman Anton Janson, who was a practicing type founder in Leipzig during the years 1668–87. However, it has been conclusively demonstrated that these types are actually the work of Nicholas Kis (1650–1702), a Hungarian, who most probably learned his trade from the master Dutch type founder Dirk Voskens. The type is an excellent example of the influential and sturdy Dutch types that prevailed in England up to the time William Caslon developed his own incomparable designs from these Dutch faces.

Composed, printed, and bound by
The Haddon Craftsmen, Inc., Scranton, Pa.